£25

Martin Goodman is Reader in Jewish Studies in the University of Oxford and Fellow of Wolfson College and the Oxford Centre for Hebrew and Jewish Studies.

MISSION AND CONVERSION

Mission and Conversion

Proselytizing in the Religious
History of the Roman Empire

MARTIN GOODMAN

CLARENDON PRESS · OXFORD
1994

Oxford University Press, Walton Street, Oxford OX2 6DP
Oxford New York Toronto
Delhi Bombay Calcutta Madras Karachi
Kuala Lumpur Singapore Hong Kong Tokyo
Nairobi Dar es Salaam Cape Town
Melbourne Auckland Madrid
and associated companies in
Berlin Ibadan

Oxford is a trade mark of Oxford University Press

Published in the United States
by Oxford University Press Inc., New York

British Library Cataloguing in Publication Data
Data available

Library of Congress Cataloging in Publication Data
Goodman, Martin, 1953–
Mission and conversion: proselytizing in the religious history of
the Roman Empire/Martin Goodman.
Includes bibliographical references and index.
1. Proselytes and proselytizing, Jewish—History. 2. Judaism—
History—Talmudic period, 10–425. 3. Missions—History—Early
church. ca. 30–600. I. Title.
BM729.P7G66 1994   291.7—dc20   93–42769
ISBN 0–19–814941–7

1 3 5 7 9 10 8 6 4 2

Typeset by Cambrian Typesetters
Frimley, Surrey
Printed in Great Britain
on acid-free paper by
Bookcraft (Bath) Ltd., Midsomer Norton

For
Joshua, Alexander,
Daisy, and Charlotte

PREFACE

THIS volume contains the Wilde Lectures in Natural and Comparative Religion, more or less in the form in which they were delivered on eight Monday afternoons in Oxford between January and March 1992. I am grateful to the electors for the opportunity they gave me to bring together studies on which I had been working for some time and which, without the deadline imposed by the lectures, might well have continued indefinitely.

My own interest in the subject of mission and conversion in late antiquity can be dated precisely to the autumn of 1985, when I applied for the Solon Fellowship in Jewish–Christian Relations in the Graeco-Roman Period at the Oxford Centre for Postgraduate Hebrew Studies and a Senior Research Fellowship at St Cross College. Asked to put forward a research topic to justify my application for this highly desirable position, I proposed an examination of Jewish and pagan proselytizing in relation to Christian mission. This book therefore constitutes the fruit of my five years as a full-time Fellow at the Centre for Hebrew Studies. I hope it may serve as a substantive memorial of my gratitude to the Centre, and to the Solon Foundation and Felix Posen, and as a reminder of congenial and stimulating company in St Cross.

During the final stages of checking the typescript I have benefited greatly from pleasant surroundings and helpful colleagues as a Fellow for six months in 1993 of the Institute for Advanced Studies at the Hebrew University of Jerusalem. I am very grateful to the Institute, and especially to Aharon Oppenheimer and Isaiah Gafni, for their invitation and hospitality.

I have been aware at all times while engaged on this research that I have strayed far outside my expertise. I am not a theologian. I am often baffled by what theologians write, and I am aware that the questions I ask often in turn seem naïve to them. Specialists in ancient philosophy, New Testament, patristics, and rabbinics may well uncover numerous errors which reveal my inadequate grasp of their disciplines. I apologize in advance, but I also plead two advantages in attempting to cover so wide a field despite my incompetence. One is the hope that a study of the religious systems of the early Roman empire alongside each other may generate interesting questions which do not usually arise when those systems are studied in isolation. My second hope, perhaps over-optimistic, is that my perspective as an outsider only vaguely aware of the debates standard within these various disciplines may enable me sometimes to broach issues which are taken for granted by scholars immersed in more traditional problems.

In an attempt to eradicate my worst blunders, I have shamelessly accepted help from very many generous colleagues. John Ashton, Louis Feldman, Paula Fredriksen, Thomas Kraabel, Simon Price, Christopher Rowland, Richard Rutherford, Ed Sanders, and Tom Wright all read all or part of the typescript at different stages. Sebastian Brock and Fergus Millar both made many useful comments and provided much moral support and encouragement during the lectures. I have been helped in various ways by Polymnia Athanassiadi, Al Baumgarten, Garth Fowden, Robin Lane Fox, Daniel Frank, Keith Grüneberg, Sam Lieu, Danny Schwartz, Norman Solomon, and Sacha Stern. Geza Vermes has provided encouragement over many years. I owe a great deal to the inspiration of the writings of Shaye Cohen and John Gager.

Earlier versions of particular chapters were presented to the Jewish History, Ancient History, New Testament, and Religions in the Mediterranean seminars in Oxford, to the Fellows' seminar at the Oxford Centre for Postgraduate Hebrew Studies, to seminars at Birmingham, Boston, Cambridge, Durham, and Princeton, and at the conference of the European Association for Jewish Studies held in Berlin in 1987. I have benefited greatly from comments made by many of the participants in these seminars. Parts of Chapters 4, 6, and 7 build upon studies published in various places between 1989 and 1992; I have referred to them at the appropriate places in each chapter.

I have retained as far as possible the style of the lectures as they were delivered, adding references in the footnotes to modern scholarship only when they seemed necessary to clarify the argument or support a contentious point. The notes should not be taken as a discussion of the history of scholarship on each question, which would have required a very much larger work. Nor does the bibliography aim at completeness, although I have included, besides the items cited in the notes, some of the more important studies which deal with the general themes I have addressed.

When so many people have helped, it is more than usually important to stress that I alone bear full responsibility for the remaining mistakes and that the willingness of friends to help and advise does not imply their approval even of my basic approach to the subject.

During the course of my research I have become aware of the significance attached to this subject by modern theologians of various persuasions. I am not perturbed by this; I am pleased if colleagues show an interest in my work, whatever the reason. But I must emphasize that, although I have an instinctive sympathy with those who advocate the greatest possible tolerance of other peoples' behaviour and beliefs, I myself have tried to approach this study simply as a historian attempting to explain a curious phenomenon in the religious mentality of past generations. I write as a Jew, which must, I assume, affect the way I understand religious history, but I have not been consciously concerned either to defend or to decry any religious tradition, nor have I sought to discern a clear theology in evidence which seemed to me ambiguous. In one area in particular I was surprised by my own conclusions. At the beginning of my investigation I took for granted the proselytizing zeal of early Christians, and only after survey-ing much evidence did I produce the present Chapter 5; indeed, I should admit that I changed my mind with some reluctance, since the more nuanced picture which resulted has somewhat complicated the argument of the book as a whole.

Emma-Jayne Muir has typed the whole manuscript and seen it through all too many drafts. I am very grateful to her for her patience and good humour.

I would never have written this book if my wife and

children had not put up with the very considerable domestic disruption caused by my acceptance of a research fellowship, and now a permanent post, in Oxford. Sarah has tried for some years to find a more attractive title for the lectures than *Mission and Conversion*, and it is with some regret that I feel unable to use either *Gone Fishing* or *Missionary Positions: Some Wilde Lectures*. I dedicate this book to my children of whom the youngest, Charlotte, arrived on the Saturday evening between the second Wilde Lecture and the third.

M.D.G.

Oriental Institute, Oxford,
Wolfson College, and
Oxford Centre for Hebrew and Jewish Studies

CONTENTS

Abbreviations   xii

1. The Significance of Proselytizing   1

2. The Diffusion of Cults and Philosophies in the
   Pagan Roman Empire   20

3. Judaism before 100 CE: Attitudes to Gentile
   Paganism   38

4. Judaism before 100 CE: Proselytes and
   Proselytizing   60

5. Mission in the Early Church   91

6. Judaism in the Talmudic Period: Attitudes to
   Gentile Paganism   109

7. Judaism in the Talmudic Period: Proselytes and
   Proselytizing   129

8. The Consequences and Origins of Proselytizing   154

Bibliography   175

Index   189

ABBREVIATIONS

AÉ	*Année Épigraphique*
AJS Review	*Association of Jewish Studies Review*
ARNB	*Aboth de Rabbi Nathan*, ed. S. Schechter (Vienna, 1887; repr. Hildesheim, 1979)
b.	*ben* (son of . . .)
b.	*Babylonian Talmud*
BAR	*Biblical Archaeology Review*
Bib.	*Biblica*
Cant. R.	*Song of Songs Rabbah*, in S. Dunsky, *Midrash Rabbah: Shir ha-Shirim* (Jerusalem and Tel Aviv, 1980).
CBQ	*Catholic Biblical Quarterly*
CD	*Damascus Rule*, in Ch. Rabin, *The Zadokite Documents*, 2nd edn. (Oxford, 1958).
CIJ	*Corpus Inscriptionum Judaicarum*, ed. J. B. Frey (2 vols.; New York and Rome, 1936–75).
CIL	*Corpus Inscriptionum Latinarum* (Berlin, 1863)
CJZC	*Corpus Jüdische Zeugnisse aus der Cyrenaika*, ed. G. Lüderitz (Wiesbaden, 1983)
CPJ	*Corpus Papyrorum Judaicarum*, ed. V. A. Tcherikover, A. Fuks, and M. Stern (3 vols.; Cambridge, Mass., 1957–64).
Deut. R.	*Deuteronomy Rabbah*, in M. A. Mirkin (ed.), *Midrash Rabbah*, vol. 11 (Tel Aviv, 1967)
Eccl. R.	*Ecclesiastes Rabbah*, in *Sefer Midrash Rabbah* (2 vols.; repr. Jerusalem, 1970)
Enc. Jud.	*Encyclopaedia Judaica* (16 vols.; Jerusalem, 1971)
ET	English translation
Exod. R.	*Exodus Rabbah*, in M. A. Mirkin (ed.), *Midrash Rabbah*, vols. 5–6 (Tel Aviv, 1959–60)
Gen. R.	*Genesis Rabbah*, in J. Theodor and Ch. Albeck, *Midrash Bereshit Rabba: Critical Edition with Notes and Commentary* (3 vols.; Jerusalem, 1965)
Heb.	Hebrew
HTR	*Harvard Theological Review*
HUCA	*Hebrew Union College Annual*

IEJ	*Israel Exploration Journal*
ILLRP	*Inscriptiones Latinae Liberae Rei Publicae*, ed. A. Degrassi, 2nd edn. (2 vols.; Florence, 1963–5)
ILS	*Inscriptiones Latinae Selectae*, ed. H. Dessau (Berlin, 1892–1916)
JBL	*Journal of Biblical Literature*
JHS	*Journal of Hellenic Studies*
JJS	*Journal of Jewish Studies*
JQR	*Jewish Quarterly Review*
JRS	*Journal of Roman Studies*
JSJ	*Journal for the Study of Judaism*
JSNT	*Journal for the Study of the New Testament*
JTS	*Journal of Theological Studies*
Lev. R.	*Leviticus Rabbah*, in M. Margulies (ed.), *Midrash Wayyikra Rabbah* (5 vols.; Jerusalem, 1953–60).
m.	*Mishnah*
MAMA	*Monumenta Asiae Minoris Antiqua* (Manchester, 1928–)
MdRi	*Mekilta de Rabbi Ishmael* (3 vols.; Philadelphia, 1933–5).
NTS	*New Testament Studies*
Num. R.	*Numbers Rabbah*, in M. A. Mirkin (ed.), *Midrash Rabbah* vols. 9–10 (Tel Aviv, 1964–5)
PCPS	*Proceedings of the Cambridge Philological Society*
PG	*Patrologia Graeca*, ed. J. P. Migne (162 vols.; Paris, 1857–66)
Pes. R.	*Pesikta Rabbati*, ed. M. Friedmann (Vienna, 1880; repr. Tel Aviv, 1963).
4 Q Flor.	*Florilegium*, in J. M. Allegro (ed.), *Qumran Cave 4* (Discoveries in the Judaean Desert of Jordan, 5; Oxford, 1968), 53–7
R.	Rabbi
REA	Revue des Études Augustiniennes
RÉJ	Revue des Études Juives
SC	*The Second Century: A Journal of Early Christian Studies*
Sifre Deut.	*Siphre ad Deuteronomium*, ed. L. Finkelstein (Berlin, 1939; repr. New York, 1969)
Sifre Num.	*Sifre to Numbers*, in H. S. Horowitz (ed.), *Siphre D'be Rab: Fasciculus primus: Siphre ad Numeros adjecto Siphre zutta*, 2nd edn. (Jerusalem, 1966)
Sifre Zuta	*Sifre Zuta*, in H. S. Horowitz (ed.), *Siphre D'be Rab: Fasciculus primus: Siphre ad Numeros adjecto Siphre zutta*, 2nd edn. (Jerusalem, 1966)

t.	*Tosefta* (ed. S. Lieberman, New York, 1955–88 (incomplete), cited as L., p. . . .; ed. M. S. Zuckermandel, repr. Jerusalem, 1970, cited as Z., p. . . .)
TAPhA	*Transactions of the American Philological Association*
VC	*Vigiliae Christianae*
y.	*Palestinian Talmud* (Krotoschin edn., 1866; repr. Jerusalem, 1969; cited by tractate, page, and column)
ZPE	*Zeitschrift für Papyrologie und Epigraphik*

Abbreviations of titles of tractates in the Mishnah, Tosefta, and Talmuds follow H. Danby, *The Mishnah Translated from the Hebrew* (Oxford, 1933), 806. References to classical texts follow the Oxford Classical Dictionary, 2nd edn., 1970.

1

The Significance of Proselytizing

TWO metaphors predominate in scholarly analyses of the religious history of late antiquity. One is the race to win souls in the first three centuries of the Christian era, in which, at least within the Roman empire, the vigour and virtue of the Church is said to have overcome the flawed competition of pagan cults and philosophies and the insufficient zeal of Judaism.[1] The other image, almost as common, is that of the market place.[2] According to this picture the consumer played a rather larger role, and more attention needs to be paid to his or her predelictions if widespread conversion is to be understood. But this metaphor shares with that of the racecourse the presupposition of a competitive attitude among adherents of religions other than Christianity. It is taken for granted that all vendors of religious truths were eager to sell their products to any customer who preferred his wares to those of rivals. It is the aim of this book to examine and challenge this assumption that all or most religions in the Roman empire were, in this sense, missionary.[3]

The investigation will be confined to the relatively small area of the Mediterranean world and the Near East, and to the 800 years or so between the conquests of Alexander the Great of Macedon and the establishment of Christianity as the predominant religion of the Roman empire. The geographical restriction has been imposed primarily because of my ignorance of affairs elsewhere, and not because I believe that,

[1] See e.g. the discussion of the various metaphors used by scholars to describe the history of early Christianity in White, 'Adolf Harnack', esp. 103, 106–7.
[2] Image of the market place in e.g. Liebeschuetz, *Continuity and Change*, 306–7 (Christianity could 'outbid' the old religion).
[3] Examples of modern scholarly works in which mission is taken for granted are too numerous to list, but Nock, *Conversion*, 16, may stand for all.

for instance, the efforts of those who promoted the spread of Buddhism in India and China in these years are totally irrelevant to my subject. For the limitation of period, the best possible justification lies in the abundance of evidence which survives from these centuries. The sources available for understanding the religious history of late antiquity are not easy to interpret (see below, p. 10), but historians cannot complain of a lack of pertinent material.

My aim is to establish a history of a religious concept. I do not thereby intend to claim that religious movements are always, or perhaps even often, motivated by, or at any rate solely by, ideas. It is entirely possible that a group of people in theory committed to a particular concept of mission may have taken no missionary action whatsoever for various psychological or social reasons. That will not be my concern, except incidentally as evidence for the existence or non-existence of the basic attitudes themselves. I intend instead to try to trace in the sources the fundamental notion of a mission to convert others. A belief that my friends and I should behave or think in a certain way does not entail a belief that others should follow suit or join our group. Nor does a belief that a god's demand for worship must be obeyed imply an assumption that worshippers of that divinity should seek more worshippers to join them. The routine ascription of such a concept by modern scholars to the religions of antiquity warrants investigation.

So far as I know there has not up to now been any study of precisely this subject. Accounts of conversion in the Roman empire have been frequent, and often illuminating, since the magisterial study by A. D. Nock in 1933.[4] I shall differ from such previous studies not by combating their arguments, except occasionally, but by posing questions which I think they were inclined to overlook. Many scholars have examined conversion from the point of view of the convert. They have asked why he or she might be prone to conversion, what argument or propaganda might be used to ensure conversion

---

[4] Nock, *Conversion*; MacMullen, *Christianizing the Roman Empire*; Lane Fox, *Pagans and Christians*. For recent studies of conversion to Judaism, see especially Cohen, 'Conversion to Judaism in Historical Perspective' and other articles by the same author listed in the bibliography.

to one cult or philosophy rather than another, what treatment or training was given to new converts, how the total change of life predicated of the committed convert differed from adhesion to a cult or philosophy, and the shades of commitment between the two such extremes. All this is very valuable, but it simply assumes a positive desire to affect outsiders as an integral part of every religion, and it is precisely that assumption that I intend to examine below— not least because such easy acceptance of the inevitability of mission in the strong sense is likely to reflect an unconscious Christianization of the study of ancient religions, a pheno- menon often noted before in other contexts.[5]

The study of mission is complicated by the variety of uses of the word 'mission' itself in modern scholarship. Such vagueness is not unreasonable: anyone sent to do anything may be said to have a mission of some sort. But I want to distinguish as clearly as possible between missions of this general type and the precise type of mission presupposed by the agonistic and market metaphors to which I have just referred.

Three attitudes in particular are worth isolating as involving considerably less than a mission to win converts, despite the fact that they are often described simply as missionary by historians of religion. Thus there is much evidence that some people in antiquity felt that they had a general message which they wished to impart to others. Such disseminators of information may have had no clear idea of the reaction they desired from their auditors. Such an attitude might be termed informative mission. Its aim was to tell people something, rather than to change their behaviour or status.

Secondly, some missionaries did intend to change recipients of their message by making them more moral or contented, but did not require that the novel behaviour and attitudes of their auditors be recognized by those auditors as part of the belief system espoused by the missionary. Such a mission to educate is easily distinguished from a desire to win converts. For instance, no recipient of Christian teachings between *c.*100 and *c.*300 CE, even if he held only correct beliefs as

---

[5] See for instance Price, *Rituals and Power*, 11–22.

defined within Christianity, could count as a Christian so long as he was unaware of the origins of those beliefs. To take a hypothetical example: if someone accepted the significance of the death and resurrection of Jesus but believed mistakenly that Jesus was an Athenian doctor who had lived in the age of Pericles, other Christians would not consider him as one of them.

Thirdly, some missionaries requested recognition by others of the power of a particular divinity without expecting their audience to devote themselves to his or her worship. Such a mission was essentially apologetic. Its aim was to protect the cult and beliefs of the missionary.

Information, education, and apologetic might or might not coexist within any one religious system, but all three can individually be distinguished from what may best be described as proselytizing. Those who approved of a proselytizing mission believed that, as members of a defined group, they should approve of those within their number who might choose to encourage outsiders not only to change their way of life but also to be incorporated within their group. It is usually proselytizing mission of this type that scholars presuppose when they use competitive metaphors to describe the religious history of antiquity.

These varieties of mission are ideal types. In practice they may be hard to distinguish because the missionary may not himself be entirely aware of the motivation for his behaviour. But one example may help to demonstrate that the distinctions are not imaginary. When I decided to write this book, I did so because I thought the information interesting; my mission was, and is, informative. If I had hoped to change my audience's behaviour (perhaps by making them more tolerant), my aim would have been educational, but I had no such intention. If I had hoped to justify the views of one religious group which I describe, my aim would have been apologetic. If I had wanted readers to join a particular religious tradition, I would have been proselytizing. It is possible, I suppose, that some readers will find their religious outlook altered by this book, or their attitudes to Jews or Christians made more friendly. It is not totally impossible that someone will find here arguments to become a Jew or a Christian. But such unintended effects are irrelevant to my mission, which has only ever been to inform. Since in this study I am discussing conscious motivation, I can in this one instance write with complete authority on the missionary attitude of myself as author.

In principle, all four types of mission—informative, educational, apologetic, and proselytizing—could be aimed either at all humans or only at a selected few. If some groups tried to inform, educate, or recruit into their membership specific individuals, such as relatives, household slaves, or friends, with whom they already had social relations, such cementing of social bonds cannot be taken as evidence that they would also have a missionary impulse towards total outsiders. On a social scale broader than that of the household, Jews, Christians, and pagans from time to time, alike took it for granted that *within* societies religious deviants had to be brought into line, if necessary by force, to avert the hostility of the divine and disaster for all. Thus Socrates was executed by the Athenians in 399 BCE on a charge of not accepting the state gods and of the introduction of new gods, an accusation which, according to Plato's *Apology*, he took sufficiently seriously to deny. The books of the Hebrew Bible contain passages of vehement condemnation of idolatry in the midst of Israel, and descriptions of the ruthless extirpation of paganism in the holy land. In the centuries after Constantine, representatives of the Christian Church were among the greatest persecutors in history, but as often as not the victims of such hostility considered themselves to be no less Christian than their persecutors. Similarly among pagan polytheists: it was to rescue the Roman empire from destruction by securing the *pax deorum* that Decius instituted his persecution of Christians in 250 CE, on the grounds that their failure to worship the gods risked divine wrath.[6] On a less violent plane, uniformity within society seemed so evidently desirable to Josephus that in addressing a readership of Greeks and Romans he praised the unanimity of the Jews in religious affairs as one of the chief Jewish virtues (*C. Ap.* 2. 179)—a surprising aspect of Judaism to be singled out by an author

[6] De Ste Croix, 'Why were Christians Persecuted?'.

who elsewhere blamed precisely the schisms within Judaean Jewry for the major catastrophe which overwhelmed his people during his lifetime.[7] The same concern for communal solidarity in the face of the divine lies behind the common phenomenon of revivalist movements, from the partially spurious claims of Augustus to have restored the ancient cults and morality of antique Rome to the calls of Hebrew prophets for Israel to worship with a purer heart. Only occasionally could be heard the voice of theological reason against such human efforts to protect the sensibilities of outraged gods. An unknown Christian forged a letter, at some time before the document was included by Eusebius in his *Ecclesiastical History*, in which the emperor Antoninus Pius was made to urge the common council of Asia not to persecute Christians when earthquakes occurred, on the grounds that the gods themselves could ensure that offenders would not escape.[8] Similarly, according to Tacitus (*Ann.* 1. 73), the pagan Roman emperor Tiberius said that any injuries suffered by the gods through perjury by men were their problem and not his concern: *deorum iniurias dis curae*.

The prevalence of what might be called inward, targeted mission of this kind has been documented in the past. But to make sense of the image (with which I began) of a cosmic struggle between religions for human souls, a missionary religion had to be universal and therefore outward-looking in its scope and inclusive in its intent. Such universal proselytizing mission must at the least have involved an acknowledgement by the members of a group, whose identity is seen by those members as precisely defined, that they approve of active efforts by members of the group to change the way of life of people seen by them as existing outside their boundaries, in order that as many such outsiders as possible, whatever their present origin and status, should become members of the group in the future. The aim of this book, then, is to investigate whether anyone in antiquity did in fact subscribe, implicitly or explicitly, to such a notion of

---

[7] Cf. Bilde, 'Causes of the Jewish War'.

[8] Eusebius, *Ecc. Hist.* 4. 13. On the history of the forgery, see Bickerman, *Studies in Jewish and Christian History*, iii. 153.

universal proselytizing mission—and, if someone did, who, when, why, and with what effect.

There is little need to justify tackling such a topic despite its complexity. The Christianization of the Roman empire had so marked an effect on the future history of Europe and the world to modern times that the causes of the Church's success are a subject of perennial fascination. I hope by concentrating on a single issue to avoid at least partially the dangers which have dogged much scholarship, either of imposing Christian presuppositions in the study of adherents of pagan or Jewish cults,[9] or of reducing religious behaviour and convictions to purely utilitarian terms, so that a decision to join one cult rather than another may seem to have had no more significance than a choice of club.[10]

Modern attitudes to mission give study of the ancient variety extra relevance. The issue of universal Christian mission, never entirely dormant but sometimes subdued within the Church, was given fresh life by the discovery of the New World and the prospect of a harvest of new souls at the beginning of the Renaissance, but it reached its acme in the missions sent to Africa and elsewhere during the last century.[11] Now, in some quarters, there has been a dramatic change, and a new desire among many Christian theologians for tolerance in a pluralistic society.[12] Supporters of both attitudes have always been able to appeal to isolated texts which were composed in antiquity. It seems pertinent to examine the ancient evidence as a whole—not just for Christian mission but for such mission in comparison with the religious attitudes of the other inhabitants of the ancient world with whom they came into contact.

A third incentive to undertake this task, and chrono-logically the first to bring my attention to the subject, is the

[9] This tendency is perhaps most noticeable in the highly influential work of Cumont, *Religions orientales*.

[10] The very useful study by MacMullen, *Paganism*, sometimes tends towards this approach.

[11] On the more recent history of Christian mission there is a large literature. See for instance Verkuyl, *Contemporary Missiology*.

[12] This motive is explicit in the introduction to Marty and Greenspahn (eds.), *Pushing the Faith*.

role often ascribed to Jews and Judaism in the history of mission. It is often asserted by scholars of early Christianity that the impulse to missionary activity in the first-century Church, and the model for its operations, lay in contemporary Judaism.[13] I shall present evidence against this view in Chapter 4, and, although in the final chapter I shall suggest ways in which the Jewish background may indeed have been an important factor, I shall be proposing a relationship very different from that normally ascribed. My scepticism is not entirely novel, for others have hinted at or asserted similar doubts in the past, though without sufficient persuasiveness to turn the tide of scholarly opinion.[14] But this is not just a question of setting the record straight, for I want to bring out also the *consequences* of denying that first-century Jews were keen to win proselytes from the gentiles.

The attribution to Jews of a missionary impulse akin to that of the early Church has created for many scholars an artificial need to explain why Christians eventually 'succeeded' and Jews did not. Thus it is sometimes argued that Jews were too demanding of converts to win more than a few[15] even though Christian taboos on sexual relations, and the extraordinary duties, culminating in social ostracism or death, which the Church expected from new members in the early centuries, were as tough on converts as anything that the Jews demanded in their circumcision, food, and purity laws.

Others claim that Judaism as a nationalistic religion was hindered from the universal mission on which Jews would otherwise have embarked,[16] an argument which contains a particularly blatant element of Christian theology: because Christians have claimed, at least at times, to champion an outward-looking universalist and therefore missionary religion in contrast to the inward-looking, nationalist, and therefore selfish Judaism which preceded Jesus, such writers assume that outward-looking universalism was inevitably missionary and that a nationalist religion could not be. In fact

[13] Most explicitly, Jeremias, *Jesus' Promise*; Georgi, *Opponents of Paul*.

[14] Munck, *Paul and the Salvation of Mankind*; Gager, *Kingdom and Community*; Rokeah, *Jews, Pagans and Christians*; McKnight, *Light among the Gentiles*. See now Will and Orrieux, *Prosélytisme juif*.

[15] So e.g. Whittaker, *Jews and Christians*, 267–8; Frend, *Rise of Christianity*, 126.

[16] Hengel, *Judaism and Hellenism*, i. 313.

neither assumption is justified. It was quite possible for individuals to uphold a universalist religious view of the eventual salvation of the whole world without any desire now to incorporate outsiders into their group: that, indeed, is the view of the Hebrew prophets often quoted as the ideological forebears of the Christian mission and therefore artificially distinguished from the rest of Jewish teaching.[17] It is worth noting that the teaching of the prophets was always canonical for Jews from the third century BCE onwards and was much quoted by even the most nationalistic Jews, without any perceived conflict between their view of universal eschatological salvation and the role of the nation.

Much of this argument is rendered otiose if in fact there was no Jewish proselytizing of the Christian type before Christianity. If Jews indeed did not win huge numbers of proselytes (which for certain periods is itself a debatable proposition (see below, p. 63)), it may have been not because they were unable but because they did not try.

In the search for universal proselytizing mission in the strong sense I have defined, much of the ensuing pages will be filled with intricate discussion of fragmentary evidence, but it would be naïve to expect the truth to emerge simply from the empirical study of a collection of quotations. Any extrapolation from a few statements in biased sources to a depiction of complete religious systems is bound to remain hypothetical. In this case, it is not even obvious quite how many religious systems ought to be analysed. Neither Christianity nor Judaism comprised a monolithic and static corpus of beliefs and attitudes in this period. On the contrary, the first three centuries CE witnessed exceptional development within both traditions.[18] Nor did the religious attitudes of pagans lack change in the same years.[19] The temptation in a study of comparative religions to assume that at least one item of

[17] Remnants of this notion are still to be found in Schürer, *History*, iii. 140: 'the stream of prophetic religion was not entirely stopped by the strict observances emphasised by the Pharisees.'

[18] For a corrective, see Segal, *Rebecca's Children*.

[19] Note the suggestive notion of a 'new paganism' in the 1st cent. CE, put forward by Veyne, 'Évolution du paganisme', 259, 279–83.

comparison was constant needs to be firmly resisted. Any claims that attitudes ascribed by Homer to the gods or prescribed in the Hebrew Bible or attributed in the Gospel to Jesus remained normative for pagans, Jews, and Christians respectively in the second to fourth centuries CE must always remain hypothetical unless there is evidence from the later period of widespread concurrence with such earlier attitudes. Ancient religions were all highly conservative and attached great value to continuity with the past. Hence all the more reason to suspect that change and innovation may have been disguised or denied by ancient writers themselves, and the need for vigilance to trace religious evolution.

It is a hazard of any comparative study that the factors investigated may seem more obviously pertinent to one system being compared than it does to the others. In theory a clear model of how religions may have worked might obviate this danger, but I am not sure that in practice such models can ever be wholly divorced from the concerns of some existent religious system. I suspect that the issues I shall raise in this book arise most naturally in a study of Judaism rather than Christianity or paganism. Thus the difference between a general educational mission to enlighten humankind and a proselytizing mission to convert all humans to membership of a specific religious group, a distinction on which I shall concentrate for much of this study, can be most clearly observed in the case of Jewish teachers and may sometimes appear artificial when applied to the doctrines of pagan philosophers or Christians. If this is indeed a distortion, it is at least distorted from a different perspective to that of previous scholars, for whom investigation of Christian and pagan evidence has been primary and the Jewish material only of interest as afterthought or background.

In any case, a bias towards *either* Jewish *or* Christian views of what matters in religion is almost inevitable in an investigation of *overt* attitudes because so much more evidence of religious thinking survives from their traditions than from ancient paganism. The concepts of pagans must usually be deduced either from the assertions of contemporary non-pagan observers or from hints—literary, archaeological, or epigraphic—about their behaviour. The clearest surviving accounts of religious attitudes written by insiders within the relevant system come from the streams of Catholic Christianity and rabbinic Judaism which have flowed unbroken to the present day. The predominance of such evidence is only partly a result of this important fact of continuity. Jews and Christians were pre-eminently and peculiarly devotees of the written word as icon,[20] and the tendency to write down their beliefs, which is often seen as evidence of a desire to persuade a literate audience and sometimes as evidence in itself of missionary intent (see below, Ch. 4), may in fact only be a form of spiritual self-communing through writing. But in any case the result is that it is much easier to hazard a guess at their theological attitudes than those of adherents of pagan cults, whose only written expression was often an uninformative dedication on stone.

Such reliance on Judaeo-Christian categories is particularly hazardous because the Jewish and Christian literatures of this period also shared peculiar notions about a future eschatological age different in kind from the present world. This belief raises a problem specific to them, which is the distinction of beliefs about a future time from desires for the present. Theological notions about the expected status and role of outsiders in the last days may have been entirely divorced from attitudes to such outsiders for the time being.[21] It is particularly difficult to make this distinction in some cases because it is probable that some Jews and Christians in fact did in some periods think they were living in the last days,[22] and indeed many of the primary texts which refer to early Christian mission were probably composed under precisely those conditions.

One further theoretical problem, which arises from the definition I have given of universal proselytizing mission,

[20] The literature on this topic is immense, but biblical scholars are perhaps not always aware of the oddity of such an attitude. See Lightstone, *Society, the Sacred and Scripture*, and my comments in 'Sacred Scripture'.

[21] See esp. Fredriksen, 'Judaism, the Circumcision of Gentiles, and Apocalyptic Hope'.

[22] See e.g. Horsley and Hanson, *Bandits, Prophets, and Messiahs*; Sanders, *Jesus and Judaism*.

applies as much to pagans as it does to Jews and Christians. In that definition I distinguished a mission to win outsiders from the imposition of order within society, and I remarked that the latter phenomenon, possibly unlike the former, was very common (above, p. 5 f). But the word 'society' is slippery. It is not always obvious to which society or societies an individual might feel that he or she belonged. It is not unreasonable to argue that the notion of society is essentially mythological, or that individuals are (within limits) free to choose whom to consider as a neighbour—hence the long debates among Jewish and Christian theologians about the precise referent of Leviticus 19: 18 ('You shall love your neighbour as yourself'). After 212 CE all Jews, Christians, and pagans alike within the empire were entitled to consider themselves as full participants in Roman society if they so wished, since they all had Roman citizenship.[23] Since in some moods or rhetorical flourishes Romans could equate their empire with the inhabited world, the *oikoumene*, what appears as universal mission *might* simply be the viewpoint of members of a universal society which they wished to see unified.

Might be—but was not necessarily. The crucial issue will be to discover whether missionaries who sought to convert others to their beliefs or groups saw themselves *at the time of their missionary activity* as members along with their auditors of such a universal society. For these purposes the social group to which an individual can be said to belong must be defined by that individual's self-perception. An inhabitant of Oxford may view him- or herself as Oxonian or British or European or, like advocates of the new paganism, as part of the natural order in which boundaries between animal species are not significant. Residents of the city of Rome in the imperial period could attribute religious significance to the *pomerium* around the city, which marked a boundary within which only approved sacred rites could be publicly established,[24] at the very time that they could see themselves as at the centre of a world state. But despite this

---

[23] See Sherwin-White, *Roman Citizenship*.
[24] Price, 'Boundaries of Roman Religion'.

fact that an individual might feel himself to be part of different social groups at the same time, and acutely aware of dual loyalties and duties when the interests of those groups came into conflict, it seems likely that *in any one transaction* involving other people he would always be able to say whether he saw those others as part of his group or as outsiders for the purpose of that transaction.

However that may be, for the historian seeking to understand the past, such multiplicity of group loyalties in any one person makes it hard to establish, simply by collecting evidence of behaviour, when missionary attitudes were aimed at perceived outsiders, and when nothing more was intended than the imposition of order within society. So, for instance, it was probably rare for any Jew to see his Roman citizenship as relevant to his religious persona, and other Romans as somehow part of his society, but it was not impossible. After all, St Paul described himself as a Roman according to Acts 16: 37, admittedly at a particularly sticky moment, and Josephus in *Against Apion* stressed to his Roman audience those qualities of Judaism that he thought might most appeal to them.[25] Even for a Jew who viewed all non-Jews as outsiders it was not always obvious who came into the latter category, since the definition of a Jew was as open to dispute in antiquity as it is now. It was not clear whether only those who professed Judaism as a religion should be urged to repent and to worship as God required, or anyone of Jewish ethnic origin. If the latter, it was hard to know whether one Jewish parent or two was the necessary condition to bring someone within Jewish society.[26]

Christians lived with similar ambiguities as to what constituted the society in which they operated. Hermas was warned in a vision, probably in the late first century CE, that he was required to suffer punishment because he had failed to prevent the sins of his household (*Shepherd*, 66. 2 (ed. Joly) = *Simil.* 7. 2). St Paul in his epistles preached the importance of good order and correct attitudes within the wider group of each city's *ecclesia*. The apostle John was so

---

[25] See Goodman, 'Roman Identity of Roman Jews'.
[26] Goodman, 'Identity and Authority'.

appalled at the presence in a bath-house of Cerinthus, the 'enemy of truth', that he fled for fear the building might collapse on all who shared with him the space within its confines (Euseb. *Hist. Eccl.* 3. 28. 6). Christian authors before Constantine often berated the Roman state for its persecution of the faithful but, although many pre-Constantinian Church fathers were Roman citizens, none of them, so far as I can discover, seems to have ascribed the troubles of the empire to the failure of sufficient Romans to recognize Christ. In other words, in religious contexts pre-Constantinian Christians apparently did not in general see their Roman-ness as relevant to their universal mission. Instead they tended to see themselves as part of a society of other Christians. If heroic enough in facing martyrdom, a Christian like a deacon from Vienne named Sanctus might even profess his faith alone in answer to an official request to name his nationality and city (Euseb. *Hist. Eccl.* 5. 1. 20). Non-Christians are usually described in the texts of the early Church as outsiders—'nations' or *ethne* (cf. Euseb. *Hist. Eccl.* 5. 7. 5), the equivalent of *goyim* for the Jews.

Faced by such ambiguities and problems I shall concentrate the investigation in this book on explicit or very strongly implied evidence of a universal mission to bring people perceived as outsiders into a particular community and to convert them to the views held by that community. Evidence that could, but need not, imply such proselytizing will be examined but will in general be discounted. Nor will even explicit statements in the sources always be taken at face value. So, for instance, not every reference by an author to the benefits of his teaching for 'everyone' or 'all men' should be read as evidence of his universal message, as is too easily done when such passages are taken out of context, for the use of such terms may conceal contrary assumptions. Thus the modern world has only recently become aware of the way that language which appears to include everyone, like the demands for universal suffrage in Britain in the nineteenth century, in fact often excludes women and children. Such exclusions in apparently universal language are possible because the perpetrators are at least temporarily unaware of the contrast between particularism and universalism which theologians take for granted. Similarly, both in antiquity and today, rabbinic sermons about moral behaviour may veer between the duties of all humans and those of adult male Jews. A female gentile seeking moral advice would have been bemused and disconcerted by such ambiguity, but since the rabbis presupposed that the audience which mattered consisted of other adult male Jews they were not concerned to distinguish which rules applied only to them and which to all humans. So it is advisable to be very cautious before concluding, for example, from a text in which Philo implied that, in contrast to exclusive pagan mysteries, the Torah was set out in the market place for the benefit of every man (*De Spec. Leg.* 1. 320), that the question of his attitude to the winning of gentile proselytes has thereby been resolved.[27]

By imposing such conditions I have clearly stacked the odds against finding evidence of an attitude which can be described as universal proselytizing mission. But such scepticism is justified not least by the probability that religion in general, apart from a new religion like early Christianity, changed more slowly in ancient societies than in contemporary life, or, indeed, in Europe since the Reformation.

One reason for this is that the concept of a separate sphere of human activity designated as 'religious' is not one easily found in antiquity before the late Hellenistic period. Even then only isolated intellectuals in late-Republican Rome, men such as Lucretius and Cicero, tried to analyse the relation of men to the divine as a general problem.[28] For ordinary people the gods were usually taken for granted and men were seen to differ only in the way they approached and placated the numinous. The religion of each society comprised the rites and rituals, the buildings, feasts, and competitions with which the benevolence of the gods was celebrated and petitioned.

Since such behaviour was an integral part of society it can be argued that it is misleading for modern scholars even to

[27] On rabbinic notions of Jewish identity as 'centripetal', see S. Stern, 'Jewish Identity in Rabbinic Writings'.

[28] See W. C. Smith, *Meaning and End*, 21–3, who brings a wider perspective to this whole question.

attempt what could only be an artificial separation between it and the other institutions and customs of ancient cultures in order to examine its function. None the less it has long been claimed, with some justification, that the rites which enshrine human attitudes to the divine played a special role in reinforcing the norms of human relations. Although ancient societies also possessed other devices to indicate the limits of membership, it was often primarily by common participation in, and adherence to, a particular series of religious rituals, that a social group defined its identity and excluded those who did not belong, and the nature of the rituals reflected or symbolized the social structure either as it was or as those responsible for such rituals believed it should be.

The great advantage of such a structuralist–functionalist view of religion as both reflecting and reinforcing social relationships is that in some societies it can be confirmed empirically.[29] Myths about the gods reflected the relationships that obtained between different groups within society; when society changed for whatever reason—external pressure, economic growth or whatever—the old myths might be abandoned and new ones adopted. At the same time both myths and rituals served a purpose by demonstrating that current society was sanctioned by divine approval: the powerful erected temples, paid for sacrifices, feasted the people in the company of the gods, and so on. To call such behaviour by ruling élites of society a manipulation of religion is too cynical, if only because, as already noted, they did not distinguish their control of religious life from their control of other spheres of life. None the less, to the friendly outsider, as Polybius, for instance, was in mid-Republican Rome, the function of the cults of the gods in preserving the social order was apparent (Polyb. 6. 56. 6–15).

Civic religion of this type flourished in the way described just as much in the early Roman empire as in classical Greece. Indeed, it can be argued that civic pagan religion fulfilled an even more central function within Greek cities of the eastern provinces in the imperial period when political autonomy no longer gave each city the separate proud identity it had

[29] See J. P. Gould in Easterling and Muir (eds.), *Greek Religion and Society*, 1–33.

boasted in the days before the rise of Macedon. There is plentiful evidence that many individuals still sought their identity not, or not only, as subjects of the great Hellenistic kingdoms or of the Roman empire but as citizens of proud *poleis* whose competition, no longer over territory and power, was confined to building programmes and other conspicuous expenditure to beautify and glorify. Among the main recipients of such expenditure were the gods. Citizens brought glory to themselves and to their fellows by erecting temples to house the gods, by funding processions, festivals, and games to please the deities. The gods brought the citizens together in a glow of proud social unity, as they had always done.[30]

If religion in antiquity had performed this function *only* as a sort of social cement, it would be hard to see how there could ever have been any possibility of a proselytizing mission to win outsiders. But the religious history of late antiquity was more complex. At some time in the period after Alexander the Great some individuals in the Mediterranean world began, perhaps for the first time in European culture, to find a different social role for religion, and to distinguish a specifically religious sphere of life from the rest of social and political behaviour. The obvious groups whose sole reason for existence was their religious function were, in fact, communities of Christians, but clubs dedicated to other cults were also increasingly found in the cities of Greece, Asia Minor, and Italy from this time. Thus the *collegia* in Italy in the second century BCE dedicated to the worship of Dionysus were seen by the Roman state not only as not integral to stable Italian society but as a positive threat.[31] Entry into such clubs was always optional and rested on a personal decision by an individual to devote himself especially to that particular deity. Except in the case of members of the exclusivist Jewish and Christian cults, which usually forbade worship of other gods, membership of such groups did not involve any disengagement from ordinary civic religion. An individual, so

---

[30] See Brown, *Making of Late Antiquity*; Lane Fox, *Pagans and Christians*.
[31] North, 'Development of Religious Pluralism'.

long as he was a polytheist, could to a large extent divorce his optional private religious life from his public persona.

Since by the third century BCE there was thus choice at least for some people between different private cults, it is true to say that there *might* have been competition, and a comparison between the missionary attitudes of Christians and those of other cults is therefore a logical possibility. But choice does not *imply* competition. Tourists with the means to travel may descend on a great variety of beauty spots and, if sufficiently attracted, may even go native. If the natives in one place are especially unwelcoming, potential visitors may choose to go elsewhere, but if the locals are neither hostile nor inviting, the traveller's decision will depend on other factors, such as the fabled delights of the landscape, the rumoured excellence of the cuisine, and the accessibility of the site. So too, *mutatis mutandis*, for religious choices.

One further complication. During the course of the fourth century CE in the Roman empire this picture of static social religion combined with a variety of optional private cults was much complicated by the elevation in the eyes of the state of one optional cult, Christianity, to a position of prime importance for the preservation of society. All religion became in some sense optional, although some religious stances were favoured with more official approval than others. Even after the attempted imposition of orthodoxy by the emperor Theodosius near the end of the century, the state still assumed (correctly) that some of its subjects chose to remain as pagans, even if many of their cult practices were forbidden. For such pagans, as for Manichees, Jews, Christian heretics, and other such deviants, their religious choices to a large extent could dictate their social status in the empire. From the point of view of orthodox Christian emperors all such subjects were ripe for conversion. But once Christianity was the religion of the state as a whole, such conversions of inhabitants of the empire could be seen as the imposition of the correct attitude to the gods on to a single society whose unity was desired, not as a mission to outsiders.

It is not easy to enter into the thought processes of ancient individuals in the way I have described as necessary to understand the origins and consequences of a universal mission to win converts. But in the chapters which follow I shall subject to scrutiny as much as possible of the evidence which has at one time or another been held up as evidence for non-Christian missions of this type. I hope that in the end the investigation may reveal those aspects of the attitudes of some early Christians to adherents of other religions which were novel in their time. In the final chapter I shall examine possible reasons for the origins of such notions within the Church and suggest some of the consequences of their emergence in late antiquity.

2

The Diffusion of Cults and Philosophies
in the Pagan Roman Empire

A TRAVELLER who visited the many thousands of towns and cities of the pagan Roman world at the height of the empire in the second century CE would have been struck by the similarities of religious and philosophical outlook to be found even in the most disparate regions. Such partial homogeneity, at least among the urban élite, was a result of the transmission and diffusion of ideas over many centuries. Most scholars believe that this entire process occurred through osmosis and imitation, and thus without regard to the desires and intentions of those who propagated such ideas. I think that they are probably right, but it is obvious that other explanations are also possible, and in this chapter I shall therefore investigate whether any pagan at any time felt a sense of mission to encourage others to share his or her beliefs; whether such mission was educational, apologetic, informative, or proselytizing; and whether it was universalistic or directed to specific groups.

Such an investigation will necessarily be far more impressionistic and speculative than the analysis of Jewish and Christian attitudes to be undertaken in later chapters, for paganism was never a single articulate system of thought; it was defined negatively by the early Church as the religion of all those inhabitants of their society who were neither Jews nor Christians. The attitudes of such polytheists can best be studied from two, quite separate perspectives, for polytheists rarely preached any doctrine or ethical code drastically separate from that of the communities in which their rituals were practised, and hence their rules for social conduct and general theories about the role of man in society usually

evolved within philosophical systems elaborated by élite
secular teachers. I shall look first at the diffusion of pagan
cults. In the second half of the chapter I shall consider the
spread of philosophical ideas.

What, then, was the attitude of the devotees of any particular
pagan cult to those outside their number? Did they feel that
such people needed to be informed or educated? Did they
believe that it was important to gain the benevolence of
outsiders towards their god? Above all, did they ever feel
themselves to be part of a defined group of worshippers into
which all humans should be drawn?

The answer to the last question will, in the end, be
'probably not'. But proving a negative is never easy, and in
this case particular problems arise. Most of the evidence about
pagan cults in general is derived from inscriptions and
buildings. Precisely because there was usually no philosophy
in paganism, rationalizations of pagan religious behaviour are
rarely to be found in ancient evidence (see above, p.15): a
writer like Varro or Plutarch discussing pagan cults was
interested in the origins of shrines and the peculiarities of
particular rituals rather than the overall justification and
meaning of such worship. Extant discussions of the theory of
pagan worship by pagans are therefore limited to the works of
a few philosophers, such as Cicero. For the rest, the rationale
of pagan worship was much discussed by Christian writers of
the time and, to a lesser extent, by Jews: thus, for instance,
one of the most important descriptions of the cult of Mithras
is that found in Tertullian.[1] But such Judaeo-Christian
discussions of 'idolatry' were of course undertaken only for
the purpose of hostile dismissal. Not only are such descriptions liable to fall into inaccuracy through polemics, but the
whole framework through which they were viewed was itself
Judaeo-Christian. These religions were shaped into an alien
and uncomfortable mould solely in order to exhibit their
shortcomings in the eyes of those for whom the mould was
natural.

There is no easy way to overcome such problems in seeking

---

[1] See Cumont, *Textes et monuments figurés*; Vermaseren, *Mithras, the Secret God*.

to discover pagan attitudes towards missionary activity. It is not to be expected that the social, political, or legal record of ancient states will often have preserved comments on, or traces of, the spread of pagan cults. Unlike Jews and Christians, the adherents of no pagan cult claimed that the worship which they advocated superseded those practised already. Since they did not attack existing cults, and since there already existed in all pagan societies a greater or less multiplicity of divinities worshipped, there was rarely any reason for the state to express opposition to or horror at the innovation which new cults represented. When such opposition was occasionally expressed, it was directed not at the cult itself but at its mode of worship: the classic example is Roman repression of the cult of Dionysus in Italy in 186 BCE (on which more below). Paucity of information in ancient sources about the spread of cults cannot, therefore, be taken to *prove* anything about the missionary zeal, or lack of it, with which such cults were spread.

Nor is much to be gained by hunting in the extant literature for a pagan justification for mission or its lack. Only very few personal accounts of the relationship between any one pagan individual and the gods survive from antiquity. These have been much studied: the last book of Apuleius' novel, *The Golden Ass*, where the fictional story of the hero's conversion to worship of Isis is recounted, or the tortured questionings of the apostate from Christianity, the emperor Julian. That they are not representative is obvious, if only because in the former case the heightened emotions are part of a novel intended to entertain and in the latter case Julian's religious mentality had been formed by the Christian education he underwent until adulthood. The only solution is to make deductions about pagan attitudes from remarks made in passing in secular literature and in religious inscriptions, and from the epigraphic and archaeological evidence for the location, spread, and popularity of particular cults. The result is not very satisfactory, but it is not entirely negligible.

That new cults *did* take root in established Mediterranean societies from the Hellenistic period onwards is beyond doubt; this fact was a prime cause of the emergence of the notion of a separate religious sphere of life which I discussed in Chapter 1. A plethora of cults could be discussed, but those best attested from inscriptions and shrines in the Roman imperial period fall into two main types. On the one hand, there were the so-called oriental cults, such as the worship of Isis and Serapis (whose mythological origins were traced by devotees back to Egypt) or Mithras (whose origins were believed to lie in Persia, although there was nothing very Persian about Mithraism in the Graeco-Roman world).[2] The appeal of such cults may have lain partly in their exotic character. Rather different were the cults which reflected the power of Rome, most obviously the goddess Roma, the personification of the city, and the worship of emperors, either dead (directly) or alive (more ambiguously).[3]

Thus it is a reasonable question to ask whether the devotees of such cults as did spread ever positively desired any outsiders to join their group and, if they did so, whether they would have been glad in principle if *all* outsiders had joined.

It can be stated immediately that, at least in theory, it was not impossible for pagan polytheists to think in this way. Some pagan intellectuals, and perhaps other pagans too by the first century BCE, seem to have understood the concept of the unity of all mankind.[4] Plutarch (*De Alex. fort.* 8; *Mor.* 330d) implied that he regretted the failure of Alexander the Great to subject all upon earth to one *logos* and one constitution as one people. The notion that a god could be all-powerful was widely expressed in ancient prayers and invocations: such language did not necessarily imply monotheism,[5] but it did imply that it would be effort well spent for any individual anywhere to worship such a divinity. Since the gods, like children, might be thought to like as much attention as possible, it could have been thought, on the face of it, a useful favour to him or her to win more worshippers; so Teiresias argued in Euripides' *Bacchae* (line 321) that Pentheus should be able to understand Dionysus' desire to be worshipped,

---

[2] See the survey of the evidence in Vermaseren, *Die orientalischen Religionen*.
[3] On the emperor cult, see especially Price, *Rituals and Power*; Fishwick, *Imperial Cult in the Latin West*.   [4] Baldry, *Unity of Mankind*.
[5] Lane Fox, *Pagans and Christians*, 34–6; Versnel, *Inconsistencies . . . Ter Unus*, 35 and *passim*.

since the gods' delight in being honoured is no different to that of men. Conversely, since the anger of the gods at insufficient attention was believed to be terrible, it might have been thought in the interests of an existing adherent of such a cult to ensure the peace of the world by forestalling divine wrath.

The problem with this theoretical model is that we do not know precisely what attitude ancient pagans ascribed to their own favourite gods when they considered the attitude of those divinities towards people who had never heard of their existence. The possible existence of such unknown gods was self-evident. The cynical view that the gods are, so to speak, created by the human societies in which they are worshipped can hardly have been generally espoused by participants in the religious communities in question. Poets might invent names for previously unidentified divinities but they could not invent the divinities themselves.[6] The argument of Euhemerus that the gods were simply ancient humans, deified by a grateful posterity for their great deeds, was branded by Plutarch (*De Is. et Os.* 23) as atheism.

But what did such deities think of those who ignored them? All pagans knew that anyone who *openly* doubted the power of a god risked exemplary punishment, even if the offended deity was as celebrated for kindness to humanity as Asclepius the healer,[7] but it was less obvious that a god would punish humans for omissions caused by unavoidable ignorance.

What, then, according to the gods, was the religious duty of all humans? On the one hand, some tendency to worship gods was reckoned to be innate in humans, and it was therefore taken for granted that the gods in general disapproved of total atheism. But divine dislike of atheists might still permit any one individual consistently to ignore any one god without expectation of retribution, if that god had not specifically demanded attention.[8] The so-called 'collegiality'

---

[6] On invention by poets, cf. West, *Hesiod Theogony*, 31–7; for the occasional argument in antiquity that men invented the gods, see the references cited by Walbank, *Historical Commentary on Polybius*, 741–2, on Polyb. 6. 56. 6–12.

[7] Pleket in Versnel (ed.), *Faith, Hope and Worship*, 181.

[8] On atheism, see Meijer in Versnel (ed.), *Faith, Hope and Worship*, 216–32, 259–62.

of the gods in late paganism[9] ensured disapproval of those who ignored the whole system, but it precluded jealousy between gods. The notion, of course, went only a certain distance. Inclusive formulas in invocations, intended to ensure that the god most interested in the prayer did not get left out, were standard in Roman state prayers from early times and were common in antiquity. The altar 'to the unknown god' alleged to have been found by St Paul in Athens (Acts 17: 23) betrayed a similar attitude, even if the story be considered an artificial invention. But on the whole late antique gods presented themselves as purveyors of benefits to those they favoured rather than as capricious, frightening forces liable to attack humans without warning.[10] Polytheists reckoned that the gods were well aware that not everyone could have a close relationship with each and every one of them. As in human friendships, not many people can strike up a close friendship with everyone they meet. Most people will remain neutral or mildly benevolent towards those with whom they have no time to forge a firmer bond. So too with gods—which was just as well for humans. For ancient pagans the world was full not just with the numerous divinities whose names survive in myth and dedications. A myriad others, of greater or less power, many yet unnamed, existed and (being immortal) always had existed. Only the most superstitious of men, as defined and derided by Plutarch in his magnificent treatise *On Superstition*, would believe that, for example, the great goddess Tyche, who presumably was reckoned to have enjoyed her power over men's lives indefinitely before men started to worship her in the Hellenistic period, felt offended at such negligence before she was 'discovered'.[11]

The best way for an individual to check which gods demanded his worship was to ask an oracle. If no heavy hint came from such a divine source, only a fool would waste time and money in prayer to a divinity proclaimed by humans

---

[9] Cf. Geffcken, *Last Days of Paganism*, 58.

[10] See Fowden, 'Between pagans and Christians'. On inclusive formulae, see Versnel in Versnel (ed.), *Faith, Hope and Worship*, 13; Veyne, 'Évolution', 275.

[11] See M. Smith, 'De Superstitione', in Betz (ed.), *Plutarch's Theological Writings*, 1–35.

alone, unless those humans came ready armed with proof of the god's power.[12] Simply to latch on to a new cult could be not only foolish but dangerous. Isis threatened with death those who came uninvited to her festivals. She preferred to issue her own instructions about who should be initiated into her mysteries. The hero of Apuleius' novel, *The Golden Ass*, had to wait impatiently at her shrine until she appeared herself in a dream for the purpose (*Met.* 11. 21–2).

Such divine initiatives were common. Veyne has argued that their frequency increased in the 'new paganism' of the early empire, unlike the old paganism of classical Greece in which humans more arbitrarily chose which gods to patronize, and the gods were in any case believed to be more capricious.[13] But greater evidence for the phenomenon may only be an accidental by-product of more extensive epigraphic survival. The demand of Dionysus for Pentheus to worship him in Euripides' *Bacchae*, a play composed at the end of the fifth century BCE, is a perfect example of this divine behaviour allegedly characteristic only of a later age. In any case, in all periods failure to obey when instructed was disastrous, as, in the play, Pentheus discovered. Penitential inscriptions which apologized for the non-worship of their author declared that his guilt lay precisely in his failure to answer the divine call.[14] According to Plato (*Resp.* 2. 7, 365a), itinerant soothsayers who offered relief in this life and after death promised terrible things for those who foolishly neglected to sacrifice in their rites.

In some ways this picture of an ancient theology with regards to those who did not worship any particular divinity seems logical enough, but it creates some difficulties of its own for those who attempt to understand pagan minds. Many complaints at the general neglect of altars and temples in particular places and periods survive from antiquity. But modern historians blithely discuss, alongside the rise to prominence of some cults in the Roman empire, the *decline* of others. What no-one stated in antiquity, so far as I know, is the attitude to such neglect which those men responsible for

---

[12] Macmullen, *Paganism*, 96.   [13] Veyne, 'Évolution'.
[14] See e.g. *MAMA* 4(1933), n. 281, cited in Burkert, *Ancient Mystery Cults*, 138 n. 55.

it, if they were conscious of it, themselves attributed to the gods thus slighted. People knew these divinities probably wanted to be worshipped—hence their existing temples and their altars. If there was any logic to the gradual lapse of worship, no polytheist is known to have discussed it. At the same time, failure to pay proper respect to those gods assumed to want such respect was a theodicy constantly available as explanation of misfortune whenever disaster struck.

Perhaps the main reason for pagans' lack of clarity about the fate they predicted for those who did not share their cult preferences is that most polytheists did not see themselves as belonging to any distinct group simply by virtue of their devotion to a particular divinity. Most of the time worshippers partook in a variety of rites without any one of them becoming the main focus of their religious self-identification; in A. D. Nock's terminology, they adhered to cults rather then converting to them.[15] However, devotees of a small number of optional cults in the early Roman empire do seem sometimes to have developed a sense of social identity which drew them together with their fellow-worshippers in contrast to the outside world. Thus the hierarchy of grades for members of Mithraic groups may have imported a powerful sense of belonging, reinforced by precise definition of status within each group. It is likely that Mithraists in one place felt a sense of communion with those elsewhere, encouraged by the relative uniformity of the detailed iconography found in Mithraea in different parts of the empire and sentiments like that apparently enunciated, if it has been deciphered correctly, on the dipinto from the Mithraeum beneath the church of Santa Prisca in Rome: 'Hail to the Fathers from East to West [under the] care of Saturn'.[16] Similarly, worshippers of Isis might sometimes feel bonds to their fellow-devotees. Thus a graffito in Pompeii alleged that the Isiaci (along with the goldsmiths and other craft groups) supported a particular candidate in the local election to the aedileship (*ILS* 6419f),

[15] Nock, *Conversion*, 15.

[16] On Mithraism, see in general Vermaseren, *Mithras, the Secret God*; on the iconography see Campbell, *Mithraic Iconography*; on the dipinto, see Vermaseren and van Essen, *Excavations in Sta Prisca*, 179–84.

and, according to the fictional account in Apuleius' novel, *The Golden Ass*, the hero Lucius was passed on, after his initiation into Isis worship in Corinth to the Isiac community in Rome (*Met*. 11. 26).

Distinctive, self-defined communities, then, but did their members want new recruits? Not necessarily. All the epigraphic evidence for the spread of new cults which *may* have been the product of deliberate proselytizing *may* also be evidence of the operation of other factors. One should allow for the movements of worshippers who took their cults with them to new places, such as those responsible for the erection of the first shrine to Serapis on Delos in the third century BCE.[17] New family members intermarried with such immigrants might become devotees. Or the name of a new divinity might be attached syncretistically to an existing native shrine, as in the adaptation of many Celtic cults to Roman religion in the northern provinces of the empire.[18]

Even when specific information happens by chance to survive about the process by which a particular cult was introduced to a certain place at a certain time, its import is often ambiguous. Thus, for example, among the many papyrus documents preserved in the Zenon archive of the mid-third century BCE was a report by a certain Zoilos in 257 BCE that he had been instructed by the god Serapis in a dream to erect a temple for him in a city far away in Asia Minor. His account has been taken by some scholars as evidence of the instinctively missionary nature of the Serapis cult. But its purport may in fact be the precise opposite. If the building of temples abroad was an obvious duty to the divinity, what need of a dream?[19] A more detailed look at two narratives composed in the early imperial period about the spread of religious cults may demonstrate the problems involved in finding evidence for proselytizing.

In the first of these narratives, the Roman historian Livy

---

[17] See Tran tam Tinh in Sanders *et al.* (eds.), *Jewish and Christian Self-Definition*, iii. 110–11.

[18] On syncretism in Romano-British religion, see Henig, *Religion in Roman Britain*, ch. 3.

[19] Tran tam Tinh in Sanders *et al.* (eds.), *Jewish and Christian Self-Definition*, iii. 110.

wrote a long account (39. 8–19) of the spread through Italy in 186 BCE of the secret rites of Dionysus.[20] His history was based on a true story, for a bronze inscription containing the decree of the Senate issued at the time of the events described happens to survive (*ILLRP* 511), but since Livy's historiographical technique entailed shaping his material to fit his own perception of how things were, his narrative may reasonably be treated as evidence of beliefs about religious behaviour in his own time also, the late first century BCE. According to Livy (39. 8. 3–4), the rites of the Bacchanalia were introduced into Etruria through the teaching of a certain 'low-born Greek', a 'mere sacrificer and fortune-teller'. This Greek was emphatically not described by Livy as a teacher who openly proclaimed his news (which Livy implies would have been all right); rather, he was a 'hierophant of nocturnal rites' which 'at first he divulged only to a few' (39. 8. 5). Only once the idea was planted did the rites begin to spread widely among both men and women 'because of the delights of wine and feasts' (ibid.). The rites diffused through Italy, according to Livy, not through the efforts or perhaps even the intention of the 'low-born Greek' or other missionaries, but 'like a contagious disease' (39. 9. 1); the image, which cropped up again in the description by Pliny the Younger of the spread of Christianity in the countryside of Pontus in the second century CE (*Ep.* 10. 96. 9), may have been standard in pagan understanding of the way that undesirable cults gained a hold on a new crop of adherents. In any case neither the episode nor Livy's description of it in themselves constitute good evidence of a proselytizing mission by worshippers of Dionysus.

The second narrative is avowedly hostile, the satirical account by Lucian of the foundation by a certain Alexander of an oracle in Paphlagonia in the middle of the second century CE.[21] Lucian claimed that this oracle, which uttered

---

[20] See North, 'Religious Toleration in Republican Rome'; Gruen, *Studies in Greek Culture*, 34–78. On Dionysiac *thiasoi*, see discussion in Burkert, *Ancient Mystery Cults*, ch. 2.

[21] See Robert, *À travers l'Asie Mineure*, 393–421, and recent discussions in Jones, *Culture and Society in Lucian*, ch. 12; Lane Fox, *Pagans and Christians*, 241–50.

prophecies on all subjects through a half-human, half-serpentine creature named Glycon who was reputed to be Asclepius reborn, was in fact a fraud, and his description of its great success was vitriolic. Such vitriol may or may not have been deserved, but since the numerous dupes castigated by Lucian evidently felt that Alexander's behaviour conformed to what they expected of advocates of new religious cults, it may in any case be possible to discover something from Lucian's narrative about some pagans' attitudes to mission.

According to Lucian, Alexander organized an energetic apologetic and propagandistic mission on behalf of his 'New Asclepius'. He raised hopes by sending men abroad to create rumours. Glycon could 'make predictions ... discover fugitive slaves ... cause treasure to be dug up ... heal the sick ... raise the dead' (24). He sent oracle-mongers everywhere in the empire to play on fears, warning the cities to be on their guard against disasters against which only Glycon could prevail (36). But Lucian did not report any proselytizing by Alexander. He did not encourage his victims to join any defined group or, indeed, to adopt any new way of life. This was not for lack of any notion of a special circle or specific teachings: Alexander had an inner coterie of noble young men known (scandalously) as 'those within the kiss' (41) and he preached a strong sexual ethic, disapproving (hypocritically) of intercourse with boys (ibid.). But, if Lucian is to be believed, the favours of the god were promised just as liberally to those outside the group as to those within: anyone with money to pay could buy divine aid. In principle, according to Lucian's Alexander, Glycon was concerned for all humans, although he did not intend to leave Abonoteichos for a further one thousand and three years; only after that time would he visit Bactria and its environs to bring profit to the barbarians as to the Greeks (43). But such barbarians, when eventually favoured by the god's visit, would be expected to bring offerings in gratitude but not to join any new group of devotees.

Of all the pagan cults known to have been widely disseminated in the early Roman empire, perhaps only one was, at least potentially, a proselytizing religion, and that was the imperial cult, the worship of emperors. Recent studies, particularly by Simon Price, have shown the importance of understanding such worship in the context of pagan theological theory, and not just as part of the manipulation of political power by the state.[22] It is likely that the main motive force for the introduction of emperor worship in some areas, particularly in the Greek-speaking East of the empire, came from the provincials themselves, but official approval must always have been implicit, since emperors were acknowledged to have the right to intervene if they disliked the building of shrines in a particular place (cf. Tac. Ann. 1. 78), and occasionally in the West encouragement was explicit: thus the altar to Rome and Augustus set up at Lyons in 12 BCE was erected, according to coins issued at the time, on the initiative of Augustus' own grandsons. Nor was this just a mission to inform, for those who participated in the cult thereby signified their membership of a quite specific group defined by fellow devotees—that is, the Roman empire. In the same way they undertook the adoption of a specific frame of mind—namely, loyalty to the Roman state.[23]

In some ways, then, the imperial cult in the early Roman empire was a fine example of a proselytizing religion, if, as some may with good reason deny, it is justified to treat the very varied forms of emperor worship found in different areas of the empire as disparate manifestations of a single cult. Matters are only slightly complicated by the fact that the individual encouraging emperor worship might also sometimes be one of the gods himself—if the emperor was seriously reckoned to be a god, and he indicated by whatever means that he wished to be worshipped, it would be as rash to disobey him as any other god. Furthermore, this proselytizing religion was at least potentially universalist in its claims, for the Roman state, of which the imperial cult was the prime religious expression, sometimes claimed sovereignty over the whole world. Thus Vergil wrote about Roman dreams of dominion without end (Aen. 1. 279) and Cassius Dio (52. 35. 5) put into the mouth of Maecenas the argument that an

---

[22] Cf. Price, *Rituals and Power*.

[23] On the altar at Lugdunum, see Fishwick, *Imperial Cult*, i. 97–149 (esp. 148), 308–16. On the imperial cult as a binding factor in the empire, see K. Hopkins, *Conquerors and Slaves*, 197–242; Gordon, 'Veil of Power", esp. 226–8.

upright emperor would be rewarded by the grant of all the earth as his precincts. But the obvious political role of emperor worship prevented any mission outside Rome's actual borders on behalf of the cult. It does not seem to have occurred to pagan Romans (in contrast to later Christian emperors) to encourage those outside their political control to join their religious community.

In sum, attitudes to mission varied greatly in ancient polytheism. When it occurred, mission was usually apologetic and propagandistic. The many inscriptions found in shrines proclaiming to passers-by the power and benevolence of the divinity may be included in these categories; their prime aim was simply to praise the god, on the assumption that the gods, like men, love to be honoured. Only occasionally did the adherents of a cult with particular awareness of the significance of its geographical spread, such as the advocates of emperor worship, indulge in proselytizing. Even in their case there is no evidence that their ambitions were universalist in scope. No pagan seriously dreamed of bringing all humankind to give worship in one body to one deity.

The search for universal proselytizing will prove equally unproductive in a scrutiny of the process by which philosophical ideas were diffused in the Roman empire. This may seem surprising, for it has been quite widely supposed that philosophers in the Hellenistic period and after were eager to convert to the tenets of their philosophy as many individuals as they could reach. In the ancient world the idea was sometimes expressed quite crudely, as in Lucian's satirical picture of 'The Sale of Lifestyles'.

There is certainly evidence that many philosophers wished to change the lives and attitudes of others. On a general level, the popular image of a philosopher in the early Roman empire was of an unkempt man with a long beard who harangued the public on street corners. A figure like Apollonius of Tyana, the archetypal wise man, visited other Greeks and barbarians in the late first century CE not only to learn but to teach (Philostr. VA 1. 26; 6. 11). Both Cynics and Epicureans, in particular, seem to have been keen to make others aware of their doctrines. Since conversions to a philosophy could involve just as radical a break with past behaviour and outlook as is ascribed to new Christians, teachers of philosophy have thus sometimes been seen as paradigms of universal proselytizing mission.[24]

With how much validity? The notion that it was a possible function of a public speaker to teach people how to live was enshrined in the rhetorical theory of Isocrates already in the fourth century BCE.[25] It was just such instruction that was widely disseminated by the followers of Epicurus so that others should benefit from the freedom of care preached by their founder;[26] similarly Cynics believed themselves to have a duty to the service of the god by going about among men as his messenger to show them good and evil (Epictetus, 3. 22. 46–7, 69). Cynics sought publicity—sometimes dramatically, as in the case of the notorious self-immolator Peregrinus— presumably to this end, for the content of their diatribes became so standard that it constituted a separate literary genre.[27] Not all Cynics wrote—perhaps not all were literate, since Cynicism was more a way of life than a philosophical system—but enough philosophical material professedly influenced by the Cynics survives to indicate the Cynics' own justification for their teaching. They were pedagogues of mankind, doctors of men's ills and so on, moved, they claimed, by philanthropy.[28]

Philosophers, then, wanted to teach; in terms of the typology outlined in Chapter 1, they had at least an educational mission. But what did they hope to achieve by such teaching? They wanted their pupils to believe in their doctrines, but did they care whether those pupils recognized the origins of those doctrines in their particular school?

Philosophers believed that they themselves belonged to select groups of the knowledgeable, those who understood what was important in life. It would be wrong to assume that they therefore necessarily felt any need for their groups to be

---

[24] Nock, *Conversion*, ch. 11.

[25] Jordan, 'Philosophic "Conversion" ', 91–3.

[26] De Witt, *Epicurus*, 329.

[27] See Dudley, *A History of Cynicism*, 110–16.

[28] On the relations of the Cynic with ordinary men, see Moles, 'Honestius quam ambitiosius', 111–16, citing earlier literature.

organized. On the contrary, the followers of most Greek philosophies do not seem to have organized themselves into groups of any kind. 'Orphic' teaching was widespread in the fifth and fourth centuries BCE, but we do not hear of Orphic groups (unless that is what the term 'Orphikos' on a recently discovered graffito in Olbia refers to);[29] despite the firm foundation of Stoicism in the doctrines of a particular group in the Stoa in the late fourth century BCE, there is no evidence that Stoic communities were identified as such in the Roman period.

None the less, at least two philosophical schools, the Pythagoreans and the Epicureans, did organize themselves into distinct communities. In both cases they presented themselves as religious fellowships dedicated to the goddesses of culture and the teachings of the founder. The Epicureans are better known than the Pythagoreans because much of the evidence about the latter derives from neo-Pythagoreans of the early fourth century CE such as Iamblichus, who, in a large-scale enterprise to revive Pythagorean philosophy, incorporated many Christian anachronisms into the master's teaching.[30] Epicureans, by contrast, in late Hellenistic times and in the early Roman empire, talked about themselves as members of a defined community, preserving the ideal of philosophical fraternities which could ensure the orthodoxy of their scattered brothers by oaths to Epicurus, worship of his image and epistles to one another to uphold the consistency of the faith. Their propaganda, mostly oral, was occasionally written down, as in the great work of Lucretius. Did Epicureans, then, want as many people as possible to join their community? And what sort of reaction did those philosophers who never formed themselves into any kind of social group, such as Stoics or, even more blatantly, Cynics, look for when they approached ordinary people with their ideas?

Historians of the philosophical schools, like Diogenes Laertius, who wrote probably in the first half of the third

---

[29] Burkert, *Ancient Mystery Cults*, 46.

[30] See Burkert in Sanders *et al.* (eds.), *Jewish and Christian Self-Definition*, iii. 13–14. On Epicurean communities see Malherbe, ibid., iii. 46–59; De Witt, 'Epicurean Contubernium'.

century CE, sometimes described philosophical conversion as a radical change which involved not only total commitment by the convert to a new way of life but also his involvement for the rest of his life in the philosophical school itself (cf., for example, *Diog. Laert.* 4. 16–17). Such a reaction to philosophical protreptic was therefore possible. But it is hard to know whether either Cynics or Epicureans would have been pleased if all of their audience had rushed to imitate them in this way.

'The aim of the [Cynic] system is not to produce little Cynics. . . . the Cynic labours not on behalf of his movement but of mankind.'[31] The listener, hearing the ragged philosopher rant as he went about his mundane business, was expected to pause, reflect and re-evaluate his role in the world, but he was not expected to adopt the Cynic way of life himself. Only professional philosophers were expected to dissociate themselves from normal society. No explicit texts show that Cynics believed that it was even *possible* for ordinary men to become full Cynic *anthropoi*. It is possible in theory that the silence of the sources about such an attitude can be explained by the assertion that it was simply assumed, but such silence would be strange, since it was precisely for their failure to care about their fellow men that some harsher Cynics were sometimes attacked.[32] For such harsh Cynics, there was no reason to approach other men at all unless it was socially necessary; the Cynic's happiness was ensured precisely by his stance somewhere outside ordinary society.[33] But what of the milder Cynics who, out of altruism, hoped to affect others? The evidence is consonant with a limited desire to change the attitudes of their audience rather than to encourage the full adoption of a Cynic lifestyle.

As for the Epicureans, the sincerity of their mission to inform cannot reasonably be doubted. Diogenes of Oenoanda spent a great deal in the late second century CE to tell his fellow citizens Epicurus' teachings and to bring them to

---

[31] Dudley, *A History of Cynicism*, 88.
[32] See discussion in Moles, 'Honestius quam ambitiosius', 113–16. Moles, however, believes that this lack of explicit evidence is not significant.
[33] Malherbe, 'Self-Definition among Epicureans and Cynics'.

happiness.[34] The motive of Epicurus, according to Lucretius, was compassion for those living without such understanding, for the unenlightened are miserable. But, despite the existence of Epicurean communities, neither author hints that the audience should strive to join such a community. That would be supererogatory.

On reflection it may seem that the logic of Cynic or Epicurean enthusiasm for teaching outsiders is not obvious. Both philosophies showed how to live without cares, how to rise above and beyond the petty concerns of ordinary mortals. It is not clear how Epicurean *apatheia* or Cynic disdain are aided by the spread of their teaching, and if no such causal link could be found it might even appear as a betrayal of principles to expend energy and raise passion precisely in the dissemination of the message that such behaviour was not worthwhile. But the existence, indeed prominence, of street-corner Cynic preachers, shows that such logic was often ignored.

Illogical behaviour should not, perhaps, surprise too much. Greater emphasis should be put on the psychological argument against a proselytizing rather than educational mission. Consciousness of their role as teachers to the unenlightened enhanced the philosophers' consciousness of their own superiority and gave extra value to their doctrines. At the same time the continued blindness of the majority of society to the truth was essential in making sense of their own stances. Both Epicureans and Cynics preached essentially negative philosophies. Happiness came through non-conformism. In a world where no one conformed, their doctrines would lack value. So, for instance, Cynic preaching against ambition and materialism would be irrelevant in a society in which neither quality was to be found.

In sum, it seems unlikely that adherents of any of the distinctive philosophies of the early Roman empire sought converts to their own self-defined groups. Their aims were much more limited. Whether from pure altruism or more mercenary motives (cf. Justin, *Dial.* 2), they tried to influence

---

[34] For the main body of the surviving material, see Chilton, *Diogenes of Oenoanda.*

the general behaviour of men for the better, to instil a little of their doctrines into the lives of others and so to improve society as a whole and make people happy. Their aim was universal in scope, but their mission was to educate rather than proselytize. According to Cicero (*Fin.* 2. 15 (49)), the influence of Epicurus was felt not only in Greece and Italy but also among all the barbarians, but how this came about, and how Cicero could know such a thing, is hard to tell. It seems probable that, if there is any truth at all in his claim, which is patently rhetorical, barbarians followed Epicurus' tenets by chance, unselfconsciously, but that raises the difficult philosophical question of the feasibility of true happiness without knowledge.

It may be significant that the two philosophical systems most widely adopted in antiquity were not those of the Epicureans or the Cynics who so keenly sought to broadcast their ideas. Both Stoicism and Platonism entered the common currency of the thought at least of the élite who produced the extant literature of the early imperial period. In neither case was any attempt made by members of any clearly designated social group to increase their membership by spreading their ideas. The last great Stoic philosopher, Marcus Aurelius, never even identified his ideas as Stoic,[35] preferring to portray himself as a philosopher *tout court*, without explicit affiliation to any particular philosophical sect. Marcus Aurelius just adopted those Stoic notions that seemed to him to be true. Thousands of others did the same, and thus philosophical notions were disseminated just as Hellenism itself spread in the eastern empire and Latin in the west in the same period— by imitation and emulation. There was no place here for the strong notion of a proselytizing mission to win converts to a particular, clearly self-defined group.

[35] See Rist, 'Are you a Stoic?'; Rutherford, *Meditations of Marcus Aurelius.*

3

Judaism before 100 CE
Attitudes to Gentile Paganism

A LOGICAL prerequisite for a universal proselytizing mission to convert others to a new religion is a belief that their present religious behaviour is unsatisfactory. Only if I believe that something is wrong with the present state of affairs can I persuade myself or others of the need for change. Such unsatisfactoriness might take any of a number of forms. The current behaviour of other people might be considered wicked or foolish or just insufficient. In this chapter I shall tackle the question of Jewish attitudes to gentile paganism as a prelude to the investigation in Chapter 4 of Jewish attitudes to proselytizing.

I am aware that anyone who begins a discussion of a complex issue such as this by defining terms risks inducing sleep in audience and readers. I must therefore apologize for my intention to devote some time to precisely such definitions. My excuse lies not only in the slipperiness of two of the main terms used in the chapter heading, but in the hope that discussion of definitions will in fact considerably advance the argument. Something needs to be said about the concepts 'Judaism' and 'gentile', and I shall spend some time trying to explain my decision to separate my studies of Judaism into attitudes before and after 100 CE. The only contentious term left undiscussed will be 'paganism', which I shall understand in the simplest way as any form of worship of divinities other than the God of the Jews and Christians.

Analysis of attitudes in 'Judaism' before 100 CE is fraught with problems. Evidence for Jewish religious concepts between 300 BCE and 100 CE has to be culled from a variety of disparate sources, each of which presents a more or less partial picture. For all Jews by this period the Pentateuch acted as a foundation document for morality, and by the late second century BCE most of the other books of the Hebrew Bible were also treated as sacred texts, but the interpretations of such writings varied widely. The extent of such variation has become vividly evident with the discovery of the peculiar writings of the sectarian Jews whose scrolls were hidden towards the end of this period in caves by the Dead Sea. In recent years it has even become fashionable in some quarters to talk about Judaisms in the plural, as if Jews shared no common core of beliefs about anything.[1] Such scepticism is probably too extreme, but the existence of such a trend should induce caution in those who are prone to quote single statements culled from the works of one or two Jewish authors of the period as if they can be taken without further argument as representative of the ideas of all or many Jews of their time. If uniformity was to be found in any area at all, it should perhaps best be sought in the publicly observable behaviour of Jews, such as the observance of the sabbath and basic food laws, rather than in theology. It is therefore important to note that, most of the time, Jews' attitudes to gentiles, which fell into the category of theoretical theology, encountered little or no pressure towards the creation of an orthodoxy.

A further spur to caution should be the inherently unrepresentative nature of the surviving evidence. Most post-biblical Jewish writings composed before 100 CE survive only through the good offices of early Christians who preserved them for their religious value. Some found their way eventually into Christian collections of the apocrypha of the Old Testament. Others, including some much quoted by the Church Fathers, are known collectively to modern scholars as the pseudepigrapha (misleadingly, since some are anonymous and others were assigned from the start to their real authors). It can reasonably be assumed that, out of the mass of Jewish literature available to them, early Christians chose those whose theological attitudes were either close to their own or

---

[1] See e.g. Neusner, Green, and and Frerichs (eds.), *Judaisms and Messiahs*. On variety, see in general, Kraft, 'Multiform Jewish Heritage'. For an attempt to define the common core of Judaism, see Sanders, *Judaism*.

in some other way pertinent to the development of the Church; it is hardly likely that Jewish literature was preserved at this early period of Christian history out of antiquarian interest alone. The survival of the contemporary Dead Sea Scrolls and of rabbinic texts of a slightly later date provide a useful insight into the sort of Jewish material that Christian copyists ignored. It is, then, reasonable to expect that the Jewish literature which was preserved by the Church might reflect something of the early Christians' interest in gentiles; conversely, it may plausibly be asserted that any lack of such material may be significant.[2]

Much the most important of the writings which survived through the Christian tradition are the works of Philo and Josephus. The temptation to treat their viewpoints as typical of all Jews, or even a large proportion of them, should be resisted. Philo was a Jewish politician in the cosmopolitan city of Alexandria in the Egyptian delta. He made a brave attempt to interpret the Torah allegorically in order to make it conform to his interpretation of Platonic philosophy. Appeal to general Greek philosophical concepts may have been quite widespread among the better-educated Jews who wrote in Greek: thus Stoic ideas were crudely incorporated into the moral exhortations of 4 Maccabees and the Wisdom of Solomon, and into the unsophisticated allegorical writings of the philosopher Aristobulus, who wrote in Alexandria in the mid-second century BCE. But, so far as is known, Philo's developed allegorical method was not paralleled, and his uniqueness may be partially confirmed by the preservation of so large a corpus of his writings. These philosophical outpourings proved so well attuned to the interests of the early Church that by the fourth century Philo was believed by some to have been a Christian. Since Christians did not preserve any other Jewish non-biblical writings in similar quantities, it is reasonable to suppose that such writings could not be found.[3]

The survival of Josephus' writings has a related but different cause. Three of his extant works dealt with Jewish

---

[2] For a survey of this literature, see Schürer, *History*, vol. iii.

[3] On Philo as atypical, see Vermes and Goodman, 'Littérature juive', 30–9.

history: the *Jewish War*, which analysed the causes and course of the Jewish war against Rome in 66–70 CE; the *Antiquities*, which recounted Jewish history from the beginnings up to 66 CE, in the process paraphrasing much of the Hebrew Bible; and the autobiographical *Life*, which was mostly concerned with his career during the war years 66–7 CE. Josephus' fourth book, *Against Apion*, constituted a detailed defence of Judaism, ostensibly against the malicious slanders of Greek writers but in fact often against straw opponents whose alleged insults could easily be controverted. Josephus' intended audience was, for the most part, gentile, and his apologetic was slanted accordingly, although the first, non-extant, edition of the *Jewish War* was written in Aramaic partly for the benefit of non-Judaean Jews, but Josephus' theological outlook, unlike Philo's, was not easily compatible with Christianity and cannot be the reason for the preservation of his work.

It seems likely that Christians who copied Josephus' writings did so not because they valued his ideas but because his narrative provided useful information for the comprehension of the life of Jesus and the story of the Old Testament in a historical narrative composed in a fairly clear Greek style with a sense (albeit a faulty sense) of chronology. Of particular importance in that narrative was the so-called *Testimonium Flavianum*, the passage in the eighteenth book of the *Antiquities* in which the Jewish historian mentioned in passing the career of Jesus in Palestine during the reign of Tiberius. The version of the *Testimonium* to be found in the medieval manuscripts of *AJ* 18. 63–4 has undoubtedly been much emended by later Christians, but the existence of *some* remarks about Jesus at this juncture in Josephus' original narrative is very plausible, not least because the preceding and subsequent passages do not fit well together without a linking episode such as the Testimonium. It is worth noting that if Josephus' writings were thus preserved by Christians, for reasons other than his theological stance, it is likely that his works will have reflected a Judaism less conforming to Christianity than Philo's.[4]

[4] See in general on Josephus, Rajak, *Josephus*; Bilde, *Flavius Josephus*.

In some contexts equally good evidence for first-century Judaism comes from the only Pharisee apart from Josephus whose first-hand account of part of his life survives—that is, St Paul. That Paul thought of himself as in some sense Jewish throughout his Christian mission is obvious from his own claim to be an 'Israelite, of the seed of Abraham, of the tribe of Benjamin' (Rom. 11: 1), and his willingness, despite being a Roman citizen, to submit to the disciplinary jurisdiction of synagogue authorities (2 Cor. 11: 24). He was patently a peculiar sort of Jew, so one can hardly deduce from his actions and attitudes what was standard for Jews in his day. But it is reasonable to seek in his writings for evidence whether he himself saw his own belief that gentiles were wicked idolaters who needed rescuing from their sin as, *mutatis mutandis*, the attitude of ordinary Jews. Converts may adopt entirely new evaluations of their past lives, but they rarely forget them altogether.[5]

Such evidence will bring the discussion of Judaism in this chapter to the end of the first century CE. Why stop there, and not 100 years before (at the birth of Jesus), 100 years later (to coincide roughly with the compilation of the Mishnah), or 400 years later (to take the discussion to the end of antiquity, and the completion of the Babylonian Talmud)? The *terminus ad quem* is not arbitrary, and the fact that it divides the discussion of Judaism in this book into two roughly equal chronological periods is no more than an accidental bonus of dividing the material in this way. Justification for stopping the discussion around 100 CE lies in the inherent likelihood of a change in Jewish attitudes to gentiles at just this time.

The most obvious reason to suspect such a change was the destruction of the Temple in Jerusalem by the Romans in 70 CE. The reason for that destruction lay primarily in the vagaries of Roman politics. Whatever the original causes of the Jewish revolt in 66 CE, the demolition of the Temple was not a natural or inevitable consequence of failure. Roman troops had conquered other rebellious peoples and yet

[5] On Paul's writings as evidence for Jewish history, see Segal, *Paul the Convert*, pp. xi, xv–xvi.

continued to treat their gods as powerful. Furthermore, when shrines were destroyed, as was a frequent occurrence, Rome expected sooner or later to rebuild them. Numerous inscriptions, and sometimes archaeological evidence, record such reconstructions. The Roman state might even provide a subvention to the cost of the new shrine, particularly when the God had enjoyed the patronage of powerful Romans in earlier times. Jews might reasonably think that their Temple, one of the wonders of the world, would receive similar treatment. After all, a Roman general like M. Vipsanius Agrippa had taken the cult sufficiently seriously to sacrifice a hecatomb there to the Jewish god, and the Roman emperors took so seriously the daily offering of a loyal sacrifice to the Jews' powerful divinity on their behalf that the cessation of those sacrifices in 66 CE had marked the beginning of revolt.[6]

For pagan polytheists, who took seriously the power of a myriad different gods, respect for existing cults, so long as they were categorized as religions rather than superstitions, was thus a self-evident norm, and what happened in Jerusalem in 70 CE was therefore a disaster that could not easily have been predicted. Vespasian, the general in command of the Roman forces sent to crush the Jewish rebels, was quite unexpectedly proclaimed emperor by his troops in 69 CE despite his humble birth and minimal military competence. Installed in power through bloody victory in civil strife, he needed a rapid, impressive and visible foreign victory to justify to the Roman people his seizure of the empire. Thus his son Titus risked—and sustained—huge loss of life among his own soldiers in a successful assault on the walls of Jerusalem in the spring of 70 CE: it would take too long to win the city in the normal way, by circumvallation and inducements to surrender. And when victory was achieved the emperor's propaganda requirements precluded portrayal of the campaign as what it really was—the suppression of insurrection in a comparatively minor provincial backwater.[7]

The new Flavian dynasty chose to make the greatest

---

[6] For my analysis of events in 66 CE, see Goodman, *Ruling Class*.
[7] See ibid. 236–9.

propaganda capital possible out of their efforts, and proclaimed the defeat of the Jews as, in effect, a victory against atheism on behalf of the gods. In the ceremonial triumph in Rome in late 70 CE Titus paraded the candelabra, incense burners, and other utensils of the Jerusalem Temple. Vespasian proclaimed the restoration of the peace of the gods.[8] By common consent the suppression of Jewish *superstitio* was to be applauded. The Jerusalem Temple, where (notoriously) no image was to be found, was easily portrayed as a mockery of religion, a cult to atheism. Only in their most philosophical moods did pagan polytheists imagine a god who not only lacked a cult statue but by definition could never be seen; it is worth recalling that the proof of a god's power often lay in his epiphany.[9] In any case, and more cynically, Titus was impelled to proclaim the Jerusalem cult illegitimate by the fact that his actions had caused its destruction, and the sacrilegious burning of the shrine of a genuine god would be the worst of omens for the new dynasty. It was obvious to everyone that, at least in the immediate future, the Jerusalem Temple could not be rebuilt.

The catastrophe deeply affected all Jews. The Temple lay at the heart of worship even for those Jews, like the Dead Sea sectarians, who believed that the priestly hierarchy of the first century invalidated the sacrifices by their wickedness. It is therefore traditionally supposed that after 70 CE Judaism changed dramatically into a personal, private religion in which individual and communal prayer and the study of Torah took the place of Temple sacrifices. The fact of such a change, which lies at the heart of the development of rabbinic Judaism between the second and fifth centuries CE, is beyond dispute, but more dubious is the precise date when Jews made the shift to a religion no longer centred on the Temple. I have already noted that the destruction of a great religious sanctuary which had previously enjoyed Roman protection, and Vespasian's refusal to permit its reconstruction, were quite abnormal in Roman history. In the late 70s CE Josephus pleaded implicitly in the *Jewish War* for the restoration of the

---

[8] Fornaro, *Flavio Giuseppe*, 71–2.
[9] So Lane Fox, *Pagans and Christians*, 102–67.

shrine, advancing the implausible claim that, despite all the imperial propaganda which revelled in the act, the destruction had occurred against the wishes of Titus (*BJ* 6. 254–66). As time passed it presumably became evident to all Jews that Flavian prestige was too bound up with the Temple's demise for rebuilding to be contemplated, but Jews could still hope for a reversion to previous policies when the dynasty came to an abrupt end with the murder of Domitian in 96 CE, particularly since the new emperor Nerva was an avowed enemy of the previous regime.

I suspect that the year of Nerva's accession witnessed a great ferment of hope and expectation among Jews, now that the family which had persecuted them was gone. Prime among their aspirations was a rebuilt shrine; plenty of priests still survived to restore the cult. Josephus' *Against Apion*, which can be firmly dated only to some time after 93 CE but which I believe best situated after the death of Domitian, pronounced the rites performed in the Jerusalem Temple as the essence of Jewish worship.[10] I think it likely that the expectation in the Epistle of Barnabas (Ep. Barn. 16. 3–4) that there will soon be a rebuilt Temple should be taken as evidence to date that work too in the same period. The detailed discussion of Temple ritual by the tannaitic rabbis of the Yabneh generations suggest that they too took for granted the restoration of the cult. Whether that was still entirely true by the end of the second century CE, when these rabbinic discussions were codified into the Mishnah, is perhaps more dubious, for by that date some of those discussions had a decidedly theoretical feel, but it seems likely that the move from discussions over Temple procedures which might any day be put into practice, to the construction of a theoretical model of Temple worship whose actual institution was not envisaged, was the result of no sudden change but a gradual process over years.

The beginning of that process, I suggest, was not in 70 CE, when the catastrophe was too recent for people to construct coherent rationales for what had happened or alternative theodicies for the future, but in 96 CE, when it became clear

---

[10] On the dating of *C. Apionem*, see Schürer, *History*, i. 54–5.

that the new dynasty began by Nerva and Trajan was not going to reverse the anti-Jewish policy of the Flavians, and that Judaism was, for the foreseeable future, a religion deprived of its central institution. By that time, too, the disaster was sufficiently distant in time for Jews to be able to take stock of what had happened. Similarly the theological implications of the Holocaust are only properly being tackled by the generation which has followed those who went through it; the sufferers themselves tended at the time to interpret events only as confirmation of their existing ideologies.

In 96 CE the process of self-evaluation was further enhanced by a new awareness of what it meant to be a Jew or a non-Jew. This awareness was impelled primarily by changes in the imposition of the Roman tax levied on Jews after 70 CE, the *fiscus Judaicus*.[11] The details of these changes I shall leave to Chapter 6. It will suffice for the moment to suggest that the desire of the Roman state to define who was Jewish for the purpose of this tax may have brought to the surface a novel concern to clarify the status of those people attached to Jewish communities who, when it came to the crunch of payment of the tax, fell on the non-Jewish side of the divide.

It is probable that before this tax reform in 96 CE neither Romans nor Jews were much concerned to define precisely who was Jewish—and, therefore, that they were equally vague about precisely who was gentile. Josephus recorded the existence in Antioch of gentiles who were 'in some way' attached to the local Jewish community (*BJ* 7. 45); whether he reckoned that they were to be considered Jews or not is unclear. In some ways such lack of clarity is rather surprising. In theory it was a matter of considerable importance for a Jew to know which of his acquaintance was not Jewish. In some circumstances a non-Jew might render unusable wine and (probably) other liquids and foodstuffs simply by touch; marriage with a non-Jew would contravene the exhortations of Ezra and Nehemiah which were carefully preserved by Jews as part of sacred scripture; the Temple priests needed to know who counted as a gentile in order to avoid pollution of

[11] See *CPJ* i. 80–2; ii. 111–16.

the shrine by the entry of such people into the Court of the Israelites. But, despite the theory, in practice there existed no central authority capable of deciding such matters. There was no census, like that in Roman society, which recorded both citizenship and social rank. There was no generally recognized *beth din*, as in later Jewish history, to clarify difficult cases.[12]

Since it was recognized by all Jews that outsiders (that is, the offspring of non-Jews or mixed marriages) *could* become proselytes and therefore in some sense Jews, one can reasonably assume that the confusion caused by this lack of an agreed authority would have created acrimonious confusion if the issue had been seen by Jews as important. But in fact, and significantly, there is no evidence of such acrimony in the sources from this period. In a malicious aside about the Samaritans, Josephus noted that they described themselves as kinsmen of the Jews when it suited them and as gentile when they preferred (Joseph. *AJ* 9. 291). Josephus' assumption seems to have been that gentiles who claimed to be Jews were entitled to have their claims taken seriously. Thus, in the extended description of the conversion of the royal house of Adiabene, Izates is portrayed as having made himself Jewish by undergoing circumcision at the hands of the court doctor (Joseph. *AJ* 20. 46). Presumably any male gentile who underwent circumcision for the purpose of keeping the Jewish law was thus to be considered as in some sense Jewish. In contrast, and despite the great volume of discussion in modern scholarship about gentile 'Godfearers' attached to Jewish synagogues,[13] there seems to me insufficient evidence to posit any formal recognition of such gentiles by Jews before the second century CE when, as I have hinted above and shall argue more fully below (Ch. 6), Jews were confronted more starkly by the need to know which members of their community were Jews and which were not.[14]

---

[12] On all this see Goodman, 'Identity and Authority'.

[13] See Feldman, 'Omnipresence of the God-Fearers'.

[14] Kraabel, 'Disappearance', argues convincingly that there is insufficient evidence of a formal category of gentile Godfearers recognized as such by Jews in the 1st cent. To my mind the inscription from Aphrodisias discussed below (Ch. 6) does not invalidate Kraabel's arguments (*contra* Schürer, *History*, iii. 168), but provides evidence that a change in Jewish attitudes had come about by the time the inscription was written.

The corollary of Jews' vagueness before 100 CE about Jewish (and, by implication, gentile) identity is that Jewish notions in this period about the moral behaviour to be required of non-Jews were probably not directed at any particular set of non-Jews close to, or involved with, Jewish communities. Speculation about gentile behaviour will have had a much vaguer basis, in the theoretical theological question of the requirements imposed by the Jewish God on those who were not part of the covenant between him and Israel.

I hope that such arguments may be sufficient to justify the division of my discussion of Judaism into two parts around the year 100 CE, for it is probably no more than chance that the same period happened also to mark a change in the nature of the surviving evidence about Judaism. No extant Greek literary or religious text written by a Jew in antiquity can be shown beyond doubt to have been composed after this date, although some texts, such as *Joseph and Asenath*, may have been:[15] the separation of Judaism and Christianity after the first century rendered Jewish Greek writings irrelevant to Christians, who therefore lacked incentive to copy them. From the medieval Jewish manuscript tradition survive only those Jewish writings, in Hebrew and Aramaic, which met the approval of the rabbis of late antiquity. Papyrological evidence of Egyptian Jews came mostly to an end after the great and destructive revolt of 116–17 CE; conversely, other parts of the Jewish diaspora produced a marked increase in epigraphic data.[16] In other circumstances such changes in the nature of the evidence might encourage an assumption that apparent changes in Jewish theology after 100 CE might reflect only the different types of material from which ancient Jewish theology is refined by modern scholars. But I hope to have established at length in the preceding discussion that the end of the first century in any case marked something more important. Real historical change produced novel theological concepts after the destruction of the Temple and engendered

---

[15] On the date of composition of *Joseph and Asenath*, see Schürer, *History*, iii. 549.
[16] The evidence is collected most conveniently in *CPJ* and *CIJ*.

recognition by Jews of a need to define more precisely who was a Jew and who was gentile.

To return (as the Talmud would say) to the main subject. What did Jews between 300 BCE and 100 CE think of gentiles who took part in pagan worship? At first glance the answer seems easy. In 300 BCE the Hebrew Bible in something like its present form was nearly complete and more or less accepted by all Jews as authoritative (see above, p. 39). The most authoritative section of the Bible, the Pentateuch, is a document replete with hostility to paganism and suspicion of gentiles. Disgust of paganism predominated, since it was reckoned the prime sin of Israelites, but the genocide of the idolatrous gentile inhabitants of the land of Israel described in Deuteronomy (e.g. Deut. 2: 30–5; cf. Deut. 20: 16–18) also makes uncomfortable reading for a modern audience. However, it is crucial to see that, for the authors and ancient readers of those texts, it was the connection between gentiles, paganism, and the *land* that aroused such violent antagonism. Gentiles were dangerous because as pagans in the same country they might lead Israelites astray and cause the latter to pollute the holy land of Israel. The polemic in Deuteronomy gave no hint of Jewish attitudes to those pagans outside the land of Israel who continued their ancestral paganism without contact with Jews.[17]

Biblical laws and prophetic adjurations were aimed at Jews alone. None the less it seems fairly clear that biblical writers assumed that gentiles also had moral duties; only on that assumption did accusations that gentiles had sinned make sense. But was one such sin reckoned to be paganism? Pharaoh in Egypt was punished for refusing to obey the Lord (Exod. 5: 2; 12: 29–30), but the implication was only that gentiles were required to be neutral and to avoid opposing Israel's God. Pagan gods were depicted as ridiculous (because powerless) and sometimes as non-existent—hence the inability of the prophets of Baal to awaken their god on Mount Carmel (1 Kgs. 18: 219). Gentiles who worshipped such

---

[17] So Novak, *Image of the Non-Jew*, 108–11. See in general ibid. 107–65, for many of the ideas expressed in the following pages.

divinities—and in practice, of course, this category included all gentiles—were therefore considered laughably foolish but not necessarily wicked. Thus paganism was not included by Amos in his list of the sins of the nations (Amos 1: 3–2: 3), and Micah took for granted that 'each of the peoples will walk in the name of its own god' just as Israel is loyal to the Lord (Mic. 4: 5). For most biblical writers Israel was required to root out pagan worship only from within the midst of the nation of Israel (cf. Deut. 12: 1–3). This was unfortunate (to put it mildly) for those non-Jews who inhabited the land where Israel settled, but it implied tolerance towards the majority of the non-Jewish world, who lived without a Jewish population in their midst.

The theology I have just described was quite coherent, but I do not wish to imply that it was in fact entirely and consistently espoused throughout the Hebrew Bible. The Bible is a complex jumble of texts composed at different periods for different audiences in a variety of genres, and the evolution of a theology about gentile behaviour was a low priority for religious enthusiasts intent on delineating the covenant between God and Israel. Within that covenant avoidance of pagan worship was so important, and the fact of gentiles' involvement with idolatry such a potential threat to weak-willed Jews who might be lured into imitation, that logic was not infrequently sacrificed to the rhetoric of hostility. On the one hand gentiles were sometimes portrayed as inherently wicked (rather than just congenitally prone to idolatry), and it was asserted that Israel can be virtuous only by total separation from non-Jews; from such an attitude derived the prohibition of intermarriage by Ezra (Ezra 9: 11–12; 10: 10–11). On the other hand paganism might in theory sometimes be seen as inherently evil, no matter by whom it was practised. But it is remarkable how little evidence survives that might conceivably testify to such an attitude. The non-Israelite setting of the book of Job was presumably intended to suggest that its hero was gentile. It may therefore be significant that at one point the author indicated clearly that if Job's heart had been 'secretly enticed' when he 'beheld the sun when it shined, or the moon walking in brightness', he would have deserved punishment (Job 31: 26–7). But since in this particular passage Job went on to assert that such idolatry would be sinful because he would have 'denied the God that is above' (Job 31: 28), it appears that at this juncture at least Job was thought of as a participant in the covenant between God and Israel—that is, as a Jew.

During the post-biblical period to the end of the first century CE Jews for the most part retained the main aspects of the biblical view of idolatry: both condemnation of Jewish idolatry and a tolerant attitude towards gentile paganism outside the land of Israel. In recent years some scholars have claimed that Jewish attitudes to *Jewish* participation in non-Jewish cults softened in the Hellenistic period, but I am unconvinced. The evidence usually cited is the undeniable fact that some Jews did participate, at least passively, in such cults. For example, some Jews in an ephebic association in Cyrene had their identifiably Jewish names (Jesus, Elazar, Judah, and so on) included on an inscription set up in a gymnasium in the early first century CE; at the bottom of the second column of one face of the stele, just below the name of Elazar, son of Elazar, was a dedication to the gods of the gymnasium, Hermes and Heracles (*CJZC* 7). Herod the Great, who liked to portray himself as a Jew however much his enemies might sneer at him as only 'half-Jewish', celebrated his accession to power as king of Judaea in 40 BCE by joining the chief magistrates of Rome in a sacrifice to Jupiter on the Capitol (Joseph. *BJ* 1. 285). But there is no evidence at all that such Jews thought they could justify their behaviour in Jewish terms. Outsiders such as Plutarch (*Quaest. Conv.* 4. 6. 2; *Mor.* 671d–2c) might syncretize the Jewish God with Dionysus but, with only a few exceptions such as the equation of God with Zeus put into the mouth of a gentile by the Jewish author of Ps.-Aristeas 16, pious Jews who remained within Judaism expressed no interest in other gods.[18] That some bad Jews went 'chasing after other gods' in post-biblical as in biblical times should not surprise. Such a tendency was indeed presupposed by the authors of the later rabbinic texts, in which the avoidance of what they called

[18] For a different view on Jewish participation in pagan cults, see Rajak, 'Jews and Christians'; for a different view on Jewish syncretism, see Lane Fox, *Pagans and Christians*, 486–7.

'alien worship' was a constant preoccupation in the definition of Jewish piety (see Ch. 6).

An indication of the continuation of Jewish tolerance of gentile paganism outside the land of Israel may be found in the interpretation of Deut. 4: 19 assumed by some Jews in pre-rabbinic writings. The biblical text states that God requires Israel to avoid all forms of idolatry (Deut. 4: 16–18): 'nor must you raise your eyes to the heavens and look up to the sun, the moon, and the stars, all the host of heaven, and be led on to bow down to them and worship them; the Lord your God assigned them for all the peoples under all the heaven' (4: 19). The clear implication is that God expects non-Jews to worship such heavenly bodies, in which case Jews are morally bound to permit such worship. Since in Jewish texts of all periods worship of the sun, moon, and stars was frequently portrayed as the archetypal form of paganism forbidden to Jews, this leniency towards gentile idolatry is quite remarkable, and in talmudic texts such tolerance caused such affront that the passage was sometimes forced into an unnatural meaning to avoid its obvious implication (see below, Ch. 6). By contrast, the masoretic text was translated literally in the Septuagint. The same attitude seems to have been enshrined in the Septuagint translation of Exodus 22: 27 (Heb.), where the Hebrew *elohim lo tekalel* was taken to mean not 'Thou shalt not revile God' but 'Thou shall not revile gods', a reading which was also presupposed by Philo (*De Spec. Leg.* 1. 53; *Vit. Mos.* 2. 205) and by Josephus (*C. Ap.* 2. 237; *AJ* 4. 207), with the argument that Jews must maintain respect for the name 'god', regardless of the being to which it was being applied.[19] The extraordinary Egyptian–Jewish writer of the third or second century BCE, Artapanus, went one step further than this liberal stance. He claimed that Moses had actually established the animal cults of the Egyptians—without in any way compromising his view that the Jewish God is master of the universe.[20]

[19] See Novak, *Image of the Non-Jew*, 121–2; Delling, 'Josephus und die heidnischen Religionen'.

[20] For the text of Artapanus, see Euseb. *Praep. Ev.* 9. 18. 23 and 27; Holladay, *Fragments*, i. 189–243.

There is little reason to suppose that such liberal attitudes in post-biblical writings constituted an element within a coherent Jewish theology about gentiles in this period any more than in earlier times. The status of gentiles was not an issue for legal debate or precision. Some of the Jewish writings from late Hellenistic and early Roman times, particularly those in Greek, were, unlike the Bible, intended at least partially for gentile readers and their authors therefore had some incentive to indicate the moral behaviour required from gentiles by Jews. Scholars have sometimes tried to read back into this literature the rabbinic concept of the Noachide Laws.[21] According to rabbis from the late second century CE and after, a small cluster of basic ethical maxims are incumbent on all descendants of Noah—that is, on all humans (see below, Ch. 6). But to my mind the pre-rabbinic passages usually cited as parallels to the Noachide laws in fact constitute evidence of the *lack* of a Jewish theology about gentiles before 100 CE. Nothing in the testament of Noah in Jubilees 7: 20–39 suggests that the ethics there urged were believed to have significance beyond the confines of Judaism. Conversely, Philo (*De Spec. Leg.* 2. 44–8) took for granted that there could exist good, wise men among the non-Jews, but the general, vague virtues he praised were those actually admired in Greek culture, not (as in the case of the Noachide laws) a Jewish blueprint for what gentile culture should be like. Whatever the historical background to the injunctions to gentile Christians in Acts 15: 29 to 'abstain from meats offered to idols, and from blood, and from things strangled, and from fornication', I see no reason to suppose that this was a simple recitation of a list of the characteristics of moral gentiles generally recognized among Jews. On the contrary, many of the problems encountered by St Paul in his dealings with Christian converts from paganism may have derived precisely from his inability to appeal to any such accepted list. Paul's determination that the rules of the Torah did not apply to non-Jewish Christians left gentile Christians uncertain where to look for ethical guidance, and Paul in effect had to invent a new morality for such people in order to prevent the

---

[21] See the literature cited by Novak, *Image of the Non-Jew*, 3–51.

moral excesses of some of his flock in Corinth and else-where.[22]

St Paul, of course, fiercely prohibited pagan idolatry to the gentiles in his communities (e.g. 1 Cor. 6: 9).[23] In contrast most of those contemporary Jewish writings which were probably aimed at a non-Jewish audience made no such demand. The author of the *Testament of Abraham* prohibited gentile homosexuality (frequently decried by Jews in antiquity) and bloodshed, but not pagan worship.[24] The Jewish writer who sheltered under the name of Phocylides, a gnomic Greek poet of the sixth century BCE, betrayed his Judaism by apparent references to moral teachings found in the Pentateuch, but presumably believed that his rather obscure gentile guise would inspire confidence and interest among gentile readers. In his text also homosexuality was attacked, but nothing was said to suggest disapproval of gentile idolatry.[25] It is worth noting that if, despite my observations above (p. 53), the ethical injunctions incorporated into the testament of Noah at Jubilees 7: 20–33 were in fact intended to apply to gentiles, they none the less included no injunction to avoid idolatry.[26]

I suspect that it simply never occurred to most Jews at this period that any gentile would consider abandoning his ancestral worship unless he was also thinking of becoming a Jew. At the point when a gentile became an exclusive monotheist, he or she in effect left gentile society. It would be an act of extraordinary folly to take such a step without at the same time entering into the alternative society of the Jews. There is no evidence that Jews expected gentiles to do anything so foolish, and no evidence that any gentile did in fact act in such a way. An inscription from Acmonia in

---

[22] See e.g. 1 Cor. 5–9; below, Chs. 5 and 8.

[23] Fredriksen, 'Judaism, Circumcision, and Apocalyptic Hope', 534, takes the attitude of Paul as evidence of general Jewish attitudes, but that begs the question.

[24] See the trans. and comm. by E. P. Sanders in Charlesworth, *Old Testament Pseudepigrapha*, i. 871–902.

[25] On this text, see Schürer, *History*, iii. 687–92.

[26] See the discussion by Collins, *Between Athens and Jerusalem*, 137–74, on the 'common ethic'. Collins, however, wishes to posit a more widespread disapproval of gentile paganism (142, 150), on the assumption that the attitude of the authors of Wisdom of Solomon and the Sibylline Oracles was standard among Jews.

Phrygia recorded the gratitude of a group of Jews in the first century CE to their benefactress, a certain Julia Severa (*CIJ* ii. 766). This woman is known to have been the priestess of a local pagan cult, but it is evident that, at least in public, the Jews who honoured her were not concerned by this fact. Her Jewish neighbours might have found her pagan practices ridiculous (although presumably it would not have been politic to say so): the emperor Claudius in the same period complained that the Jews 'set at nought the superstitions of other people' (Joseph. *AJ* 19. 290), and that such behaviour is annoying. Jews would confidently expect that in the last days Julia Severa, like all gentiles, would bury her idols (cf. Tobit 14. 6) and come to recognize the Lord alone, but such behaviour belonged to the eschatological era, not the present.[27] No non-Christian Jew in this period is known to have claimed that gentile renunciation of paganism now would hasten the arrival of future bliss. That was a doctrine unique to the Church.

The lack of a coherent doctrine about gentiles in this period as in biblical times left room for the expression by some Jewish writers of views which deviated from this tolerant norm. It has been seen above that, despite this theoretical possibility, it was hard to find in biblical texts any condemnation of gentile paganism outside the Holy Land (above, p. 49), but rather more evidence for such condemnation can be found in post-biblical texts.

The most violent attack can be found in Wisdom of Solomon, chapters 13–15, which constitutes a sustained polemic against the foolishness of Egyptian idolatry.[28] Wisdom is a strange work preserved within the Septuagint manuscript tradition. With advice familiar from biblical wisdom literature, but with a vocabulary often culled from popular Hellenistic philosophy, the anonymous author donned the persona of a Jewish king (presumably, though not explicitly, Solomon) to admonish his fellow monarchs. Those

[27] The important distinction between quotidian and eschatological Jewish views of gentiles is made by Fredriksen, 'Judaism, Circumcision, and Apocalyptic Hope', 533–48.

[28] For discussion and bibliography on Wisdom of Solomon, see Schürer, *History*, iii. 568–79.

monarchs must presumably be reckoned gentile, so in one sense the intended audience of the attack on pagan practices was non-Jewish and Wisdom looks like a fine example of protreptic intended to turn gentiles from idolatry. On the other hand it could be argued that the presumed audience was as blatantly a literary device as the assumed persona of the author, and that in fact the allusions to biblical history and the theme of the sovereignty of the Torah could only have been intended for the appreciation of Jews. But it may be wisest to leave the question of the intended readership of Wisdom unresolved, since it must be admitted that only a small proportion of its audience, Jew or gentile, would ever have appreciated it fully. In any case, Wisdom seems to have been entirely unknown to, or ignored by, all Jewish authors in antiquity outside the Christian tradition. In contrast the work was very popular within the early Church. Since Christians were strongly hostile to gentile paganism from the beginning (see below, Ch. 5), the preservation and use of Wisdom by Christians, who certainly did read it as an attack on gentile paganism, may suggest that, within the Jewish literary tradition available to the early Church, Wisdom was exceptional in providing a foothold for such an interpretation.

A similarly uncharacteristic passage is found in the writings of the anonymous Jew who composed the passages of the Sibylline Oracles which decry all worship of idols, no matter by whom (*Orac. Sib.* 3. 545–9, 601–7).[29] This author, who probably wrote in Egypt in the second century BCE, clearly intended to reach a gentile readership with his message, but it may be wondered how typical was the peculiar individual or individuals who invented oracles under the name of a pagan prophetess and succeeded in passing them off as genuine. In any case it must be emphasized that the diatribe in all such works tended to stress the foolish stupidity rather than the moral wickedness of gentile idolatry; a particularly clear example of such scorn can be found in the speech put into the mouth of the Jewish high priest by the author of Ps.-Aristeas 134–9.

In favour of viewing a tolerant attitude to gentile paganism

[29] See Collins, *Sibylline Oracles*; Schürer, *History*, iii. 618–54.

as prevalent rather than exceptional among Jews down to 100 CE some general observations may be put forward. Thus, in all the extant pagan literature referring to Jews and composed before that date, much hostile comment is to be found, but the notion that Jews object to pagans continuing their ancestral religious practices in their own lands is almost never included.[30]

The failure of anti-Semitic writers regularly to use such a powerful charge in their attacks on Jews is striking, as may be seen from the one extant passage by a gentile writer in which the charge was employed. In *Contra Apionem* 1. 248–50, Josephus reported an accusation by the anti-Jewish Egyptian author Manetho in the third century BCE that the Solymites (the inhabitants of Jerusalem) were impious (*anhosioi*) because they had pillaged Egyptian temples impiously (*anhosios*) in alliance with polluted Egyptians in the time of king Amenophis—that is, in distant antiquity. In his long polemic against Manetho's views (251–87), Josephus turned briefly to the charge that Jews had attacked pagan shrines in Egypt (264, 269, 275). The shape of his response is curious. He claimed that Manetho's story was implausible, but that in any case the Jews' actions, if they had taken place, would have been justified. Such acts were terrible (*deina*), but the invaders from Jerusalem were not to blame because they were only joining in the attacks on Egyptian shrines which had been begun by disgruntled native Egyptians. By implication, if natives had turned against their gods, it was reasonable for outsiders to join with them. This is a curious argument, and it is interesting that Josephus did not here use the argument found elsewhere (see above, p. 52) that Jews would not behave in such a way. The most significant fact to note may be that such an accusation could be made about Jews in the distant past but does not seem to have been made about Jews in the present.[31] It would surely have added greatly to the

---

[30] See the texts collected by M. Stern, *Greek and Latin Authors*.

[31] Frankfurter, 'Lest Egypt's City', 210–11, argues from this text and others that native Egyptians saw Jews as enemies of their gods from the 3rd cent. BCE. If he is correct that Jews were simply slotted into a pre-existing mythology of 'Typhonian' opponents of Egyptian divinities, Egyptian stereotypes about Jewish behaviour may have borne little connection to Jews' actual attitudes.

armoury of Apion in the struggles of Greeks against Jews in first-century Alexandria if he could plausibly have claimed that Alexandrian Jews attacked the cults of the pagan community.

The scarcity of evidence from the Hellenistic and early Roman periods for Jewish hostility to gentile paganism within gentile societies stands in marked contrast to the plentiful and unabashed information, from both Jewish and non-Jewish sources, about Jewish antagonism to idolatry in the land of Israel. Josephus recorded without apology in the *Antiquities* the actions of the Hasmonaeans in the destruction of pagan shrines and sacred precincts (e.g. *AJ* 12. 344). More positively, Jews were said by Josephus to have objected violently to the infiltration of emblems of idolatry, in the form of Roman military standards, into the land of Israel (*AJ* 18. 121), and even more against such pollution of the holy city of Jerusalem (*BJ* 2. 170). By implication they must have felt less strongly when their own sacred space was not thus invaded. According to Josephus (*C. Ap.* 1. 193), the Greek author Hecataeus of Abdera, who flourished *c.*300 BCE, even expressed *approval* of the Jews' destruction of pagan temples and altars *erected in their country*, which he saw as an instance of the Jews' admirable tenacity in upholding their laws. Even if this passage is judged to have been either part of a pseudonymous Jewish composition or the work of a Jewish reviser of Hecataeus' words, it remains significant that Josephus was evidently able to imagine a gentile Greek viewing such Jewish behaviour with favour, which would surely have been impossible if Josephus had attributed to Hecataeus a belief that Jews liked to destroy pagan cult places wherever they found them.[32]

It seems, to put the conclusion at its weakest, unlikely that many Jews in this period perceived any justification for them or their compatriots to object to the pagan idolatry assiduously practised by the non-Jews with whom they came into contact, so long as such practices did not take place in the holy land of

---

[32] On different views about the genuineness of the passage of Hecataeus quoted by Josephus in *C. Ap.* 1. 183–204, see M. Stern, *Greek and Latin Authors*, i. 22–4; Schürer, *History*, iii. 672–3.

Israel or lure Jews into an abrogation of their special covenant with their God. The implications of this tolerance for Jewish attitudes towards potential proselytes will be explored in the next chapter.

4

Judaism before 100 CE
Proselytes and Proselytizing

SINCE the work of Schürer and Juster at the beginning of this century, most scholars have subscribed to the view that Jewish proselytizing in antiquity reacted a peak of intensity in the first century of the Christian era at the time of the emergence of Christianity. This consensus has been re-inforced in recent years by some of the most influential contemporary students of Jewish history in the period, such as Menahem Stern and Joachim Jeremias.[1] Dissent, which has been expressed only rarely, has not often been argued with any great cogency. Thus the assertions of, for instance, Johannes Munck and David Rokeah have been generally ignored by mainstream scholars.[2] Despite this, I hope to show in this chapter the flimsiness of the hypothesis on which the mainstream consensus is based.

I should make it clear that I do not doubt either that Jews firmly believed in their role as religious mentors of the gentile world (so Wisdom of Solomon 18: 4), or that Jews expected that in the last days the gentiles would in fact come to recognize the glory of God and divine rule on earth (cf. Isa. 66: 19; 2 Baruch 68: 5).[3] But the desire to encourage

---

[1] Schürer, *Geschichte*: Juster, *Juifs*; M. Stern, *Greek and Latin Authors*; Jeremias, *Jesus' Promise*.

[2] Munck, *Paul and the Salvation of Mankind*; Rokeah, *Jews, Pagans and Christians*. See now McKnight, *Light*; Cohen, 'Was Judaism Missionary?'; Will and Orrieux, *Prosélytisme juif*. Much of this chapter repeats my arguments in 'Jewish Proselytizing in the First Century'.

[3] McKnight, *Light*, 47–8, emphasizes the expectation of a mass conversion of gentiles in the eschatological age. Fredriksen, *From Jesus to Christ*, 149–50, 166, and 'Judaism, Circumcision and Apocalyptic Hope', 547, by contrast emphasizes that gentiles will recognise the power of God *as gentiles*. Cf. also Donaldson, 'Proselytes or "Righteous Gentiles"?'.

admiration of the Jewish way of life or respect for the Jewish God (that is, apologetic mission) (cf. Psalm 117), or to inculcate general ethical behaviour in other peoples (educational mission), or pious hope for the possibly distant eschatological future, should be clearly distinguished from an impulse to draw non-Jews into Judaism in the present.[4]

I shall begin by laying out as clearly as possible the evidence which has been used in the past to support the view that Jews in the first century sought proselytes. In the second section of the chapter I shall try to expose the weakness of the evidence. Finally I shall offer some general reasons to doubt that Jews of any variety apart from Christianity saw value before 100 CE in a mission to convert outsiders to the faith.

To begin, then, with the evidence generally put forward to show that Jews had an active proselytizing mission in the first century. For many historians Jewish proselytizing has been seen simply as a natural corollary to the existence of proselytes.[5] In the context of the ancient world, the whole concept of proselytism was indeed highly peculiar. Jews constituted a nation which at some time before the Hellenistic period had accepted the principle that it was open to anyone to integrate him or herself into its political and social community simply by acceptance of Jewish religious customs. The potential flexing of communal boundaries entailed by such a notion is quite astounding. It is in marked contrast to the jealous preservation of the rights of individual citizens by Greek city states and the frequent exclusion of outsiders from such rights. The difference was particularly marked because, like Romans but unlike Greeks, Jews accepted the notion that their *politeia* was not fixed to any particular locality.

There is no good reason to doubt that the possibility of such conversion was generally accepted by Jews in this period regardless of the manifold problems that arose in establishing the status of particular individuals. It is true that not all those

---

[4] The distinction is drawn with admirable clarity by Bowers, 'Paul and Religious Propaganda', 316–18.

[5] See e.g. Cohen, 'Conversion to Judaism', 36. Cohen, 'Was Judaism Missionary?', 17–21, reverses his earlier position with a critique of the standard arguments similar to that offered here.

said to have 'Judaized' were reckoned at the time to be proselytes[6] and that precise markers to distinguish the boundary between gentile sympathizers to Judaism and converts could not be drawn (see above, Ch. 3, p. 46).[7] Haziness in this regard was particularly likely in considering the status of women who were putative proselytes, since there is no evidence of any ceremony taken to mark female conversion in this period (apart, perhaps, from marriage to a Jew).[8] It is possible to construct an ideal type of a proselyte as a gentile who committed himself or herself to the practice of Jewish laws, exclusive devotion to the Jewish God and integration into the (or a) Jewish community, like Achior the Ammonite who, according to Judith 14: 10, saw the power of the Lord, believed and was converted,[9] but we do not know whether all these elements were generally considered to be necessary conditions for valid conversion or only the expected norm. Native-born Jews, after all, might not always commit themselves to the laws, or to the exclusive worship of the God of Israel, but did not through their failure cease to be Jews (see Ch. 3). Separation from the community might be considered wicked but it did not in itself invalidate a person's Jewishness.

I suspect that ancient Jews were simply vague about such questions. Thus Josephus in one work (*BJ*) seems not to have distinguished a general adherence to Jews or Judaism from full conversion, whereas in the *Antiquities* at least sometimes he did so.[10] In his last work, *Against Apion*, denial of the past (but not explicitly past paganism) was explicitly predicated of (some?) converts,[11] but this was a self-consciously apologetic work about Judaism as a religion, and greater precision was called for by the literary genre. In general, Jewish writing was more prone to rhetoric than to law on the subject. The author of 2 Baruch described such gentiles as 'those who have left behind their vanity and fled under your wings', who 'first did

---

[6] Cohen, 'Respect', 416.

[7] Cohen, 'Crossing', 13; Goodman, 'Identity and Authority'.

[8] Cohen, 'Respect', 430; 'Matrilineal Principle', 29.

[9] Cohen, 'Crossing', 26.   [10] Cohen, 'Respect', 419.

[11] Cohen, 'Respect', 411–12. Cf. Cohen, 'Crossing', 27: Josephus was never explicit that proselytes were required to reject paganism.

not know life and who later knew it exactly' (41: 4; 42: 5). Shaye Cohen has pointed out that Jewish authors did not ever state as a Jewish view that proselytes become Jews (rather than just proselytes, conceived as a special sort of gentile), although the assertion that such converts become full Jews was not infrequently ascribed by Jews to gentile observers.[12] There is much evidence that Jews held a variety of opinions in antiquity about the extent to which proselytes became like the native born. In some ways even the emphasis by Jewish writers on the respect to be awarded the outsider who was joined to the community only served to stress the stance of such friendly outsiders as a separate group alongside the main congregation (so, for instance, the warning in Ps.-Phocylides 39 that the *epelys* should be held in equal honour with citizens).

However, all that is really important for the present argument was the recognition by all Jews that such a separate group could and did exist. When Tobit (Tobit 1: 8) was said to have given a tithe to needy people, including 'proselytes who attached themselves to the sons of Israel', no Jew of the Second Temple period would have wondered who those proselytes were. Even at Qumran, where the attitude to proselytes was in general rather frosty, the category itself was still recognized.[13]

Nor was the category simply theoretical. We have evidence of at least some such converts during the Hellenistic period and early Roman empire. Josephus provided a detailed description of the conversion of famous royal proselytes from Adiabene (*AJ* 20. 34–48). Acts 6: 5 refers to a proselyte of Antioch. The semi-technical use of the term 'proselytos' in the Septuagint (see below, p. 72) suggests that the right of such converts to be considered as part of the house of Israel was widely recognized by Jews. There is no evidence positively to refute the hypothesis, which has been widely canvassed, that converts made up a great proportion of the Jewish population.[14]

Both Josephus and Philo seem in general to have assumed

---

[12] Cohen, 'Crossing', 14 and 29.   [13] *4 Q Flor.* 1. 4; McKnight, *Light*, 38.
[14] So e.g. Baron, *Social and Religious History*, i. 171–3, 181.

that proselytes are to be welcomed. Philo's ethical platitude that proper nobility is not a corollary of good birth (*De Virt.* 187–91) may have implied that anyone could acquire the virtues enshrined in the Jewish Law. The author of 2 Maccabees 9: 17 rejoiced that the wicked king Antiochus Epiphanes on his deathbed promised to become a Jew. Similarly Josephus was clearly proud of the converts in Adiabene (*AJ* 20. 17–96), and he stated explicitly that Jews were happy to accept committed converts (*C. Ap.* 2. 210). The activities of some of the earliest Jewish believers in Jesus have been adduced as in themselves indirect evidence that some non-Christian Jews must have done the same thing.[15] The probable growth of the Jewish population in the period, as evidenced by the remarkable spread of Jewish settlement in the diaspora, the size of some of the communities there, and the increase in the population of Palestine apparent from archaeological survey of settlements, has been adduced as a proof that Jewish mission was successful in winning large numbers for the faith.[16]

Furthermore those who believe that Jews were keen to win proselytes point out that in certain circumstances some Jews may have insisted on gentiles' conversion. In the most dramatic instances, whole populations of gentiles are said to have been incorporated within the Jewish nation by the militant Hasmonaean dynasty. Thus, according to Josephus, the Idumaeans of southern Palestine were forced by the Hasmonaeans to convert *en masse* in the 120s BCE, and some of the Ituraeans of the northern part of the country were compelled to submit to circumcision in 104–103 BCE (Joseph. *AJ* 13. 257–8; 319). Both the Bible and the Apocrypha record with some glee how gentiles at moments of Jewish glory converted to Judaism out of fear of the Jews. The word *mityahadim*, or 'act like Jews' in Esther 8: 17, was translated in the Septuagint Greek as *perietemnonto*, or 'they were circumcised'.

More generally, even Jews as lax in their religious observance as the female members of the Herodian dynasty insisted

---

[15] Georgi, *Opponents*, 101.
[16] Feldman, 'Omnipresence of the God-Fearers', 59.

that their gentile marriage partners should be initiated into Judaism before marriage (Joseph. *AJ* 20. 139, 145). All Jews accepted the metaphor of the nation as a family into which outsiders had to be adopted to be accepted, and when a fiancé refused to take up Jewish customs, the wedding was liable to be cancelled. It is also possible, although not certain, that at this period, as later, some Jews still expected that their male slaves would submit to circumcision as stipulated in Genesis 17: 12–13. The Damascus Document of the Qumran sectarians prohibited the sale to gentiles of foreign servants converted to Judaism (*CD* 12. 10–11, Rabin p. 61). Conversion would at any rate be desirable if the slave was to be used for domestic purposes, since only if the slave was considered in some sense Jewish (or at least not an idolater) could the danger of pollution to food be avoided.[17]

Since it is possible that Jews thus sometimes insisted on conversion when they had the power to enforce their will, it has been suggested that they used persuasion when that was the only weapon available to them. Proselytes were sometimes instructed in Judaism by some Jew before conversion: the name of the teacher of the future king of Adiabene, Izates, in Charax Spasini, a certain Ananias, was preserved by Josephus (*AJ* 20. 34–42), and the traveller Eleazar who insisted that Izates should be circumcised if he wanted to follow Jewish law is often portrayed in modern scholarship as a missionary (Joseph. *AJ* 20. 43–5).

Yet more alleged evidence for Jews as proselytes has been culled from the literature written by Jews in Greek in this period. Such literature, it has been claimed, may reflect the arguments and methods used by missionaries to win converts. This literature is somewhat heterogeneous. The writings of Demetrius the Chronographer comprise a rather dry analysis of the time periods given in the biblical narrative. Philo the Elder, Eupolemus, and Artapanus rewrote the biblical stories in prose with considerable embellishments. Ezekiel the Tragedian did much the same with the narrative of the Exodus but in his case produced his reinterpretation in

---

[17] On pollution by gentiles, see Goodman, 'Kosher Olive Oil'. On slaves in Jewish law in general, see Flesher, *Oxen, Women or Citizens* (1988), citing earlier literature.

dramatic form. Ps.-Hecataeus and Ps.-Aristeas wrote glowing accounts of Judaism as a way of life and of Jews as a people, presenting themselves in the guise of non-Jewish writers. The Jewish authors of parts of the corpus of Sibylline Oracles similarly slipped comments about Judaism into the oracles they forged. Finally, at least three authors attempted to produce a version of Judaism that would fit more or less comfortably with contemporary Greek philosophy. Of these, the author of the Wisdom of Solomon made the fewest concessions to the rigours of philosophical analysis, Philo made the most. Aristobulus, who wrote in the second century BCE, lay somewhere between the two. The intended audience of such writings is not always obvious, but at the least it can be asserted that there is no proof that such literature was not meant for outsiders, and it is not totally impossible that any gentiles who read such literature were expected to react by considering conversion to Judaism.

But if it was indeed true that Jews wrote such propaganda literature in order to win proselytes, how did they expect to make sure that their propaganda was read or heard? In a time before mass printing books would only spread in single, rare copies. Enthusiasts would have to employ slaves to produce their own copies. Scholars have therefore suggested that the literature enshrines material that was disseminated more widely by oral means. It has been alleged that Jews invited pagans into their synagogues to hear displays of preaching along the same lines as the extant writings, hence Philo's statement (*De Vita Mosis*, 2. 216) that 'each seventh day . . . the places of prayer in every city' are 'schools of good sense' and other virtues, while Philo's denial (*De Vita Mosis*, 2. 211) that Jews on the sabbath attended performances in the theatre has been taken to suggest that a comparison between synagogues and theatres was possible.[18] Josephus wrote of the Jews of Antioch that they had brought into their rites (*threskeiai*) in the first century CE many Greeks and (presumably by this means) made them 'in some sense part of themselves' (*BJ* 7. 45). The use of the verb *prosago* in the middle form implied action by the Antiochene Jews on their

---

[18] Georgi, *Opponents*, 113–14.

own behalf, so it may be surmised that they wanted such gentiles to join their rites and to become 'in some way' attached to their community.[19] Not enough survives of first-century synagogues to tell whether they allowed easy access to casual outsiders to listen from the street, but it is possible: in Caesarea in 66 CE one synagogue was down an alleyway next to pagan houses, though in this case not conversion but antagonism resulted (Joseph. *BJ* 2. 285–6).

If Jews were really eager to win converts, the easiest way to increase their number might have been to remove some of the more onerous requirements laid upon proselytes. It has therefore been vehemently argued by some scholars that some Jews in the diaspora were prepared to allow some male gentiles to be treated as Jews even without undergoing circumcision.[20] It is certain that an uncircumcised Jew was not a logical impossibility. Later rabbis contrasted the alien, whose 'heart is not towards heaven' to an uncircumcised man whose heart is 'towards heaven'; they seem to have had in mind haemophiliac Jews for whom the operation would endanger life and could therefore be forgone (*b. Pes.* 96a). When other rituals, including the bringing of an offering to the Temple, were also required of converts, the question also arose of the religious status of a proselyte who had fulfilled some of the initiation procedures but not (yet?) all of them.[21] Philo in one passage referred to a small group of Jews— 'extreme allegorists'—who believed that only the inner meaning of the Torah matters and that its actual observance was therefore irrelevant (*De Migr.* 89–90). Such Jews might perhaps forgo circumcision for their sons and stress instead a moral allegory such as that propounded for the operation by Philo himself in his explanation of the difficult text of Exod. 22. 20 (Heb.), in which (in the Septuagint Greek) the Israelites were described as *proselytoi* (*Quaest. Ex.* 2. 2). Finally, Epictetus wrote in the early second century as if the ultimate sign of dedication to Judaism by a convert was baptism (ap. Arrian, *Diss.* 2. 9. 20), and the same seems also to have been implied by the (probably Jewish) author of *Orac. Sib.* 4. 165,

---

[19] Sevenster, *Roots of Pagan Anti-Semitism*, 206.
[20] McEleney, 'Conversion, Circumcision and the Law'.
[21] Cf. Nolland, 'Uncircumcised Proselytes?'.

who wrote in *c*.80 CE, although this latter passage may refer not to a baptism for converts but just a bath for purification.

If Jews were keen to win converts, they will, according to the ideal model of the proselyte, have been eager also to lure pagans away from their customary worship. As such, any Jewish mission for converts was likely to provoke opposition from the gentile society in which it operated. So modern authors who believe that Jews proselytized have pointed out that Jews were expelled from the city of Rome in 139 BCE and 19 CE and have asserted that this was as a punishment for seeking proselytes.[22] In the former case one of the Byzantine epitomators of the first-century CE writer Valerius Maximus implied that the Jews' crime was that they 'tried to transmit their sacred rites to the Romans'. In the latter case Cassius Dio (57. 18. 5a) is said by John of Antioch to have written (in the early third century CE) that the Jews were 'converting many of the natives to their ways', an explanation which is missing in the earlier historians Josephus and Tacitus, who related instead a curious story of the duping of an aristocratic Roman lady proselyte by unscrupulous Jews intent on her money. It has been argued that Tacitus was ignorant and that Josephus (*AJ* 18. 81–3) hid the truth because it embarrassed him in his apologetic aim of reconciling the Romans to the Jews.[23]

The case for believing in a mission to win proselytes may reasonably be ended with three of the most striking categories of literary evidence. First, Horace, *Sat.* 1. 4. 142–3, *veluti te | Iudaei cogemus in hanc concedere turbam*, has been interpreted to mean that 'like the Jews, we will compel you to join our throng', that is, to convert.[24] A second piece of evidence much cited is Philo's description of the translation of the Septuagint, in which he expressed a hope that all the human race might be profited by it (Philo, *De Vita Mosis*, 2. 36) and 'each nation (person) might abandon its (his) peculiar ways and, bidding farewell to its (his) ancestral customs, turn to our laws alone' (*De Vita Mosis*, 2. 44).[25] Third, and most

[22] See M. Stern, *Greek and Latin Authors*, i. 357–60; ii. 70.
[23] Thus Georgi, *Opponents*, 92–6; Cohen, 'Respect', 424.
[24] See text and comm. in M. Stern, *Greek and Latin Authors*, i. 323.
[25] Georgi, *Opponents*, 84–118, esp. 109–11, cited by McKnight, *Light*, 39–40.

striking, is the text of Matt. 23: 15, which reads 'Woe to thee, scribes and Pharisees, that you cross land and sea to make one proselyte', a phrase which to most scholars seems to imply that scribes and Pharisees did indeed travel in such a way to win converts to Judaism.[26]

Such is the considerable body of evidence generally marshalled to suggest that Jews were keen to win proselytes in the first century. Scholars who argue that this was the case are surely right that it would be naïve to expect Jews to have had no interest whatsoever in those non-Jews who elected to join them and their religion. But it is one thing to agree that it is likely that proselytes provided reaffirmation of the values of Judaism for those born into the fold. It is altogether different to claim, simply on the basis of the evidence just outlined, that Jews, unlike their pagan contemporaries, positively wished to win converts whenever the opportunity offered. In this section I shall therefore examine all this evidence just cited, and the conjoined arguments, in an attempt to demonstrate why it seems to me deficient. The last text cited, from the Gospel of St Matthew, has often been taken as the starting point for discussions of the Jewish attitude to mission in the first century CE, and it seems fitting to begin with this passage scrutiny of all the arguments and evidence for such a mission which I have laid out.

The imprecation against the scribes and Pharisees ascribed to Jesus by the author of Matt. 23: 15 is one of a series of attacks on the alleged hypocrisy of these religious leaders. The polemic is directed not so much against their religious practices, as against the value they placed on those practices and their failure to pay sufficient attention to other matters seen by Jesus as of greater importance. Some at least of the woes put into the mouth of Jesus by Matthew probably originated in the Palestinian stratum of the tradition about him, if not indeed from Jesus himself—the accusation that Pharisees tithed agricultural produce but did not keep the weightier matters of the law (Matt. 23: 23) can only have

---

[26] The bibliography of works in which the text is understood in this way is huge. See Garland, *Intention of Matthew 23*; McKnight, *Light*, 106–8, with bibliography.

applied in the land of Israel—but there is no agreement among scholars on the origin of the specific woe in Matt. 23: 15. The saying incorporates various semitisms, including the Aramaic term 'Gehinnom', but the fact that it was omitted by Luke may suggest that it reflected the special interests of Matthew or his source.[27] Fortunately for the present argument, the issue may be left unresolved, for in any case it is overwhelmingly likely that the phrase was, like the rest of the woes, believed by the author to reflect the actual practices of 'scribes and Pharisees' and that it was expected to make sense to Matthew's audience at the end of the first century. By that date, therefore, if not before, 'scribes and Pharisees' were believed to cross land and sea to make one proselyte.

The crucial issue is quite simply the meaning of the imprecation. The collocation 'scribes and Pharisees' here, as elsewhere in Matthew's Gospel, almost certainly referred to Pharisees alone; in one of the following imprecations, in verse 26, the word 'scribe' was dropped altogether.[28] The expression 'one proselyte' is peculiar, since it is not clear whether the reader was meant to supply an extra word to make the phrase 'even one proselyte',[29] but I cannot see how to make any useful deduction from this oddity. Thus the word which deserves most investigation is the term *proselytos*. In the ensuing pages I shall study in some detail the uses of this word in extant Jewish literature composed before 100 CE. In the end I shall suggest that in this verse Jesus (or Matthew) was attacking Pharisees for their eagerness in trying to persuade *other Jews* to follow Pharisaic halakha.[30]

It seems clear that the *proselytos* to whom Matthew referred became a Pharisee or a follower of Pharisaic teaching as a

---

[27] See now the discussion of the origin of the saying, and the citation of earlier literature, in McKnight, *Light*, 106–7, 154.

[28] Precisely what group was intended by Matthew when he used the word *grammateis* is not clear. Cf. Garland, *Intention of Matthew 23*, 41–6; Saldarini, *Pharisees, Scribes and Sadducees*, 157–73, with references to older literature.

[29] Munck, *Paul*, 266, suggested that Matthew had in mind a particular instance of a gentile converted by a Pharisee.

[30] This notion was floated by Munck, *Paul*, 267 in one paragraph, but it has never been properly argued, so far as I know. Despite this it is regularly dismissed out of hand without discussion, cf. Jeremias, *Jesus' Promise*, 18 n. 1; Garland, *Intention*, 129; Cohen, 'Conversion', 44 n. 16; McKnight, *Light*, 107.

result of the Pharisees' efforts. He became 'twice the son of Gehinnom' that the Pharisee was, which is not an expression which Matthew was likely to use about Jews *qua* Jews.[31] Is the conversion of Jews to Pharisaism something that Pharisees would have found desirable in the first century? There is little explicit evidence, but it seems at least possible. If Pharisees believed that they alone could interpret the Torah correctly, it would seem obvious that, like the prophets of old calling the people to repent, they should feel a duty to teach the rest of the Jews how to live righteously and bring divine blessings onto the community. Similarly those members of the Essene sect who were celibate may have adopted a missionary stance in order to survive for their divinely ordained mission, since no children could be born within the group. The only figure given in any ancient text for the size of the Pharisees' sect is Josephus' reference to the 'more than six thousand' individuals who identified themselves as Pharisees at the end of the first century BCE when they refused to take an oath to Herod (*AJ* 17. 41–5). There is no evidence that there were any more followers of the sect than that number, even though they were widely influential, persuading the people about prayers and sacrifices (Joseph. *AJ* 18. 15). It is reasonable to suppose that they might wish as many Jews as possible to 'become Pharisees', although precisely how such a conversion would be marked (other than by the self-description of the convert) is unclear.

That Matthew should find such missionary behaviour by Pharisees objectionable is also unsurprising. For much of the first century the followers of Jesus may have been competing against Pharisees and other interpreters of Judaism to win Jews as converts to Christianity. More of a problem is the implication of the phrase 'across land and sea' that Pharisees sought followers outside Palestine, for which there is no other firm evidence: the diaspora Jew St Paul claimed to have been a Pharisee, but he may have been trained in Jerusalem rather than Tarsus, and Josephus, who said that he followed Pharisaic teachings when in Rome, made no explicit mention of Pharisaic teachers outside the land of Israel. But the

---

[31] See already Allen, *Commentary on Matthew*, 246.

teachings of the rabbis, who were in some ways the successors of the Pharisees after 70 CE, did in time spread to Babylonia and elsewhere and eventually were to become normative among Jews of the western diaspora as well. In any case, the same objection applies whatever interpretation of the term *proselytos* is preferred, since there is also no other good evidence for Pharisees seeking to convert gentiles to Judaism outside Palestine.[32]

In sum, Matt: 23. 15 makes good sense—indeed, better sense—if *proselytos* has the meaning I have suggested rather than that traditionally attributed to it. Is such a meaning possible? There are a number of factors in its favour. First, it should be noted that the term *proselytos* is very rare in the first century CE and earlier except in quotations from the Septuagint. It was hardly used by Philo and never used by Josephus. Apart from the passage in Matthew, the only book of the whole New Testament where it is found is Acts, where it occurs three times (Acts 2: 11; 6: 5; 13: 43), with the meaning of 'a gentile who has become Jewish'. I suggest that the word was *becoming* a technical term among Jews for a converted gentile, and had been doing so since the time of the Septuagint translation of the third and second centuries BCE, but that its meaning was not yet confined to this sense alone.

An examination of Philo's use of the term may illustrate this continuing flexibility. In referring to gentile converts to Judaism, Philo preferred to use the word *epelys*. *Proselytos* appears only when it is already found in the passage of the Septuagint which Philo was quoting. In the Septuagint itself *proselytos* undoubtedly *usually* meant a gentile convert: the Hebrew word *ger*, which means 'immigrant' or 'resident alien' in the earlier layers of the Pentateuch and 'gentile who has become Jewish' only in the latest layer, was always translated by *proselytos* in the Septuagint when it has the latter meaning (except once, when it was transliterated as *geioras*),

---

[32] Baumgarten, 'The Name of the Pharisees', 414 n. 10, argues that Eleazar, who converted the king of Adiabene, Izates, may have been a Pharisee because he was described by Josephus (*AJ* 20. 43) as *akribes* ('accurate') in the law. But *akribeia* in Josephus' writings cannot always be equated with Pharisaism: in Joseph. *C. Ap.* 2. 227 the Spartans are said to have observed *their* laws *akribos* (as noted by Baumgarten himself, op. cit. 413 n. 6).

whereas other terms, such as *paroikos*, were usually used for those places where *ger* appears in the Hebrew with one of its earlier meanings. But 'gentile convert' cannot have been the *only* acceptable meaning of *proselytos* for the Septuagint translators for, just occasionally, this term also was used to mean a resident alien (e.g. Lev. 19: 10: 'to the beggar and the stranger (*proselytos*) you will leave them (i.e. unharvested grapes)').

This latter use is striking in the Greek of Exod. 22: 20 (Heb.), where *proselytoi* is found, as a translation of *gerim*, to refer not to gentiles but to the Israelites in Egypt. Philo evidently found such a usage strange but not impossible, since he did not choose to substitute one of the other Septuagintal translations of *ger* at this point, as he could have done. In *Quaest. Ex.* 2. 2 he commented that what makes a *proselytos* is not circumcision (which, he therefore implied, is what one might have expected), since the Israelites were not circumcised until they began their wanderings in the desert; what matters is turning to God for salvation. He made the same observations at *De Spec.* 1. 51, pointing there to the etymology of the word, which suggests that the *proselytos* has come to a holy life from a different one. This sense of *proserchesthai* as the approach to something sacred can also be found in the general use of the verb in the Gospel of Matthew[33] and in 1 Timothy 6: 3; Hebrews 7: 25; 11: 6; 12: 22, and especially 1 Peter 2: 4. In the works of Josephus the closest parallel may be found in Joseph. *BJ* 2. 142, where those who join the sect of the Essenes are described as *tous prosiontas*, a participial form of the same verb.[34]

What I suggest, therefore, is that *proselytos* in the first century had both a technical and a non-technical sense, and that in that latter sense it could quite easily be applied to Jews. This usage is precisely parallel to that long ago noted for the term 'Godfearer' in this period, which also often, sometimes apparently as a semi-technical term, referred to gentiles but was also, perhaps metaphorically, used to describe Jews.[35] In

---

[33] Edwards, 'Use of προσέρχεσθαι'. On the term *proselytos* in the Septuagint, see Allen, 'Meaning'.   [34] See Munck, *Paul*, 267.

[35] Feldman, ' "Jewish Sympathisers" in Classical Literature'; Cohen, 'Respect', 419.

a Christian text written probably some time in the fourth century CE, the *Acts of Pilate*, the Jewish High Priest was portrayed as providing a definition of 'proselytos' for the Roman governor Pilate. The definition by this date and in this context was unambiguous: 'They were children of the Greeks and now they have become Jews' (*Acta Pilati*, 2. 4, Tischendorf, p. 226). I assume that the same definition was accepted by those Jews to whose names on epitaphs the designation 'proselyte' was attached (as an honorific) in the second century CE and after.[36] But the clarity of such usage in the middle and later Roman empire does not show that the term had always had this meaning. On the contrary, it emphasizes by contrast the vagueness of the usage of the first century and before. If this argument is accepted, then it will no longer be possible to use Matt. 23: 15 as a proof-text—often *the* proof-text—for a mission by Pharisees and other Jews to win converts to Judaism from the gentile world.

So too with the other literary 'evidence' cited as part of the argument for a proselytizing mission in the first section of this chapter. The text in Horace, *Sat.* 1. 4. 142–3, *veluti te | Iudaei cogemus in hanc concedere turbam*, need not refer to Jewish eagerness to proselytize at all: Horace certainly portrayed the Jews as prone to use pressure to achieve their ends but he implied nothing about gentiles being compelled to become Jewish nor about the corollary of such conversion, that such converts learn to despise their own gods. The Jewish crowd was notorious in Roman politics, at least in the previous generation when Cicero referred to them (*Flac.* 28 (66)) as prone to use mass intimidation to get their way when law suits were in progress, and that may be all that is at issue here.[37] Alternatively, Horace may have been referring to the forced conversions of the Idumaeans and Ituraeans by the Hasmonaeans in the previous century. The verb *cogere*, 'to compel', seems too strong a word for an allusion to conversion by persuasion.

The passages in Philo, *De Vita Mosis*, 2. 25–44 which have been taken as evidence of a hope for conversions are better explained as part of Philo's rhetorical exaggeration in his

---

[36] Cohen, 'Crossing', 28–9.
[37] See Nolland, 'Proselytism or Politics in Horace'.

eulogy of the Torah. Philo chose to discuss the translation by the Seventy in order to illustrate the excellence of the legislator Moses, whose laws are not only permanent (2. 12–16) but have won the respect of other nations (17–24). It was the fame of these laws, widespread because of the impressive practices of the Jews who observed them, that led the worthy king Ptolemy Philadelphus to organize a translation into Greek (27–30). The translators' prayer that their version be perfect was answered by God, who wanted thereby to profit all humans, not just those who understood Chaldaic writing (36). The excellence of the whole project was proved by the admiration of gentiles for the Jewish law. It was true that not all gentiles shared in this adulation but this was only because the political fortunes of the Jews were at a low ebb. If only (and here comes the rhetorical exaggeration) the Jews' political prospects were brighter, Philo believed (or claimed) that each individual or nation would leave his or its own ancestral customs and 'convert (*metabalein*) to our customs alone, which shine so much brighter than those of other peoples (44)'. The crucial word is 'would'. The nations *would* convert if all these conditions were met. There is no hint here that the nations *should* convert now.

It is unlikely that any of the residual arguments for a Jewish mission in the first century would ever have been proposed if such a mission had not already been presupposed. In recent years even the mass conversions to Judaism said by Josephus to have been forced by the Hasmonaeans have been thrown into doubt, with the ingenious argument that the allegation that the Hasmonaeans used force was fabricated by gentile anti-Hasmonaean propagandists, and that more truth is to be found in Strabo's view that the Idumaeans were originally Nabataeans who just elected to join the Judaeans and share in Jewish customs (Strabo, *Geog.* 16. 2. 34), perhaps as part of a confederation based on a common link of circumcision. Strabo's account made no mention of the use of force by the Jews, although it did not preclude the possibility that force had been used.[38]

---

[38] Kasher, *Jews, Idumaeans and Ancient Arabs*, 46–83, esp. 46–8; accepted by Cohen, 'Was Judaism missionary?', 16.

This argument is certainly not impossible, but I confess that it does not seem to me very plausible. It is hard to explain why Josephus, who was proud of his own Hasmonaean lineage (Joseph. *Vita*, 2–4), would have included such propaganda in his history, and I am unable to perceive any condemnation of the Hasmonaeans' actions in the historian's dry account.[39] It may be preferable to accept the hypothesis that those conversions were a political gambit which may have owed something to the example set by the Roman Republic in the spread of Roman citizenship over Italy: the notion, at least in theory, of an indefinite expansion of citizenship in this way was found in the ancient world only among Jews and Romans and, since the latter had found it strikingly advantageous in the centuries immediately preceding the Hasmonaean dynasty, it would not be all that surprising if the Jewish monarchs, who were eager to maintain contact with the Romans, followed suit. The recent suggestion that the Hasmonaeans were imitating Greek attitudes in treating their (Jewish) citizenship (*politeia*) in the same way that Greeks viewed Hellenism, as a culture which others could adopt, will explain their assumption that mass conversions were possible, but not that they were desirable.[40] A gentile observer such as Timagenes (cited by Strabo) accepted such conversions as standard political incorporation of a neighbouring people (Joseph. *AJ* 13. 319).

At any rate, if the Hasmonaeans wanted a *theological* justification—and it is quite possible that by the 120s BCE they had so far assumed the characteristics of a normal Hellenistic state that they saw no need for one—they could find it in the notion that the land of Israel must be purified by the exclusion of idolatry (see above, Ch. 3, pp. 49–50). Despite the location of Pella just east of the Jordan, such an attitude would best explain the treatment of the inhabitants of that place: because they did not promise to go over to the national customs of the Jews, their city was destroyed (Joseph. *AJ* 13.

[39] Cohen, 'Respect', 423, claims that there is no explicit condemnation of the compulsory conversions in Josephus' writings, but that implicit condemnation was likely. This is, however, only speculation.

[40] Cf. M. Smith, 'Rome and the Maccabean Conversions'; Cohen, 'Religion, Ethnicity, and "Hellenism" '.

397).[41] So too the Galileans who were intent on the enforced circumcision of two of Agrippa II's gentile courtiers whom they caught in their territory in 67 CE argued that 'those who wished to live among the Jews' must needs be circumcised (Joseph. *Vita*, 113).

If this distinction was generally made by Jews, it provides of course an argument *against* any universal proselytizing mission, since it suggests that gentiles were welcome to remain uncircumcised provided that they lived outside the holy land. As for the conversion of the Idumaeans, it is true that biblical Edom was not part of the biblical land of Israel, but in Maccabaean times the story of the relationship between Jacob and Esau (ancestor of Edom) was rewritten in the Book of Jubilees to emphasize both their fraternal origins and the justified domination of the latter by the former. In any case the area inhabited by Idumaeans by the 120s BCE was north of biblical Edom and in fact lay within the southern part of the old kingdom of Judah.[42]

The assumption by Jews that marriage partners should convert before union does indeed seem to have been general by the first century. As evidence can be cited the very public insistence to this effect by the women of the Herodian family. Against such a view, it has been argued that the term *memigmenon* at Joseph. *BJ* 2. 463 may refer to Jews who have intermarried with the unconverted gentile population.[43] But it must be assumed that many Jews viewed such liaisons with distaste, for the actions of the Herodians would otherwise be inexplicable. It is, however, hard to see how such insistence on conversion for marriage can be seen as missionary. It might even be suggested that opportunities for mission were lessened by such a custom since a Jew was not expected to seek to convert his or her partner after marriage, as was permitted among Christians (1 Cor. 7: 12–16). That Jews in general preferred to portray themselves as marrying only within the fold was common knowledge (cf. Tac. *Hist.* 5. 5: *discreti cubilibus*). When an outsider was allowed in, he or she would have to be initiated into the community; such

---

[41] Kasher, *Jews and Hellenistic Cities*, 156–7.
[42] See Mendels, *Land of Israel*, 75–81; Selzer, 'Joining', 48.
[43] M. Smith, *Palestinian Parties*, 65–6, 182 n. 33.

behaviour was calculated to reinforce the group's boundary and solidarity, not to open it up to the outside. All this needs emphasis because, despite the lack of explicit evidence outside the family of Herod, it is *a priori* probable that in antiquity, as now, at least some conversions to Judaism took place to facilitate a marriage.[44] Marriage as a motive for conversion was not mentioned by gentile authors who attacked Judaism, but it is noteworthy that in *Joseph and Asenath* the heroine was portrayed as the paradigm of the proselyte, but that the main theme of the story was that she could not marry Joseph while she was heathen whereas she could and did as soon as she had been initiated into Judaism.[45]

Little need be said about the other group on whose circumcision Jews may have insisted, namely their male slaves. I have already suggested (above, p. 65) that this may have been partly for domestic convenience, and it is likely that almost all slaves owned by Jews, at least in Palestine, will have served primarily as domestic servants since that was their normal function in the Near East. Such insistence must be understood in a similar way to conversion for marriage. The slave became by force a member of the family group and circumcision established him as part of that group. Such an attitude reveals nothing at all about Jews' expectations and hopes for those whose economic circumstances did not bring them into this sort of close social relationship with a Jewish family.

What explanation should be offered for the fragments of the large Jewish literature in Greek which, it is claimed, was produced to win converts to Judaism? The argument, it will be recalled, was roughly as follows (above, p. 65 f.). Some Jews wrote a number of religious tracts in Greek during the first century CE and the two centuries before. Such works would have been more or less readily comprehensible to non-Jews.

---

[44] Cohen, 'From the Bible to the Talmud', suggests that intermarriage was uncommon in 1st-cent. Judaea and in rabbinic society, but 'perhaps not uncommon in Rome and Alexandria'. I do not know any evidence for this distinction.

[45] Cohen, 'Crossing', 21, denies that Asenath was seen as a full proselyte, on the grounds that the text says nothing about her observance of Jewish laws or her inclusion in a Jewish community. It is odd thus to make a substantive conclusion from silence when Cohen himself notes (26) that descriptions of conversion in antiquity rarely included all the elements of the process.

Since the main burden of such writings was praise of Judaism and the Jewish God, it is assumed that those gentiles who read such material were expected or hoped to become proselytes.

The fallacies in this assumption are evident and have been often demonstrated since the pioneering work of Tcherikover.[46] It is more than likely that most Jewish literature in Greek was composed primarily for Greek-speaking Jews. This seems fairly certain for the greatest product of that literature, the Septuagint translation of the Bible and the revisions of the Septuagint by Aquila and others, even if the brief quotation of the opening verse of Genesis by the anonymous gentile author of the rhetorical treatise *On the Sublime* demonstrates that at least one non-Jew did come across the text.[47] A Jewish audience is probable also for all the other Jewish texts which both proclaimed their Jewishness and stressed the need to keep the Law. There is no evidence at all of any non-Christian gentile interest in, for example, the Wisdom of Solomon or the Fourth Book of Maccabees. It is highly unlikely that any non-Jew would have been interested in the dry chronological calculations of Demetrius. The novelistic *Joseph and Asenath* was not a plausible missionary tract, since the text assumed the reader's familiarity with the biblical story of Joseph.[48] Even those writings masquerading under gentile authorship, such as the works of Ps.-Hecataeus and Ps.-Aristeas, may have been intended primarily for Jews: Jews steeped in the surrounding Greek culture as well as their own religious traditions will have taken comfort from such testimony by respected gentiles to the truth of their faith, much as more recent rabbis appeal on occasion to modern science as support for the wisdom of traditional Jewish customs.

It is of course *possible* that some of these works were read by gentiles as well as by Jews, and that this was intended by their authors, even though the only gentile known to have taken any interest in any of these writings before Christians adopted them was the polymath Alexander Polyhistor, who collected such material in the first century BCE for his own

---

[46] Tcherikover, 'Jewish Apologetic Literature'.
[47] See comm. in M. Stern, *Greek and Latin Authors*, i. 361–5.
[48] Chestnutt, 'Social Setting of Joseph and Asenath'.

work *On the Jews*. But, if so, it is hard to see what gentiles were to make of such literature. The status of gentiles in the cosmic order was referred to on occasions, particularly in the Sibylline Oracles, but this question was decidedly not the main focus of the bulk of these works. On the contrary, their main theme was the excellence of Judaism. When the writings urged specifically Jewish customs, such as the observance of the sabbath, they tended to be pseudonymous: thus, the fact that Orpheus was portrayed by a Jewish forger as approving of Jewish morality was likely to be comforting for a Jew who was impressed by Orpheus but was not likely to persuade a gentile to become Jewish. By contrast, those writings which were openly Jewish often urged not conversion to Judaism but a more general ethic. The themes which crop up in, for instance, the Testament of Abraham are moral ones: charity, hospitality, the avoidance of adultery and homosexuality, the shunning of infantidice, and so on.[49] Even in a work like the Third Book of the Sibylline Oracles, where the fact that it was the Jewish cult that was being praised was only thinly disguised and one could argue that such a disguise was a necessary part of the oracular form, there was no suggestion that gentiles should immediately rush to convert, or, indeed, that the covenant of Judaism (including circumcision) had anything to do with them—at least, until the final reckoning at the end of days.[50]

One might have expected that literature which was intended as its primary function to persuade gentiles to abandon their social customs and enter a new society in Judaism would be far more direct than this, even if the impact of the Septuagint on the Christian writer Tatian, who according to his own account was converted to Christianity while reading it (*Oratio c. Graecos*, 29), shows that even quite unlikely texts could have a profound impact at times. It is only because some modern scholars have assumed (wrongly) that Jews sought proselytes of some sort that they have sometimes attributed to such writings an *intention* to attract proselytes who would observe only a select few of the

---

[49] See Collins, *Between Athens and Jerusalem*, 137–74, on the 'common ethic'.
[50] Collins, 'Symbol of Otherness', 165–6.

commandments.[51] For Josephus, the matter was simple: those proselytes who found it beyond their endurance to keep the laws properly were considered to be apostates (*C. Ap*. 2. 123).

And yet, as has been seen (above, p. 67), many have argued that one religious duty in particular was often waived by Jewish missionaries in their eagerness to win proselytes. It was possible, so it is claimed, for gentile males to become Jewish without undergoing circumcision. Why this particular duty rather than any other? To be sure, circumcision is a painful business and cases are recorded from the ancient world of this being the sticking point for would-be converts: Izates of Adiabene hesitated to undertake an act which might prove disastrously unpopular with his subjects (Joseph. *AJ* 20. 38–9). But the main reason for modern scholarly interest in this particular religious duty is the emphasis laid upon it by St Paul in his attacks on 'those of the circumcision' and his insistence that it was not required for entrance into the Church. The operation is no more painful or dangerous than that in initiation rites in other periods and places, although it did differ from other contemporary rites in so far as it was painful and (more or less) irreversible. It could even be argued that the discomfort caused constituted part of its efficacy for initiation. Many peoples other than Jews practised (and practise) the same custom. It seems naïve to suggest that dropping this one requirement could bring a flood of proselytes to join the Jewish fold. The physical discomfort would be negligible compared to the social problems faced by the new convert.

But in fact the evidence for uncircumcised proselytes is anyway minimal and should be discounted.[52] Epictetus, assuming baptism as the main sign of initiation (ap. Arrian, *Diss*. 2. 9. 20), may simply have been confused or taking a part of the initiation ceremony to stand for all. The rabbinic texts said to consider the possibility of a proselyte who has not (yet?) been circumcised discussed the case only as part of a gradual unveiling of a complex theoretical argument. An examination of Philo's allegorical method and its application

[51] McEleney, 'Conversion, Circumcision and the Law', *passim*, esp. 323–4.
[52] See Nolland, 'Uncircumcised Proselytes?', for the following arguments.

to the significance of circumcision makes it highly implausible that he suggested the abolition of this law any more than any other. It needs to be recognized how far-reaching such an abolition would be. Circumcision was the symbol of the Jew (for outsiders as well as for Jews themselves), however many other peoples did it and regardless of the occasional Jew who, for whatever reason, did not carry out the Law. The attitude of Metilius, the Roman garrison commander in Jerusalem in 66 CE, can be taken as indication of the importance of the rite. He was prepared, he said, to behave as a Jew (*ioudaisein*) 'even as far as undergoing circumcision' (Joseph. *BJ* 2. 454).

One final serious claim needs to be countered, namely, that the expulsion of the Jews from the city of Rome in 139 BCE and 19 CE was in retaliation for the vehemence of their proselytizing (above, p. 68). Neither case is as well documented as is often assumed. The affair in 139 BCE was referred to only by Valerius Maximus, an author of the late first century BCE whose remarks survive only in two Byzantine epitomators, Julius Paris (*c*.400 CE) and Nepotianus (*c*.500 CE). Since the two accounts differ, they are clearly not preserved verbatim, and the confused nature of the reference to Jupiter Sabazius in Julius Paris has been well clarified by Lane.[53] According to Nepotianus, the Jews were banished, along with astrologers, for 'trying to transmit their sacred rites (*sacra*) to the Romans'; private altars were therefore removed by the Roman authorities from public places, and they were expelled from the city. Various peculiarities about this story have been noted. Most significant is the odd description of the Jews' alleged crime. It seems difficult in the context of Judaism in the second century BCE to imagine a new convert being recommended to set up altars of any kind. Jews did countenance the setting up of a temple at Leontopolis in this period by priests who had come from Jerusalem, but no Jews are recorded as having approved of the use of private altars by Jews in this way. What was at issue here, then, if the account is not totally confused or these Jews were not so syncretistic in their religious attitude that they were genuinely engaged in the worship of Jupiter Sabazius, was something

---

[53] Lane, 'Sabazius and the Jews'.

rather less than the conversion of proselytes to Judaism. I suggest that the Jews were accused not of teaching Romans to despise their native cults, which would be the most obvious and objectionable effect of conversion, but simply of bringing in a new cult into public places without authority, a practice which the Romans traditionally deprecated, as they had shown recently in their opposition to the spread of the cult of Dionysus. What may have happened is that some Romans, impressed by Jews, chose to express their admiration in conventional Roman fashion by the setting up of altars within the city. How pleased Jews might be about this it is impossible to say, but they would certainly distinguish it quite clearly from the conversion of Romans to Judaism.[54]

As for the expulsion from Rome in 19 CE, I have already noted that neither Tacitus nor Josephus gave missionary activity as an explanation (see above, p. 68). The suggestion that Josephus might have been prepared to hide the truth is somewhat implausible: if the Jews' missionary activity was well known, Josephus would have been better advised to try to justify such behaviour than to try to pretend it did not happen. It seems to me better to explain the motive for the expulsion, which is first found in a fragment of Cassius Dio's history which is preserved not in the manuscript traditions but in a solitary quotation (not necessarily verbatim?) by the seventh-century Christian writer John of Antioch, in terms of a new Roman awareness of the possibility of proselytism since the end of the first century, and perhaps as evidence for a real proselytizing mission in Cassius Dio's day, the third century CE (see below, p. 144).

What is left of the arguments customarily arrayed to demonstrate an extensive proselytizing mission by Jews in this period may be dismissed quite rapidly. The argument from the proportion of proselytes within Jewish society is irrelevant, both because any estimate of such numbers is in fact pure guesswork and because the existence of proselytes is not in itself an indication of a mission to win them. The missionary impulse of early Christianity could have arisen regardless of the attitude to proselytizing in contemporary

[54] See Bickerman, 'Altars of Gentiles'.

Jewish society, since allowance must be made for the possibility, indeed probability, of unique circumstances in the early Church which led to a proselytizing mission.

Nor should any conclusions about proselytizing be made from the general growth of the Jewish population in this period, which can be fully explained in other ways. Ancient writers explained the Jewish diaspora by the overpopulation of the home country (cf. Philo, *De Vita Mosis*, 2. 232) and Jewish fertility by the Jews' strange ideological opposition to abortion, infanticide, and contraception (cf. Tac. *Hist.* 5. 5). To this one could add the Jewish concept of charity, unique in the ancient world until Christianity, which made it a religious duty to prevent the children of the poor from dying in infancy, so that the main natural inhibition on population growth was at least partially stifled.[55] The theory that a massive surge of proselytes to Judaism accounted for this population growth is thus not impossible, but it is implausible, and it runs up against the curious fact that no ancient Jewish writer claimed that such widespread conversion had taken place, although it would have been an obvious source of pride.

Finally, the conversion of the royal family of Adiabene. Josephus in *AJ* 20. 34–46 alone provided an account of the process of the conversion, although the later rabbinic texts demonstrate wider awareness of the fact that it had happened.[56] In describing the two Jewish teachers of the Adiabeneans, Ananias and Eleazar, Josephus made no suggestion that any such teachers travelled abroad specifically in order to win converts or even to provide instruction. On the contrary, Josephus made it clear that Eleazar's intention in coming to Adiabene was not to convert anyone but simply to pay his respects to the royal family. The initative in this, as in all cases, came from the would-be converts, not the converter.

[55] See my argument in Goodman, *Ruling Class*, 61, but note that rabbinic references to Jewish foundlings (e.g. *m. Kidd.* 4. 2) suggest that some Jews may have adopted the standard gentile custom of exposing unwanted children, as Sacha Stern has pointed out to me.

[56] Cohen, 'Respect', 417, notes that Josephus in BJ and rabbinic sages in tannaitic literature referred to Adiabeneans without mentioning the fact they were converts. In contrast, Josephus in *AJ* and amoraic rabbis made much of the conversions. Cf. Schiffman, 'Conversion of the Royal House of Adiabene'.

In the final section of this chapter I propose to examine some positive reasons for denying that Jews sought proselytes in this period. So, for instance, the name of no Jewish missionary from antiquity is known (except for St Paul), and the survival of detailed accounts of early Christian missionary efforts points up the lack of Jewish parallels. Since conversion to Judaism and to the new social group which went with it was a major undertaking, one would expect much negative comment about such proselytizing in the anti-Semitic literature which survives, but it is not to be found before the end of the first century CE. One would also expect riots and expulsions from the other great centres of Jewish life such as Antioch and Alexandria, giving proselytizing as justification, but, again, and despite the survival of much evidence from elsewhere in the empire, only in the city of Rome is this said to have happened, and even there the evidence seems doubtful. One would expect a great deal to be said about such a mission in the works of Philo and Josephus if Jews wished all gentiles to take so momentous a step. But in fact these authors have little about proselytes and nothing about a mission to win them. Indeed Josephus is explicit that those outsiders who only flirt with Judaism will not be accepted as proselytes (*C. Ap.* 2. 210). A full commitment was needed, and if this diminished the number of conversions no contemporary Jewish author expressed any regret. It should be recognized that the suggestion that Josephus deliberately hid the fact that Jews believed that they had a mission to convert the world is a major, and most implausible claim.[57] How could he hope to escape undetected with such a lie?

The ambiguous status of proselytes in the eyes of Jews is itself evidence that the winning of more was not seen as a religious duty. I noted at the beginning of this chapter that Jews were remarkable in espousing the whole notion of permitting converts to enter the body politic (above, p. 61), but this should not prevent awareness of the limitations in the

[57] See Delling, 'Josephus und die heidnischer Religionen', 51. Cohen, 'Respect', puts forward a more sophisticated version of the same argument, in which he attempts, for instance, to explain away Josephus' emphasis on the Adiabenean conversions on the grounds that Romans would not find conversions threatening if they happened on Parthian territory. I am not persuaded.

openness to outsiders thus expressed. If Jewish attitudes to proselytes are compared not to contemporary pagans but to the early Church, those limitations will rapidly become clear.

In the early Church, a convert to Christianity was in essence equal to his fellows. There is no evidence of prejudice against those who had formerly been in darkness, except in so far as they needed to heed the teachings of the more enlightened. In the early years, of course, all Christians had been converts. By contrast, a proselyte to Judaism became in religious terms a member of a clearly defined, separate, and in a few cases mostly concerned with marriage, less privileged group within the Jewish commonwealth. That this was so was doubtless due to the dual function of conversion as entry into a political and social as well as into a religious entity, but it is significant that the distinct definition of a proselyte as a particular *sort* of Jew was retained throughout antiquity. It was even possible to describe the descendants of the Idumaeans who had converted to Judaism as 'half-Jews' (Joseph. *AJ* 14. 403).

It would be wrong to suggest that a negative attitude towards proselytes predominated in the Jewish texts of the first century—in so far as converts were discussed at all, it was usually with sympathy and sometimes with admiration. But even the possibility of such ambivalent attitudes is enough to show how unlikely the picture is of a Jewish mission to win converts. If gentiles wished to come to (*proserchesthai*) Israel, the commandments, and God, they were welcome, but the etymology of the word 'proselyte' implies movement by the gentile concerned, from darkness into light, not the changing of his nature as simple repentance might be termed, and not a bringing in by the body of the Jews as the model of mission would require. For the most part the role of the Jews was simply passively to bear witness through their existence and piety.

I should stress that I do not wish to imply that Jews therefore had no interest in such gentiles as accreted to their communities. Scraps of evidence can be found for active Jewish enthusiasm for gentile recognition of the power of the Jewish God, what I defined as apologetic mission. Thus according to

Josephus the merchant Ananias was eager to persuade the royal family at Charax Spasini 'to revere the god'—in marked contrast to his reluctance to let them become proselytes (*AJ* 20. 34, 40–42). Josephus claimed that Solomon built the Jerusalem Temple precisely in order to persuade all men to serve God (Joseph. *AJ* 8. 117). The same author described how the Jews of Antioch in 67 CE had for many years been bringing into their cult practices (*threskeiai*) many Greeks whom they had thus quite deliberately made 'in some way' a part of themselves (*BJ* 7. 45).[58] I think it likely that such gentiles filled a role equivalent to that filled in later centuries by 'Godfearers' attached to synagogues with a status formally recognized by the Jews among whom they lived (see below, Ch. 6), although there is no evidence from this early date that Jews anywhere yet treated such gentile hangers-on as a defined and honoured *group*.

There is, then, some evidence of a Jewish mission to win gentile *sympathizers* in the first century. It must be presumed that, as with all missionary activity, the intensity of this mission varied from place to place and period to period. There is strikingly little evidence for such sympathizers in the evidence from Alexandria and the rest of Egypt. But that some Jews felt able to justify it to themselves seems clear. The way in which they found justification is however quite inexplicit and it may well have been political or social rather than theological. It might be suggested that such sympathizers were simply those who had established social links with the local Jewish community, and from other *Jews'* point of view this would certainly make sense, although the incentive for gentiles in a pagan city like Antioch publicly to identify themselves with a minority group in this way is obscure. It could perhaps be argued that these gentiles themselves believed that they would receive tangible advantages in this world or the next from their allegiance to the Jewish community and that the Jews encouraged them in this belief

---

[58] Cohen, 'Respect'; 417 and 'Crossing', 27 asserts that this passage must refer to the full conversion of the gentiles concerned, because it implies their social integration into the Jewish community. However, in neither discussion does he make any attempt to explain the phrase *tropo tini*, by which Josephus explicitly modified the description of their incorporation.

in order to win political support from influential friends for their independent existence in a pagan environment. Accounts of inter-communal rivalry between Jews and Greeks in Alexandria in particular and, to a lesser extent, in Antioch suggest that the Jews needed all the help they could get in their demand for *isopoliteia*, which has been persuasively translated in some contexts as the right to follow their own customs within their own polity.[59] It may be that it was only when such a support group was found both useful and viable, as at Antioch, that Jews urged forward their mission to win gentiles to fear God.

This partial mission to win gentile adherents to the Jewish cult is far from the universal proselytizing mission with the portrayal of which this chapter began and which it has been the aim of this chapter to examine. The significance of such apologetic mission lies precisely in its *negative* implications for claims that there was a mission by Jews to win proselytes. Such sympathizers have sometimes been portrayed as half-way between gentile and proselyte or even as 'semi-proselytes'.[60] Sociologically this may sometimes have been an accurate description. Thus Juvenal described how the son of a man who fears the Jewish God, keeping the sabbath and some food laws, carried to extremes his father's habits by denying pagan cult and undergoing circumcision (*Sat.* 14. 96–106). But theologically it is without foundation. Unlike Christian *catechumens* who were expected to baptize, there is no evidence that a pious sympathizer was *expected* to undergo the initiation of circumcision and to become Jewish. To the extent, therefore, that Jews apparently openly through the synagogues in this period offered a hope of God's blessing to gentiles who did not convert, they undermined any effort they might wish to make to win such converts.

In any case, the generally relaxed attitude of Jews to unconverted gentiles outside the land of Israel (see above, Ch. 3) meant that Jews lacked an incentive for proselytizing, and it could be argued that in theological logic arguments against winning converts could even have been brought forward. If

[59] Kasher, *Jews in Hellenistic and Roman Egypt.*
[60] Feldman, 'Omnipresence of God-Fearers', 60.

many Jews believed at this time as did some rabbis in the second and third centuries, that the imminent arrival of the last days could best be facilitated by the repentance and righteous behaviour of Jews (cf. *b. Sanh.* 97b), it might seem a retrograde step to produce more Jews who, through human nature and the difficulties inherent in full observance of the Jewish way of life, were liable to add to the number of Jewish sinners. But such arguments are only found in later periods and even then have an air of justification after the event—no one seems to have urged the corollary, that producing children should also be avoided.

The lack of proselytizing attitudes in first-century Judaism seems to me all the more striking when it is contrasted not just with the early Church but with the developments within Judaism later in antiquity, to be considered below, in Chapter 7. By the third century CE, the patriarch Abraham was described as being so good a proselytizer that he caused God to be known as king of earth as well as heaven, and this prowess in winning proselytes was one of the main features of the career of Abraham singled out for praise in later rabbinic writings. By contrast, it was Abraham's piety as a convert, not a converter, that was stressed by Philo, Josephus, and other writers of earlier periods.[61] What might appear to be an exception on closer inspection proves the rule. Josephus wrote that Abraham went to Egypt 'intending, if he found their doctrine more excellent than his own, to conform to it, or else to rearrange them to a better mind should his own beliefs prove superior' (*AJ* 1. 161). But what he taught was not, it seems, Judaism or even monotheism or anything like it.[62] The burden of his teaching emerges unexpectedly as arithmetic and astronomy (*AJ* 1. 167), while the Jew Artapanus in the second century BCE envisaged Abraham, as the bearer of culture, teaching the Egyptian Pharaoh astrology (Euseb. *Praep. ev.* 9. 18. 1).

[61] Philo, *De Abr.* 60–7; *De Virt.* 212–19; Joseph. *AJ* 1. 154–7; cf. Sandmel, *Philo's Place in Judaism*, 200.

[62] The content of the religious system into which Abraham himself converted and to which he converted others received little attention in Jewish writings in antiquity. Jews knew, of course, that his career predated the covenant on Sinai, but this was a fact that could be ignored in practice.

The missionary hero in search for converts to Judaism is a phenomenon first approved by Jews well after the start of the Christian mission, not before it. There is no good reason to suppose that any Jew would have seen value in seeking proselytes in the first century with an enthusiasm like that of the Christian apostles. The origins of the proselytizing impulse within the Church should be sought elsewhere.

5

Mission in the Early Church

To what extent was the attitude of Jews to non-Jews reflected in the attitude of early Christians to those outside their faith? The question is not as simple as it sounds, and no plausible answer is likely to be straightforward. Firstly, many different groups and individuals claimed in the early centuries to represent the true voice of Christianity, even when designated by their opponents as heretical. I have followed the policy, as with the Jewish material, of accepting the self-designations adopted by individuals in antiquity—thus, anyone who thought of himself or herself as within the community of those who worshipped Christ will be treated as a Christian. Secondly, many Christians in the first decades were Jews (not least, Jesus, Peter, and Paul), and this led from the start to deep controversy about whether one kind of non-Christian (non-Christian Jews) should be treated differently from another kind of non-Christian (non-Christian gentiles). Thirdly, the years after the crucifixion were a time of great eschatological fervour which was inherently likely to have affected all aspects of Christian life, including attitudes to mission. Attitudes which emerged under such eschatological impulses may need to be distinguished from those prevalent in more settled times.

In some ways the easiest aspect of Christian mission to explain was the mission to the Jews. As Jews one would expect the apostles to believe that their interpretation of God's will should be preached to their fellow Jews for the sake of all Israel, who had jointly entered a covenant with God. If my interpretation of Matt. 23: 15 is correct (above, p. 70), it was in just such prophetic mission to other Jews that Pharisees engaged, hence it was this sort of mission that the author of Matthew opposed. The evidence for such a mission to the Jews (albeit not always successful) runs right through the variegated texts of the New Testament. The only real problem in understanding such a mission is to know whether such Jews were really thought of as converts, for their new faith proclaimed itself as the natural, true continuation of their old religion (e.g. Phil. 3: 3). It is not likely that all Jewish Christians underwent the thorough reorientation of religious outlook undergone by St Paul according to his own evaluation of his prophetic calling on the road to Damascus (Gal. 1: 12–24).[1] The idea that Jews should be preserved in their own, non-Christian faith as *testes veritatis*—that is, witnesses to Jewish suffering for the rejection of Christ—is not to be found in Christian writings before Augustine, and I am not convinced by the eirenic view that St Paul preached a dual route to salvation (Mosaic for Jews, through Christ for gentiles).[2]

Much more complex is the origin of the Christian mission to the gentiles. If I am right (above, Ch. 4), Jews in the first century might have favoured an apologetic mission to win gentile sympathizers, but they would have seen no point in a proselytizing mission to win new Jews. According to some texts preserved in the Christian tradition, at least some Christians at some times took a very different attitude. They believed that it was desirable for as many humans as possible to be brought within the fold of the Church.

The text most often used by theologians as a classic statement of Christian universal proselytizing mission is the so-called great commission addressed by Jesus after the resurrection to the apostles at the end of the Gospel of Matthew (Matt. 28: 18–20): 'Go and teach all nations, baptizing them and bringing them instruction.'[3] According to Mark 13: 10, Jesus stated that the Gospel must be preached among all nations before the end comes. St Paul claimed of

[1] On Paul's view of his experience as a religious conversion, see Segal, *Paul the Convert*.

[2] Gaston, *Paul and the Torah*, quoted with approval by Gager, 'Proselytism and exclusivity', 75. For arguments against Gaston's view of Paul, see Sanders, *Paul, the Law and the Jewish People*, 171–9. For the claim that *ethne* in Matt. 28: 18–20 means *goyim*, and thus excludes Jews, see Harrington, *Light of All Nations*, 110–23. On Jews as *testes veritates*, see Juster, *Juifs*, i. 227–30.

[3] See e.g. Blauw, *Missionary Nature of the Church*, 86.

himself that he felt under such a compulsion to preach the good news that it shaped his whole life (1 Cor. 9: 16–23).[4] This self-image is confirmed by the early Christian traditions about Paul and others as missionaries to the gentiles. According to the Acts of the Apostles, a series of brave individuals travelled widely in those years to tell both Jews and gentiles the good news. Acts 11: 19–20 states specifically that after persecution arose in Jerusalem, some of the scattered brethren in Phoenicia and elsewhere preached only to the Jews, but 'men of Cyprus and Cyrene' on coming to Antioch 'spoke to the Greeks also, preaching the Lord Jesus'. The historicity of Acts is dubious, but the narrative of the spread of the Church must have been credible to Christians at the time of the composition of the work—still disputed, but certainly before the end of the first century—and it is therefore certain that by that date the Christians for whom Acts was written found it praiseworthy, at the least, that someone in the past had carried out an active mission in the style portrayed by that work. The disciples were to be witnesses 'to the ends of the earth' (Acts 1: 8), testifying to the Gospel (Acts 20: 24) until it has been preached 'in all the creation under heaven' (Col. 1: 23). The travelling apostle became a literary type incorporated into extra-canonical Christian literature, such as the Acts of Thomas, a work composed some time before the mid-third century. Paul became the hero who had proclaimed justice to the whole cosmos (1 Clement 5: 7). For Eusebius in the fourth century, the Christian message was now being announced to 'all men and to every nation' (Euseb. *Hist. Eccl.* 1. 2. 17).

The problems arise when one asks the content of the message and the effect it was expected to have on its auditors. Many modern students of contemporary Christian mission distinguish clearly the type of mission they find desirable from proselytizing. Naturally enough, they seek to base their own notions of (usually) educational mission on biblical texts.[5] It is axiomatic for such students that the preconceptions of the stalwarts of the great missionary movements of the nineteenth century were in fact the product of distinct

---

[4] See e.g. Senior and Stuhlmueller, *Biblical Foundations*, 161.   [5] ibid. 2–3.

historical circumstances, despite the belief of those missionaries at the time that they were fulfilling biblical commands.[6]
Such disagreements are fomented by the remarkable scarcity
of teachings in the New Testament about the way the Gospel
should be spread. It is likely that this scarcity reflected not the
unimportance of the subject but the fact that, for early
Christians themselves, the preaching of the Gospel was too
obvious to need detailed injunctions.[7] But whatever its cause,
this phenomenon has much stimulated later dispute about the
correct aims of Christian mission, in the present as well as the
past.

So far as I know, no early Christian text states explicitly
that it is desirable to turn non-Christians into Christians by
converting them and enrolling them as members of their local
churches. The notion may be implied by the ubiquitous
assumption in such texts that it is desirable to preach the
Gospel of Christ (e.g. Rom. 10: 14–17), but it is not *stated*.
Various explanations of this fact can be suggested. Perhaps
the Christian message at the beginning said nothing at all
about incorporating outsiders into any institution, and the
institutionalized Church, and local churches, were only
originally intended as a temporary, historical phenomenon to
help prevent backsliding by those who had seen the light in
the short period between the incarnation and the second
coming,[8] but this explanation presupposes that the expectation of an imminent end, to be found, for instance, in 1 Thess.
4: 16–5: 11 and 1 Cor. 7: 29–31, was prevalent in the first
generation of Christians which, though likely, is disputed.[9]
Perhaps the earliest Christians, with their eagerness to spread
the Gospel, lacked interest in institutions, and their
successors, who took the institutions for granted, lacked
interest in mission. If that is so, perhaps the concern of much
New Testament literature with the health of church communities can be explained simply as the product of the
epistolary and homiletic genres in which they were written,
rather than as a reflection of the concerns of their authors and

---

[6] Blauw, *Missionary Nature*, 9.   [7] So Blauw, ibid. 102.

[8] See Markus, *Saeculum*, 180.

[9] For the view that early Christians believed that the end had already come, so
there was no sense of waiting, see Wright, *New Testament and People of God*, 459–64.

readers. Even in a writing as late as the *Epistle to Diognetus*, composed in the second or third century CE, a Christian rhetorically addressing a pagan could describe Christianity as if it lacked institutionalized forms: Christians were to be found in no special place, with no special customs or lifestyle, but 'spread throughout the world, like the soul through the body' (*Ep. Diog.* 5–6, esp. 6.1–2).

It may prove helpful at this juncture to reiterate the various elements of the full-blown concept of proselytizing mission which I laid out in the first chapter and whose applicability to early Christians I wish to scrutinize. It will be recalled that a proselytizing mission was defined as the approval by the members of a self-aware organization of efforts to bring as many people as possible into that organization, when by so doing they expected to change the lives of the newcomers in such a way that they would conform more closely to the attitudes and beliefs of the existing members (see above, pp. 3–4, 6). The doubts expressed above suggest two areas in which the early Christian mission to the gentiles may seem to have differed from this ideal type. First, did those Christians who reached out to others think of themselves as belonging to a specific, self-defined group? Secondly, if they did so, did they believe that it was desirable to incorporate all other humans into that group?

One reason to suppose that some early Christian mission was not intent on proselytizing is that Christian authors sometimes enunciated hopes for what sounds like an educational mission. Thus Luke in Acts quoted Isaiah's description of Israel as the light to the gentiles (Acts 13: 46–7), and a desire to educate by example was also sometimes reflected elsewhere in the early Church (cf. 1 Pet. 2: 12; Matt. 5: 16). It is also possible, but hard to demonstrate from the surviving evidence, that some missionaries were concerned primarily to encourage the simple recognition of Christ as a powerful deity, that is, intent on apologetic mission. This, after all, was the most likely effect of the witnessing of miracles and healing, for which there is much evidence.[10] Peter in Rome

---

[10] On the role of miracles, see MacMullen, *Christianizing*, 25–30, 40–1, and *passim*.

was said to have rejoiced at the 'mass of people daily called to the holy name' (*Acta Petri Cum Simone* 33, ed. Lipsius, 85). It is mistaken to assume that all who called themselves Christians were wholly devoted to their new cult alone. Some Gnostic followers of Jesus shared the official Roman view that an offering of incense to other gods was not so drastic an act that it must be avoided even at the cost of persecution.[11]

Such apologetic and educational mission will not have presupposed that the audience to whom the missionaries preached should join any new community. According to Acts 8: 36–9, the Ethiopian eunuch baptized by Philip proclaimed his belief that Jesus was the son of God, but afterwards simply 'went on his way rejoicing'. Presumably there did not yet exist any church community in Ethiopia into which he could enter, but the author of Acts left open the crucial question whether missionaries would be happy to allow a new convert not to join an *ecclesia* when an appropriate local community was available. Since St Paul at least was capable of thinking in such representative terms that he could claim to have 'completed the Gospel from Jerusalem and in a circle as far as Illyricum' simply on the grounds that some of the citizens there had set up churches (Rom. 15: 19),[12] the decision of any particular individual who heard the Gospel to exclude him or herself from any community might seem to be a matter of indifference. On the other hand, it is hard to reconcile such indifference with Paul's evident concern to define Christian communities in relation to Judaism and paganism (cf. 1 Cor. 8–10).

Such arguments suggest that some Christians at some times did not view an active mission to convert as obviously desirable, but do not show that no Christians ever espoused such a mission. What, then, is the positive evidence that some early Christians sometimes approved of a policy of proselytizing the world?

It may be best to begin with the frequent (if, as I have just noted, not universal) vehemence of Christian opposition to paganism, wherever and by whomsoever it was practised.

---

[11] Gager, *Kingdom and Community*, 124.
[12] For Paul's treatment of churches as 'representative', see Sanders, *Paul, the Law and the Jewish People*, 189.

Such opposition, which contrasts markedly with the general trend in Judaism before 100 CE to tolerance of gentile paganism outside the land of Israel (see above, Ch. 3), was presupposed by most early Christian literature and by many pagan observers of the Church; most Christians who compromised by offering incense to the gods will have accepted that their actions were sinful but claimed that the sin was venial. Paul urged the Corinthians to flee idolatry (1 Cor. 10: 14), which he considered the primary sin (cf. 1 Cor. 5: 10; 6: 9–11). In 1 Thess. 1: 9 and Rom 1: 18–25 he implied that he would appeal to all gentiles to abjure paganism.[13] Similar sentiments were ascribed in the New Testament to John (1 John 5: 21). The suggestion that St Paul posed no threat to the cult of Artemis of the Ephesians was put by the author of Acts 19: 23–40 into the mouth of the pagan city clerk. It may be assumed that Paul himself would have been delighted to be seen as such a threat.[14] According to 2 Clement 3: 1, Christ has saved Christians from idolatry.

From the point of view of non-Christians, such opposition to pagan worship was both noticeable and reprehensible. It was their neglect of the sacred rites in the temples that brought Christians in the Pontic countryside to the notice of Pliny the Younger in the early second century CE (Pliny, *Ep.* 10. 96). The pagan philosopher Celsus, in his attacks on Christianity composed in the mid-second century CE, complained that Christians 'cannot bear to see temples and altars and images' (Origen, *C. Celsum*, 7. 62). Christian martyrs were killed not so much for their championing of Christ as their refusal to worship other gods. If indeed some Christians were the first individuals in the ancient world to preach, not that gentile pagan idolatry was foolish (as did Epicureans and Jews), but that it was immoral, the antagonism of pagan society to their teachings is hardly difficult to comprehend.

---

[13] Senior and Stuhlmueller, *Biblical Foundations*, 186, note the latter passage but ascribe it, wrongly in my view, to 'standard Jewish teaching'. Fredriksen, 'Judaism, Circumcision and Apocalyptic Hope', 553, describes Paul's demand as standard for Jews in the eschatological age, but the Jewish texts provide evidence of *expectation* of the end of gentile paganism, not a Jewish *demand* for it.

[14] *Contra* Schussler-Fiorenza (ed.),, *Aspects of Religious Propaganda*, 18.

At the same time, the idea that there is no salvation outside the Church was early embedded in some streams of Christianity, in particular those which lay behind the Fourth Gospel and the letters of Paul. The concept was not explicitly enunciated until Cyprian in 256 CE (*Ep.* 73. 21; *De Cath. Eccl. Unitate* 6), after which it became a commonplace quoted, for example, by Augustine in the late fourth century (*De Baptismo*, 4. 17 (24), Petschenig, p. 250). But it is implicit in Jesus' assertion to the disciples at the end of Mark's Gospel in the longer, and probably inauthentic version, that 'he that believes and is baptised shall be saved, but he that believes not shall be damned' (Mark 16: 16). Paul preached to the Romans that the only way to be saved is by faith in Christ (Rom. 11: 13–36), and in the similitudes of the Shepherd of Hermas, which may well have been composed later in the first century, it was implied that to be numbered with the gentiles (meaning non-Christians) is to be damned (*Shepherd* 75. 3, ed. Joly = *Simil.* 8. 9. 3).[15] In the mid-second century Justin Martyr contrasted the eternal punishment of the wicked to the bliss of the virtuous, 'by which we mean those who have become Christians' (*II Apol.* 1).

Such a doctrine left (and still leaves) a difficult theological problem in accounting for the fate of the unconverted who remain ignorant of the Gospel.[16] One way around the problem is that attributed to Jesus in Mark 9: 40: 'He that is not against us is on our side.' But elsewhere the view expressed is harsher. According to 2 Thessalonians 1: 8–9, in the last days all those who know not God and obey not the gospel of Christ will suffer eternal destruction. Hence the altruistic sense of responsibility for the unevangelized world. The general picture of such people untouched by the Gospel is that they are hopeless sinners: in the imagery of the Shepherd of Hermas (*Shepherd*, 53. 4, ed. Joly = *Simil.* 4. 4), they are sprouting, withered trees. They are of course potential converts, but they are generally seen as outsiders beyond the frontiers of the community that matters (that is,

[15] On the date of composition of the *Shepherd of Hermas*, see Lane Fox, *Pagans and Christians*, 331–90.

[16] For the continuing problem, see Senior and Stuhlmueller, *Biblical Foundations*, 187.

the Church), rather than errant members of the (whole human) community. Christian writers in the early centuries often, though not always, took for granted that knowledge of, and assent to, particular metaphysical propositions about Christ and his relationship to the divine and human orders are conditions to be expected, and perhaps required, of those who wish to find favour in the eyes of God.

It is worth stressing this attitude to the unevangelized because early Christians sometimes presupposed that it is better not to have heard the Gospel at all than to have heard it and rejected. A similar principle seems to lie behind a passage in the Gospel of Matthew, where Chorazin, Bethsaida, and Capernaum are cursed for their unwillingness to recognize Jesus' manifold miracles, and compared unfavourably with the inhabitants of Tyre and Sidon, who at least have the excuse that they have not seen the mighty works in question (Matt. 11: 21–4), but early Christian attitudes towards those who had failed to recognize the power of Jesus during his lifetime may have been different from their attitudes towards those who did not accept the Gospel. In the Gospel of John the same sort of argument was put differently: 'if I had not come and spoken to them, they had not had sin: but now they have no cloak for their sin' (John 15: 22). So too Paul claimed that ignorance was a valid excuse, and that he has therefore been forgiven his blasphemies done 'ignorantly in unbelief' (1 Tim. 1: 13). According to the Shepherd of Hermas, those who sin knowingly receive double the punishment of those who sin in ignorance, although the difference is oddly described: the former die eternally, the latter just die (*Shepherd*, 95. 2, ed. Joly = *Simil.* 9. 18. 2). Against the background of this theology, the argument of the apocryphal writing *Kerygma Petri* reads rather grimly. According to this work (Fragment 3, ed. Klostermann, p. 15, lines 19–24), the apostles were sent out partly to remove from their auditors the excuse (*apologia*) that they had not heard the Gospel.

Some Christians were thus strikingly clear that all humans must convert. But it is less clear to what they thought people should convert, or, more precisely, into what group. Many early Christians would have been horrified at the suggestion that the aim of their struggle was only to increase the number of subscribers to a particular religious denomination. For Paul, his theology was not a type of, or an alternative to, Judaism; it was the single correct and obvious creed which should transform the whole world; thus in theory the only group to which he felt himself to belong and to which he appealed was coextensive with humanity. But despite such logic, Christian behaviour, vocabulary and religious concerns often revealed from St Paul onwards a clear notion that they belonged to a specific, well-defined group, the Church.[17]

The reasons for the emergence of the Church as an institution are fiercely debated and not here my concern.[18] It will suffice to show how soon after the crucifixion the notion existed, and therefore to place it firmly in the period of greatest missionary activity. The concept of the *ecclesia* as a 'pure and uncorrupted virgin' until the advent of heresy after the apostolic age can be found in its clearest form in the fourth century, in the Church History of Eusebius (*Hist. Eccl.* 3. 32. 7), but a similar image was already applied by Paul to the Corinthians (2 Cor. 11: 2–4) and, the word *ecclesia* ('assembly') to define all those who believe in Christ, wherever they may live, is already familiar in the New Testament. Thus the author of Ephesians urged in Eph. 5: 25: 'Husbands, love your wives, even as Christ also loved the Church, and gave himself for it . . .'. The crucifixion, according to this understanding, occurred not to save the world but the Church. It is of course likely that many different groups claimed in opposition to each other that they constituted *the* Church. But such conflicting claims demonstrate only the value of the claim for each party.

The notion that Christians were a race set apart was implicit in all early Christian literature. The name 'Christian' was not itself attested before the composition of the Acts of the Apostles (Acts 11: 26), and, despite the claim of the author of Acts that it came into use during Paul's mission, the term may not have become current until the end of the first century, when Acts was written.[19] None the less the teachings of St Paul already implied that Christians constituted a 'third

---

[17] See Meeks, *First Urban Christians*, ch. 3.
[18] See e.g. Blauw, *Missionary Nature*, 79, and the large literature on ecclesiology.
[19] See the arguments of Georgi, *Opponents*, 347.

race' (cf. 1 Cor. 10: 32).[20] Christians were a group with special entrance requirements (faith and baptism). They were the chosen, the elect (1 Pet. 1: 1–2), with whom other Christians could identify by using the first person plural (e.g. Justin, *I Apol.* 14). Hence the emphasis on the need for harmony within the Christian community which is such a feature of Christian writing from Paul to the Council of Nicaea. In the visions of the Shepherd of Hermas, the Church was personified as an aged woman (*Shepherd*, 8. 1, ed. Joly = *Vis.* 2. 4. 1), then as a great tower which is still under construction (*Shepherd*, 13, ed. Joly = *Vis.* 3. 5. 1–5). In the *Kerygma Petri* (Fragment 2, ed. Klostermann, p. 15, line 8), Christians were explicitly described as a third race who worship God in a new way.[21] The terminology used by Eusebius in the early fourth century was marvellously fluid. Christians were a 'new nation' (*Hist. Eccl.* 1. 4. 2), which extended to wherever the sun shines (10. 4. 19). They were 'the believers', 'the saints' (cf. Acts 9: 13) and so on. The martyr who, when questioned by an official as to his nation and city, responded simply that he was a Christian (Euseb. *Hist. Eccl.* 5. 1. 20) (see above, Ch. 1), provided thereby both an answer and an evasion, for outsiders too were at a loss how to categorize the Church. Josephus (*AJ* 18. 64) described Christians as a tribe. In one single imperial edict cited by Eusebius, they were defined successively as a nation (*ethnos*), a superstition (*deisidaimonia*) and a cult (*threskeia*) (*Hist. Eccl.* 9. 9a. 1–6).

Christians also had a clear concept of individual churches within the Church. These communities were sociologically distinct once they had set up their own meeting places separate from those of synagogues. The members had no need of elaborate doctrines or hierarchies to give them a sense of their identity, although in fact both developed quite early.[22] None the less they early developed a communal vocabulary, as brothers and sisters in Christ, fellow citizens of the same household (Eph. 2: 19), blessed, like a mundane happy family, with children (2 Clement 2: 1).

[20] See the arguments of Sanders, *Paul, the Law and the Jewish People*, 172, 176.
[21] For the literature on Christians as a 'third race', see Harnack, *Die Mission und Ausbreitung*, 259–81.   [22] Markus, 'Problem of Self-Definition', 3.

Christians preferred to marry within their community.[23] They gave help to each other in times of adversity before offering aid to outsiders: when in the late third century Alexandria came under siege, the bishop Anatolius first ensured the escape of 'those from the *ecclesia*' and only later gave succour to others, Eusebius in his narration of these events implicitly approved the attitude thus displayed (*Hist. Eccl.* 7. 32. 11). Christians expelled undesirables from their number so that the divine name might not be blasphemed (cf. 2 Clement 13: 1–3); presumably their fear was that outsiders might be misled by the actions of such perverts into denigrating Christianity as a whole. Ignatius in the early second century produced a fine picture of a model *ecclesia*, which must have deacons, bishop, and presbyters to deserve the name (*Ignatius to the Trallians*, 3. 1). Each community was sufficiently separate from the others for Paul to be able to expect gratitude from the Corinthians because, as he claimed, he had robbed other churches to do them service (2 Cor. 11: 8). The martyr Polycarp prayed for the churches (rather than the Church) throughout the inhabited world (Euseb. *Hist. Eccl.* 4. 15. 9). The precise relationship between Church and churches was left unclear.

To some extent, then, and despite the lack of such a clear-cut theological basis, some early Christian institutions mirrored those in contemporary Jewish society. From a very early date there existed self-aware Christian communities into which an outsider could be inducted. Conversely, it was in theory just as possible to be a sympathizer close to, but outside, a Christian *ecclesia* as it was to be a sympathizer on the fringes of Judaism. The story of the freelance exorcist in Mark 9: 38–40 suggests that the notion was not always ruled out. According to the story, an exorcist who had not followed the disciples had none the less cast out devils in Jesus' name. The disciples' reaction was to forbid him, 'because he follows not us', but Jesus gave them instructions to leave him alone: 'for there is no man which shall do a miracle in my name, that can lightly speak evil of me.' The crucial question is whether any Christians wanted all outsiders to become full converts or

---

[23] Schoedel, 'Theological Norms', 50.

all would be satisfied, like Jews before 100 CE, with sympathetic support and appreciation.

The predictions of some early Christians about the awful fate of those who did not believe suggest that those Christians at least would be satisfied with nothing less than full conversion. Precisely what they meant by 'full conversion' doubtless varied, but there can be little doubt that they sometimes expected the convert to enter a new community.[24] The images used by the Gospel writers were of fishing for men (Mark 1: 17; Luke 5: 10) and of inviting strangers to a wedding feast (Luke 14: 16–24). Paul wrote that any method is permissible to gain souls: the image he used was of heaping up wealth (1 Cor. 9: 20–1).[25] Those thus gained were the husbandry of the apostle (1 Cor. 3: 9), his work in the Lord (1 Cor. 9: 1). As often, the image was presented most clearly in the Shepherd of Hermas. Much of the work is based on a parable which emphasised the importance of getting into the tower which explicitly symbolized the Church. The visions were made to begin with Hermas' awareness of his sin, which was simply his failure to convert his own household as he could, and should, have done (*Shepherd*, 3. 1, ed. Joly = *Vis.* 1. 3. 1) (see above, Ch. 1).

Christians thus sought new members for the wider Church, but they did not necessarily therefore also expect them to become part of a local Christian community. When many individuals in a particular place believed, it was normal for the successful missionary to found a church, as, for example, Peter is said to have done in Sidon (*Ps. Clementines, Homilies*, 7. 8), appointing religious leaders to guide the new converts (cf. 1 Clement 42. 3–4). Early Christian writers often simply assumed that believers belonged to local communities, not least perhaps because that was reckoned the ideal type of Christian living. So, for instance, Paul after his baptism stayed with the disciples in Damascus according to Acts 9: 18–19, and the spread of the Gospel could be measured by the spread of church communities (Acts 16: 5; Euseb. *Hist. Eccl.* 2. 3. 1–2). In practice there must have been some Christians in the

---

[24] Lane Fox, *Pagans and Christians*, 314–17.
[25] On rabbinic parallels to the phrase see Daube, *New Testament and Rabbinic Judaism*, 352–61.

first centuries who lived in the countryside or for other reasons were unable to participate fully in Christian communities. It can be argued that Christian missionaries, who were presumably aware of this possibility, therefore only set up churches as centres from which the rest of humanity could receive enlightenment, without the concomitant obligations which fell upon full church members.[26] But such rationalizations of missionary activity seem to me unlikely, and can certainly not be proved from anything written by early Christians themselves. I think that it is more likely that the position mirrored that of Jews. Ancient writers, both Jews and non-Jews, assumed that Jews lived in communities which were subjected to internal self-regulation. Usually, indeed, they did so, but sometimes they did not. (Consider, for example, the solitary John the Baptist, or Josephus' friend Bannus, who lived alone in the Judaean desert (Joseph. *Vita*, 11) .) In ancient (and most modern) descriptions of Jews and Judaism these exceptions were not explained away. They were just ignored.

Christians assumed, correctly, that the lives of those who joined their churches would be transformed. As Hermas proclaimed, there is no other conversion (*metanoia*) than when we went down into the water (*Shepherd*, 31. 1–2 ed. Joly = *Mand*. 4. 3. 1–2). Ignatius implied that Christianity is a way of life (*Ignatius to Magnesians*, 10. 1). In this respect it was like Judaism (and unlike other cults). Christians thus hoped to teach every man to become 'perfect' in Christ (Col. 1: 28). After all, Jesus according to the great commission to the apostles in the Gospel of Matthew, had demanded total submission to *all* his commands (Matt. 28: 18–20).[27] Obedience was complicated by variations in the tradition about precisely what Jesus had taught. Even the minimal rules of the so-called Apostolic Decree contained in Acts 15: 19–20 were preserved in different wordings in the different manuscript traditions of the New Testament and left much unclear. None the less it was not long before a host of taboos specific to Christians emerged, every bit as restrictive as the dietary rules which confined Jews but in the case of Christians mostly

[26] So Senior and Stuhlmueller, *Biblical Foundations*, 184.
[27] See the interpretation of Blauw, *Missionary Nature*, 87.

concerned with the governance of, or abstention from, sexual relations.[28]

The biggest agent of transformation for the convert was negative: withdrawal from pagan worship. Withdrawal from cult immediately separated Christians from the surrounding society. Each day they marked their difference from their non-Christian neighbours simply by abstention, for pagan cult infringed upon every aspect of life. It was probably precisely the pressure of such separation from ordinary people that led Christians to stick together to form their alternative communities. The position of an isolated atheist (as pagans would have viewed solitary Christians) was well-nigh insupportable.

In any case Christians welcomed converts into their communities with a warmth far distinguished from the ambivalence of contemporary Jews. Converts were given immediately a status equal in theory to that of existing members of the community: people were either entirely outside the Church or entirely inside it. No extant early Christian text refers to sympathizers on the fringe of Christianity. The catechumen, a category found in churches from the second century onwards, was from the start expected to proceed to baptism and full conversion. Any delay, as urged for example by Tertullian in his treatise on baptism, was simply intended to ensure a more efficacious rite of passage: for him, baptism must be undergone only by a convert properly instructed in the meaning of the ceremony, so that in effect education became part of the process of initiation. The practice of delaying baptism altogether until near death to avoid sinning after it, probably, despite the possible implications of Heb. 6: 4–6, did not become common until after Constantine, who was one of its first practitioners.[29]

Such a proselytizing mission was a shocking novelty in the ancient world. The amazed reactions of Jews to the policy of making gentiles 'members of the same body' (Eph. 2: 11–3: 21) show that Paul was not seen by them as simply continuing Jewish proselytizing in a special form. If he had been only the

[28] See Meeks, *First Urban Christians*, 97–103; Brown, *Body and Society*.

[29] Lane Fox, *Pagans and Christians*, 338–9, citing Tertullian, *De Bapt.* 18. 5–6.

Christian inheritor of a Jewish concept of mission he would have had no call to speak so emotionally about his calling as the apostle to the gentiles.[30] Only familiarity makes us fail to appreciate the extraordinary ambition of the single apostle who invented the whole idea of a systematic conversion of the world, area by geographical area.[31]

It is therefore a moot, and important, question whether Paul was alone in thinking of himself as apostle to the gentiles. He did, after all, portray his own calling as divinely vouchsafed in a time of eschatological fervour, and he stated clearly (1 Cor. 12. 28–9) that 'not all can be apostles'. The evidence is remarkably exiguous, but there is just enough to suggest that some, if not necessarily many, Christians *in Paul's time* shared his missionary assumptions, even if they rarely (if ever) took such active steps as he did to win proselytes to the Christian faith. Thus from occasional hints in Paul's own writings it seems likely that not all the missionaries to the gentiles were under his control: for example, in Romans 16: 3–4, Paul sent greetings to Prisca and Aquila, his 'fellow-workers in Christ Jesus' who are greeted by 'all the churches of the gentiles'. According to Acts 11: 20 unnamed Christians, not including Paul since they came from Cyprus and Cyrene, 'took the Gospel to the Greeks in Antioch'.[32]

But it is a separate question how many Christians believed a proselytizing mission to be desirable after the eschatological fervour of the first generations. Against any view that such a mission was generally seen by Christians as applicable in later times is the treatment of the texts of Jesus' commission to the apostles (Matt. 28: 19–20; Mark 16: 15–16) in patristic writings of the second to fourth centuries. By most of the Church Fathers these texts were treated historically (for example, Euseb. *Hist. Eccl.* 3. 5. 2): the Gospels recorded the teaching given at that time to the apostles, and by implication the injunction to spread the gospel and baptize the world was not understood to apply to later generations. So far as I can

---

[30] Blauw, *Missionary Nature*, 96–8.

[31] Cf. Bowers, 'Paul and Religious Propaganda'.

[32] On a pre-Pauline gentile mission, see Hengel, *Between Jesus and Paul*; Hengel, *Acts and Earliest Christianity*; Sanders, *Paul, Law and Jewish People*, 191–2.

discover, when these texts were interpreted to apply to their own day, the religious messages which early Christian writers derived from them did not include an injunction to missionary activity. Thus Eusebius (*Dem. Ev.* 1. 6. 74–5) cited Matthew 28: 19–20 to show that 'Christianity' was what Christ told the apostles to teach. Epiphanius (*Ancoratus*, 7. 1; 8. 7) quoted the same text to illustrate the concept of the Trinity. Tertullian (*De Bapt.* 13. 3) and Cyprian (*Epp.* 27. 3) quoted it for the concept of baptism. Elsewhere Cyprian also used the commission text as an example of the desirability of obeying Christ's commands (*Epp.* 63. 18).[33]

Such silence about Gospel passages used as prime proof texts in later Christian missionary theology is striking but it is also important to note that no early Church Father (so far as I know) positively *denied* that Christ's commission to convert all humanity still applied in their time. Indeed the notion that the commission might still apply seems to be implicit in the argument of at least one patristic text. In *De Fuga*, 6. 2, Tertullian was explicitly concerned with the relevance of Gospel passages to his own day. He asserted that injunctions in some passages in the Gospels to restrict mission to Israel and to flee in time of persecution were no longer valid for the post-apostolic generations.

It is remarkable that the missionary assumptions taken for granted by most historians of the early Church prove to be based on such tenuous evidence, but the negative picture I have given, that Christians did not deny the desirability of mission, but nor did they generally affirm it, seems to reflect the general attitude of patristic authors. In a striking passage of *Contra Celsum* (3: 9), Origen replied to an attack by the pagan Celsus, that 'if all men (*anthropoi*) wished to be Christians, the Christians would not want it', by asserting that this was a lie. Origen cited as evidence the fact that Christians travel as far as they can go all over the inhabited world to spread the word, spurred on by the fact (3: 8) that

[33] The scarcity of quotations of Matt. 28: 18–20 in writings of the 2nd cent. is noted also by Green, *Evangelism*, 290, who deduces from this that mission was not seen as a duty but as a spiritual rather than legal command. The distinction seems to me dubious, but it reflects quite well the lack of a clear theology about mission in patristic texts.

God wants the whole world to be filled with Christian piety. This seems a peculiarly clear statement of universal proselytizing mission, but it must be significant that Celsus could have made his charge. If the apostolic commission had been generally and explicitly taken by second-century Christians as an important element in their religious self-perception, one might have expected precisely their universal missionary ambitions to be the main butt of criticism from such hostile observers as Celsus.

Thus we shall never know for certain how clear a notion of his proselytizing aims was in the mind of Celsus' contemporary in the second half of the second century CE, the missionary Pantaenus, when he set off on his great journey to bring the Gospel to the nations of the East as far as India (Euseb. *Hist. Eccl.* 5. 10. 2), nor how accurate a picture of the Church is provided by Eusebius' claim in the same passage that before the time of Pantaenus there were many 'evangelists of the word . . . on the apostolic model'. But from the point of view of the present study such uncertainties may not be very important. What is crucial is not that the notion of universal proselytizing *was* often adduced by Christians after the apostolic age (which is dubious), but that it *could* be, as it was (polemically) by Origen and as it has been by Christians of much more recent times. In the rest of this book, I shall try to trace the impact of this novel and powerful concept on the religious history of late antiquity. In the final chapter I shall make some tentative suggestions about its possible origins.

6

Judaism in the Talmudic Period
Attitudes to Gentile Paganism

IN the final three chapters of this book I shall examine the possibility that the novel policy of a universal proselytizing mission found in early Christianity provoked not just attention and opposition in the late antique world, but also imitation. I shall begin the investigation in this and the next chapter by scrutinizing the comparatively large body of evidence which survives to testify to the attitudes of Jews in this period.

Judaism in the talmudic period (broadly defined, for these purposes, as from c.100 CE to c.500 CE) was probably hardly less diverse than it had been before 70 CE. At the very end of the first century Josephus still wrote about the three distinct *haireseis* of the Jews (Pharisees, Sadducees, and Essenes) as existing groups (*AJ* 18. 12–22), and the common assumption of modern scholars that Sadducees and Essenes simply disappeared soon after the Jerusalem Temple is only a hypothesis and not in fact very plausible.[1] Variety was slow to disappear.

Rabbinic Judaism had some connection to Pharisaism, but modern ignorance about the latter precludes too accurate a description of the relationship.[2] In any case, the concepts and concerns of the rabbis evolved rapidly in the second and third centuries CE through the efforts of small, intensive coteries of

---

[1] For the assumption, see e.g. the important study by Cohen, 'Significance of Yavneh', esp. 31–6.

[2] On the relationship of rabbinic to Pharisaic Judaism, compare Neusner, *Rabbinic Traditions about the Pharisees*, with the critique by Sanders, *Jewish Law*, 166–254.

religious enthusiasts who produced in *c.*200 CE the Mishnah and in the following centuries a mass of legal and homiletic material.[3] However, at some time before antiquity merged into the Middle Ages, rabbinic Judaism became normative among the Jews who lived within the boundaries of the Roman empire and its successor states, although this process may have been both gradual and slow.

Rabbinic texts of the second and third centuries, such as the Mishnah and Tosefta, still presupposed that much of the Jewish population, even in close proximity to rabbinic academies, was indifferent to the rabbis' religious concerns.[4] Explicit evidence for rabbinic influence in the Mediterranean diaspora is negligible until the late fourth century. It is possible that rabbis were accorded no authority whatsoever in such centres of Jewish settlement as Rome, Greece, and Asia Minor until the rabbinic *nasi*, called in the Roman law codes the 'patriarch of the Jews', was accorded by the Roman government, probably in the late 380s CE or soon after under Theodosius the Great, something akin to the status of a Roman magistrate.[5] Thus in 404 CE the *nasi*'s efforts to raise funds for his own purposes from diaspora communities was recognized by the Roman authorities as legitimate (*Cod. Theod.* 16. 8. 17) after its temporary suppression since 399 CE (*Cod. Theod.* 16. 8. 14); in a law of 429 CE after its cessation, this tax was described as the payment which the patriarchs had once demanded as 'crown gold' (*Cod. Theod.* 16. 8. 29). In 392 CE the emperors confirmed the devolved authority of the *nasi* over excommunications from Jewish communities throughout the empire (*Cod. Theod.* 16. 8. 8). On the deposition of Gamaliel VI from his honorary prefecture in 415 CE, it was taken for granted that he had the ability to found and dismantle synagogues (*Cod. Theod.* 16. 8. 22). This transformation of the leading rabbi into an empire-wide autocrat parallel to the most powerful bishops within the Christian Church probably did not survive more than a

[3] Introduction to this material in Strack and Stemberger, *Introduction*. On the rabbinic schools, see Levine, *Rabbinic Class*.

[4] Oppenheimer, *Am Ha-aretz*; Goodman, *State and Society*, 102–4.

[5] On this and the following argument, see Goodman, 'Roman State and Jewish Patriarch'.

generation (cf. *Cod. Theod.* 16. 8. 29), but this may have been the catalyst that finally enshrined the rabbinic religious values of the *nasi* firmly in the centre of Jewish life, marking an important stage in the process by which rabbinic Judaism became normative.

If this analysis is correct, religious variety within Judaism will have continued to be taken for granted before the 380s among most inhabitants of the Roman empire who described themselves as Jews. However, if non-rabbinic Jews produced religious writings most—perhaps all—of them have disappeared, and hints about the nature of non-rabbinic Judaism thus have to be gleaned from the hostile comments of rabbis, from the architecture of synagogues, such as the great building at Sardis, from the iconography of the frescoes on the walls of the Dura Europus synagogue, and from the contents of, and assumptions revealed by, the numerous inscriptions set up by Jews all over the empire in the late-Roman period.[6] Such hints can never be entirely satisfactory as evidence, but they can be combined into quite a detailed picture. It is noticeable and helpful that, unless the pattern of survival is deeply misleading, diaspora Jews seem to have espoused the epigraphic habit increasingly as the Roman imperial period progressed.

In all this varied evidence about rabbinic and other forms of Judaism one might reasonably expect to find a variety of attitudes to gentile paganism outside the land of Israel. Such variety will indeed emerge, and each distinct view, as it was stated or implied, will be examined in some detail below. But of greatest interest will be the evidence that seems to show a shift by most rabbis and some other Jews away from the tolerance towards such paganism which, I argued in Chapter 3, was characteristic in the first century not just of Josephus and Philo but of most Jews. The incentive to examine this evidence in detail is all the greater because of the claim in a recent study devoted to this topic that 'Jewish thinking about gentile pagans becomes milder as one gets later'. I shall argue

---

[6] On synagogue architecture, see Levine, *Synagogue in Late Antiquity*; on Sardis, see Hanfmann, *Sardis*; on Dura-Europus, see Kraeling, *Excavations at Dura-Europus*; for inscriptions, see *CIJ*, with extra material in *AÉ*.

in this chapter that this evaluation should be precisely reversed.[7]

The evidence that by the mid third century CE some Jews at least had given up the tolerance characteristic of earlier periods lies most clearly in the first extant appearance in a rabbinic text of the laws prescribing gentile behaviour which were later to be codified as the Noachide laws. According to the Tosefta (*A. Zar.* 8 (9). 4, Z. p. 473), the children of Noah were admonished concerning seven religious requirements of which one was idolatry; the term used, as throughout the tractate, was *avodah zarah*, literally 'alien worship'. From the ensuing discussion in the text it is clear that these rabbis took the rulings to apply not just to the distant past but to non-Jews in the present: thus, in the discussion of the injunction to set up courts of justice (ibid.), the sons of Noah were contrasted to Israelites despite the fact that Jews as much as gentiles are by definition descended from Noah. It is striking that these rabbis do not seem to have found the prohibition of 'alien worship' contentious. They did debate possible additional prohibitions, and in later versions of the code came up with up to thirty laws, but this particular issue was seen as obvious.[8]

The extant Tosefta text lacks any explanation for the interdict on alien worship, presumably because of a lacuna in the transmitted text, but it may be assumed that the original justification proffered was of the same type as that given for other rulings, namely, a more or less plausible exegesis of a biblical passage. Since no such passage *requires* an exegesis forbidding all gentile idolatry, the impulse to the prohibition

---

[7] The quotation is from Goldenberg, 'Other Religions', 34–5. For another recent discussion, see Novak, *Image of the Non-Jew*, ch. 4. Porton, *Goyim*, ch. 9, is entitled 'Gentiles as Idolaters' but, correctly following the main emphasis of the rabbinic texts themselves, this chapter deals only with the effect on Jews of contact with gentile paganism, not the morality of gentile idolatry in itself.

[8] This fact is ignored by Goldenberg, 'Other Religions', 38, which explains his quite different evaluation. Cohen, 'Crossing', 22 n. 26, asserts that *most* versions of the Noachide laws prohibit idolatry, rather than all. He gives a reference to Novak, *Image of the Non-Jew*, 3–51, 107–65, but I am not able to find there any version that does *not* prohibit idolatry. Novak himself documents the change in attitude to gentile idolatry but does not try to explain it. Porton, *Goyim*, does not deal with the Noachide laws at all.

must have come from other considerations. The problem is to discover what those considerations are likely to have been.

Of crucial importance in seeking a plausible answer is the identity of the people referred to by the rabbis as sons of Noah. The logic of the biblical story of Noah requires that all humanity be included among his descendants and nothing in the discussion in the Tosefta narrows this definition any further. In the later rabbinic compilation, the Babylonian Talmud, the evolution of the Noachide laws was in one passage (*b. A. Zar.* 64b) linked to the biblical institution of the *ger toshab*. Since the *ger toshab* was perceived in the Talmuds, as in the Bible, as a non-Jew living among Jews in the land of Israel, prohibiting him from idolatrous practices which might infect the Jewish population would be entirely in keeping with the biblical concept of purifying Israel from contact with such pollution.[9] But it is evident that the motivation for this link by the rabbis involved in the discussion was a desire to elucidate the meaning of *ger toshab* (about which there was some disagreement), not the Noachide laws. Thus it is not possible to argue that the rabbis considered as sons of Noah only gentiles who lived in the Holy Land. Later rabbinic tradition followed the more obvious understanding of the Tosefta passage, that the laws apply to gentiles wherever they may live.[10]

There is also nothing in the Tosefta passage, or in later rabbinic references to Noachides, to suggest that the gentiles in mind were those who had expressed some sort of devotion to the Jewish God without becoming Jews. The rabbis acknowledged that such a fearer of heaven (*yirei shamayim*) should be accorded special recognition by Jews, and in the early third century the Jews of Aphrodisias included the names of large numbers of such gentile Godfearers (*theosebeis*) on an honorary inscription (see below). But worship of, and even respect for, the Jewish God was not one of the requirements of the Noachide laws, which simply insisted on the negative attribute of non-interference by gentiles in

---

[9] Cohen, 'Crossing', 22 n. 25.
[10] The relationship of the concept of *ger toshav* to the concept of the Noachide is discussed by Novak, *Image of the Non-Jew*, 14–19.

Jewish cult—that is, the prohibition of blasphemy (*kilelat ha-Shem*).

The Noachide laws were thus apparently perceived as the rules incumbent on all gentiles wherever they might live. The notion that alien worship (*avodah zarah*) was forbidden for all non-Jews would, in the second and third centuries CE, imply that almost all non-Jews were sinners in the eyes of the Jewish God. For most people in the ancient world, religious cult consisted precisely in the offering of sacrifices and libations before images.[11] The pagan concerned might, if philosophically inclined, claim that the image was only a symbol of the divinity worshipped, but such arguments would not acquit him or her of the charge of *avodah zarah* as defined by the rabbis, according to which any action that even appeared to be according cult to a manufactured object was to be prohibited. The rabbis did not often leave any doubt about what they were forbidding. The treatise *Avodah Zarah* in the Mishnah was complemented by extensive commentary and additions in the Tosefta and both Talmuds with the purpose of clarifying what fell into this category. These tractates were undoubtedly primarily intended to warn Jews rather than non-Jews about the practices to be avoided, but this mass of discussion provided any rabbis with a ready answer in the (unlikely) event that a gentile should happen to ask him precisely what he should not do if he wished to be virtuous in the eyes of Jews.

In practice, the rabbis simply assumed most of the time that gentiles were inveterate idolaters.[12] The principle of *yayin nesekh*, which was presupposed and elaborated in the Mishnah, forbade all wine touched by a gentile on the grounds that any gentile is automatically suspect of pouring an idolatrous libation from any wine in his care. According to *b.Meg.* 13a R. Yohanan b. Nappaha even claimed that by

[11] Lane Fox, *Pagans and Christians*, 64–167, esp. 69–72, 133–7. The arguments of Novak, *Image of the Non-Jew*, 124–6, that rabbis saw gentile pagans outside the Holy Land not as idolaters but as traditionalists, is eirenic but specious; his view is based on one tradition, attributed to R. Yohanan in 3rd cent. Palestine (*b. Hull.* 13b).

[12] See, Porton, *Goyim*, 241–58. See also Alon, *Jews, Judaism and Classical World*, 146–9, 181, on the resulting impurity of gentiles, despite the ability of rabbis to take up quite a sophisticated stance with regard to *Jewish* uses of images without idolatry; cf. Urbach, 'Rabbinical Laws of Idolatry'.

definition any gentile who renounced idolatry became a Jew—a statement than can hardly have carried any legal weight but which nicely emphasized rabbinic assumptions about gentiles' idolatrous predelictions.[13] Thus, it is not surprising that it was taken for granted in various rabbinic texts (e.g. *b. B.K.* 38a) that gentiles did not in fact keep the laws laid down for the descendants of Noah. This assumption may have been no more than a rhetorical flourish: according to R. Joseph in this passage and in the parallel in *b. A. Zar.* 2b, gentiles were so incapable of keeping the laws that they were released from them, but this was derived from a pun on *vayater* in Habakkuk 3: 6, which may have conditioned the exegesis.

If the failure of gentiles to keep the Noachide laws was seriously envisaged, the assumption may have fulfilled a useful function within the Jewish religious system to explain in Jewish terms why misfortune sometimes struck individual gentiles. The theodicy which explained the problems of Jews was clear-cut: God punishes Israel when they break the terms of the covenant they had made with him. But according to the Bible gentiles had made no such agreement, so it was less clear why they should also sometimes suffer and be punished. The Noachide laws, and the perception that they were regularly infringed by the non-Jews on whom they were incumbent, provided a ready answer. Sometimes indeed talmudic texts described the Noachide precepts as the rules that Noah's sons 'accepted', on the model of the Sinaitic covenant, although in other passages the laws were said simply to have been 'commanded' by God.[14]

A theodicy to explain gentiles' misfortunes of course did not necessarily condemn all sinning gentiles to ultimate perdition, an attitude which rabbinic Judaism at least came in the end to renounce quite clearly.[15] In any case the rabbis of late antiquity held divergent views even about whether *righteous* gentiles would be 'saved', from the cheerful assumption of R. Joshua b. Hananiah reported in *t. Sanh.* 13. 2 (Z., p. 434) that 'the righteous of all nations have a share in

---

[13] On this passage see Cohen, 'Crossing', 22 n. 24.
[14] See Novak, *Image of the Non-Jew*, 3, 257–63.
[15] This is noted correctly by Goldenberg, 'Other Religions', 30.

the world to come' to the assumption of R. Judah in *t. Sot.* 8: 6 (L., p. 205) that the gentiles really know the Torah (in seventy languages!) and have chosen to ignore it, thus meriting their damnation in hell.[16] An explanation of such varied attitudes is easily found. Rabbinic discussions about membership of the world to come in passages such as *t. Sanh.* 13 (Z., pp. 434–5) were concerned to define which Jews would be excluded and had no interest in gentiles.

Confirmation that rabbinic hostility to gentile paganism even outside the land of Israel was not confined to clauses in the various versions of the theoretical Noachide laws may be found in the interpretation of Deuteronomy 4: 19 and 17: 3 given at *b.Meg.* 9a–b. It will be recalled that in the Septuagint the first of these passages was translated literally, thus implying that God gave the heavenly bodies to non-Jews for them to worship (see above, Ch. 3). In contrast, the rabbinic text asserts that in the version commissioned by Ptolemy the King, the translators inserted into the biblical verse that God gave them the sun and moon 'to give light'. The translation to which the rabbis referred was presumably the Septuagint, but since in fact this addition is found neither in any extant text of the Septuagint nor in any reference to the Septuagint in a Greek source, it is most likely that this interpretation of the Bible should be attributed to the rabbis themselves. As for Josephus' and Philo's exegesis of Exod. 22: 27 (Heb.), according to which the *elohim* whom Jews were enjoined not to curse were the pagan divinities of the gentiles (see above, p. 52), rabbinic literature seems to have been unaware of any such interpretation. On the contrary, according to *b.Meg.* 25b Jews are positively permitted to mock idolatrous worship.[17] On the same lines, the prohibition on returning runaway slaves to a heathen master, found in *Sifre Deut.* 259, seems to presuppose, if the slave in question was assumed to be non-Jewish, the undesirability of gentiles practising paganism even if they are gentiles.

How, then, had these rabbis come to take up this illiberal stance? It is possible of course that they reflected a long

---

[16] On this divergence of views, see Lieberman, *Greek in Jewish Palestine*, 78–81.
[17] Cf. Goldenberg, 'Other Religions', 169 n. 23.

tradition which had originated many centuries before the first attestation in the Tosefta, in which case Josephus and Philo simply represented different strands of Jewish thinking; in that case, the rabbis' attitude was presumably espoused only by a minority of Jews before 70 CE, since I argued in Chapter 3 that Josephus' and Philo's attitude was standard among Jews at that time. But the evidence also allows for the possibility that these rabbis' view was novel and first adopted only after 70 CE, and, if that was indeed what happened, the question of greatest interest in assessing the significance of this development is the reason for the change. Did it arise simply from theoretical speculation by the rabbis? Or was it engendered by events in the outside world?

One clue to a possible answer to such questions lies in the evidence that the illiberal attitude towards gentile paganism just described was not universally adopted by Jews in this period, and therefore that it cannot have been theologically necessary as a reaction by Jews to their predicament. The persistence of diverse views on the subject will not cause surprise after my remarks at the beginning of this chapter about the probable diversity of late antique Judaism. Much, although not all, of the evidence for the continuation of a more liberal stance comes from Jewish milieux which probably fell during the relevant years outside rabbinic sway.

The clearest such evidence comes from the now famous inscription which was set up, probably in the synagogue and probably in the early third century, in Aphrodisias in Asia Minor and which was published in 1987.[18] The inscription consists of a list of the names of 125 individuals (originally more), 71 of them Jews, who were thus honoured for their connection with an institution described as a *patella*, whose purpose is now obscure. Of the Jews three were explicitly described as proselytes (face *a* lines 13, 17, and 22). The remaining 52 individuals were listed on face *b* under a separate heading. A slight gap was left on the stone to distinguish them from the first group of people. The heading reads: 'And as many as are Godfearers (*theosebis*)'. None of the names on this list is distinctively Jewish, in marked

---

[18] Reynolds and Tannenbaum, *Jews and God-Fearers*.

contrast to the Jewish names to be found on face *a* and in the list of Jews at the top of the face *b*. Clearly, too, the Jews of Aphrodisias at this time treated the term 'Godfearer' as at the very least a semi-technical term for a gentile who revered the Jewish God without converting to Judaism.[19] The significant factor for the present argument is the social standing of some of the godfearers whose names were given on face *b*. Nine of these individuals were described as *bouleutai* or 'councillors'. The most plausible inference is that they were councillors of the city of Aphrodisias.[20] In that case these gentiles who sympathized with Judaism and who were honoured on an inscription set up by the Jewish community must necessarily have participated in pagan cult, since such involvement was unavoidable for all city councillors unless, like fully committed Jews, they were specially absolved by order of the Roman state.

Partly in reaction to this inscription, many scholars in recent years have collected and analysed the rest of the evidence from antiquity about Godfearers. It is noticeable that much of this evidence comes from Asia Minor and its environs—not just from Aphrodisias, but from Miletus, Tralles, Sardis, Deliler, and Panticapaeum on the north coast of the Black Sea.[21] One extra item of evidence from the same region may be worth adding, since this particular implication of the passage has not, I think, previously been noted. According to the *Martyrdom of Pionios*, a literary and highly coloured description of the execution of the bishop of Smyrna in 250 CE, Jews in Smyrna had invited Christians into their synagogues and some Christians had been tempted to accede to the invitation (*Mart. Pion.* 13. 1). The passage has sometimes been taken to mean that Christians converted to Judaism to avoid the hostility of the Roman state,[22] but that interpretation is impossible: conversion by male gentiles to Judaism was just as much a crime in the eyes of the Roman state in this period as their adoption of, or continuation in,

[19] On the double meaning of *theosebes* in earlier texts, see Feldman, ' "Jewish sympathisers" in Classical Literature'.

[20] So Reynolds and Tannenbaum, *Jews and God-Fearers*, 55, 58, 66–7.

[21] For the evidence, see Trebilco, *Jewish Communities in Asia Minor*, 145–66.

[22] See Lane Fox, *Pagans and Christians*, 479–80.

Christianity. If the martyrdom account reflected historical reality at all, the Christians thus suborned must have been either ethnic Jews returning to their roots or, perhaps more plausibly, gentiles who became not Jewish proselytes but Godfearers. As such, the Roman state would have given them no licence to refuse to worship in pagan cults, but this might be of less concern if the Jews of Smyrna, like those of Aphrodisias, expressed no disapproval of the pagan practices of the gentile sympathizers to whom they accorded formal recognition within their community. Such an attitude seems likely if, as this passage implies, the Jews of Smyrna welcomed newcomers into their synagogues even when they continued to attend as Christians the meetings addressed by Pionios.

Despite the concentration of this inscriptional and literary evidence from Asia Minor, it is unlikely that such Jewish tolerance of gentile paganism was confined to that region.[23] In Africa, in 197 CE, Tertullian remarked that some gentiles kept customs similar to the sabbath and Passover, while presumably continuing to worship at pagan altars (*Ad Nat.* 1. 13), although the attitude of the local Jews to the behaviour of these gentiles is unknown. Later in the third century CE (probably), the Christian writer Commodian, who may have had some connection with Gaza, remarked with hostility on the tolerance of Jews towards the pagan worship of the gentiles who came to them to be taught the precepts of true religion (*Instructiones*, 1. 37. 10–11).

But particularly significant is the fact that, unlike the Jews of Asia Minor, some of the other Jews who appear to have retained the old liberalism quite certainly operated from securely within the rabbinic tradition. At *b. Hull.* 13b, the opinion was ascribed to R. Hiyya b. Abba in the name of R. Yohanan that gentiles outside the land of Israel are not idolaters but simply follow their ancestral customs, which seems to imply that such gentiles should be allowed to practise paganism so long as they are outside the holy land. The blessing prescribed at *t. Ber.* 6 (7): 2 (L., p. 33) to be

---

[23] Cohen, 'Crossing', 32, suggests that it was an attitude specifically localized in Asia Minor.

uttered on seeing a destroyed site of pagan worship presupposed that only idolatry by Jews or in Jewish territory
was of concern. The existence of long amoraic discussions as
to how the Mishnah could have permitted a gentile to render
null and void an idol which, according to the later rulings, he
should not have owned in the first place revealed the tenacity
of the assumption even among rabbis that gentiles had a right
to their paganism.[24] Rabbinic tradition ascribed to Yohanan
ben Zakkai a warning that destroying pagan altars could only
lead to unfortunate consequences.[25] Some rabbis apparently
taught that Jews might even manufacture the appurtenances
of idolatry for gentiles to worship; the issue was of course not
purely theoretical for Jewish craftsmen offered such employ-
ment.[26]

Lack of rabbinic consistency on this issue, as on others not
central to the rabbinic world-view, need not surprise, but the
imperfect integration into rabbinic halakha of the illiberal
notions about correct gentile religious behaviour enshrined in
the Noachide laws may at least suggest that those notions
were not halakhically generated in the first place. If that is the
case, it may seem more plausible that the antagonism towards
gentile paganism found in the Noachide laws marked part of a
more general shift by Jews away from religious liberalism. I
shall try to show in the remainder of this chapter that such a
general shift might have been precipitated by a process to
which I alluded only briefly in Chapter 3: an increased
awareness among Jews of the sharp theological distinction
between Jews and non-Jews, which in turn was precipitated
by the altered definition of Jewish status espoused by the
Roman state after 96 CE.

I argued in Chapter 3 that Jewish vagueness about who was
or was not a Jew was endemic in the period before 100 CE. By
contrast tannaitic rabbinic texts revealed at the least an
attempt to produce a coherent definition. It was in the
Mishnah that for the first time was enunciated the matrilineal

---

[24] See the discussion of these texts in Novak, *Image of the Non-Jew*, 117–23.
[25] Goldenberg, 'Other Religions', 170 n. 27, quoting Lieberman, 'Palestine in the
Third and Fourth Centuries', 366 n. 363; Urbach, 'Rabbinical Laws of Idolatry', 156.
[26] See Urbach, 'Rabbinical Laws of Idolatry', 158–65.

principle which has become standard in orthodox rabbinic Judaism to the present day.[27] Whether this codified an attitude already found among some Jewish groups before the redaction of the Mishnah in the second century CE is a hotly disputed and, in the final analysis, unanswerable question. But it is worth noting that the principle was evidently still being discussed and refined by the tannaitic rabbis themselves, since the record of their disputes survives. Thus if the tannaim inherited any criteria about how to establish Jewish status, those criteria were not clear-cut. According to the Mishnah, for instance, the child of a Jewish mother and gentile father is a *mamzer*, a Jew indeed but of seriously blemished birth (*m. Yeb.* 7. 5), a view eventually to be firmly rejected by the amoraim.[28]

Rabbinic interest in defining Jewish status did not come from a fascination with the topic for its own sake. It is notable that the interest of the contributors to the Mishnah in 'diverse kinds' of animals and plants, which encompassed a sizeable proportion of the corpus, did not extend to an interest in 'mixed' humans, the offspring of Jews and gentiles.[29] The impetus to define Jewish status clearly came from elsewhere. Perhaps behind it lay the actions of the Roman state in picking out the inhabitants of the empire who were liable to the Jewish tax.

The Roman state created for itself the problem of defining who was Jewish by the decision of Vespasian, after the destruction of the Jewish Temple in Jerusalem, to impose a tax of two denarii on Jews, to go to the rebuilding of the Temple of Jupiter Capitolinus in Rome, burnt down in the previous year. Contemporary sources make clear who was liable to pay: an *amphodarches* in Arsinoe in 73 CE drew up a list of Jews for the purpose (*CPJ* 421), and ostraca from Edfu reveal payment by women, children and slaves as well as adult males (*CPJ* 160–229). Josephus wrote in *BJ* 7. 218, a passage probably composed by the early 80s CE at the latest, that all Jews now pay to the Capitol what they had previously paid to

---

[27] Cohen, 'Matrilineal Principle', esp. 29–37.   [28] Ibid. 32.

[29] Ibid. 48. For the arguments in the next few paragraphs, see Goodman, 'Nerva, the *fiscus Judaicus*, and Jewish Identity'.

the Jerusalem Temple. As Suetonius stated (*Dom.* 12. 2: '*imposita genti tributa*'), Jews paid the tax because of their religion, but they were defined as Jews by their ethnic origin. It was simply assumed that all ethnic Jews subscribed to the national cult. Vespasian's definition of a Jew ought to have been clear, for the Roman state was usually precise about who paid what taxes, and those paying at Edfu in the 70s probably included Roman citizens, if it is possible to judge their status from their names (*CPJ* 162, 174). Collection was taken seriously from the start, with the establishment of a separate *fiscus* and a special *praktor* in charge of its administration evident at Edfu by 80 CE (*CPJ* 181). The assumption that ethnic origin presupposed religious practices is entirely in accordance with standard pagan use of the Greek term *ioudaios*, Latin *Judaeus*, before 70 CE. Nor is this very surprising, since it was also the standard Jewish assumption as found in Philo and Josephus.

In 96 CE Nerva courted popularity in Rome for his new regime by changing the way in which this special tax on Jews was exacted. The reform was widely advertised by the issue of coins from the Rome mint under the auspices of the senate, with the proclamation '*fisci Judaici calumnia sublata*'. Precisely how Nerva removed the *calumnia* no source states, but it can be surmised. The tax did not cease to be collected, for its imposition was still in operation in the time of Origen and possibly down to the fourth century CE (cf. Origen, *Ep. ad Africanum*, 20 (14)). It is a reasonable hypothesis that Nerva's intention was to demonstrate publicly his opposition to the way in which his hated predecessor, Domitian, had levied the tax, and to procure release for those described by Suetonius (*Dom.* 12. 2) as particular victims of Domitian's tendency to exact the tax '*acerbissime*'. According to Suetonius, these unfortunates were those who either '*inprofessi*' lived a '*iudaicam vitam*' or '*origine dissimulata*' refused to pay the tax: the people thus trapped by Domitian and, if the hypothesis is correct, exempted by Nerva were those who failed to admit openly to their Jewish practices and/or those who hid their origins (presumably as Jews).

What then, was Domitian doing with the exaction of the tax which caused such an uproar? No source suggests any change in the formal definition of the tax, only in who was affected when it was exacted *acerbissime*. It was long assumed that the vulnerable who suffered with regard to the tax under Domitian were gentiles who had taken up Jewish practices,[30] but such a reading of Suetonius creates problems: in these years such gentiles were accused of *atheotes* and executed, so they could not have been given legal recognition by a tax at the same time. It seems more likely that those at risk were ethnic Jews who had given up public identification with their religion either by hiding their continued Jewish practices or by pretending that their customs had nothing to do with their Jewish ethnic origins, which they dissimulated.[31] Thus Suetonius (*Dom.* 12. 2) narrated the story of an old man of 90 who was stripped before a court to see whether he was circumcised: he could hide all other aspects of his Jewishness, but not this.

If it was this group of non-religious ethnic Jews who were persecuted for the tax by Domitian, it is a reasonable hypothesis that what Nerva did to end the *calumnia* was to release such people from payment. It is certain that such individuals no longer paid by the early third century, for, according to Cassius Dio (66. 7. 2), who characteristically back-dated his definition to 70 CE, the tax was levied (presumably in his day) from those Jews who still observed their ancestral customs (so presumably not from those who had ceased such observances); the disapproval of Domitian implicit in Suetonius' account suggests further that this reform had come about at least by the date of the composition of the biography of that emperor, in the 120s CE or earlier. It can be readily appreciated that the removal of such men from liability to the tax might be considered by Nerva as a means to court popularity in the city of Rome. Such apostate Jews would include men like Tiberius Iulius Alexander, the former prefect of Egypt, who was described by Tacitus (*Ann.* 15. 28. 3) with no mention of his Jewish ethnic origin. It may be assumed that Romans accepted the right of ethnic Jews like other people to assimilate into the Roman citizen community

[30] Smallwood, 'Domitian's Attitude'.
[31] Cf. Thompson, 'Domitian and the Jewish Tax'.

or other peregrine communities so long as they gave up their peculiar customs, and Domitian's behaviour was an affront to this attitude.

If it is correct to interpret Nerva's removal of the *calumnia* in this way, his reform will have restricted liability for the tax to those who practised Judaism *professi*, i.e. openly. But such a solution to Domitian's excesses brought its own problems, for it was not easy for the state to recognize when a Jew was living a Jewish life. Simple observation of which individuals had Jewish customs would not suffice, for far too many gentiles in Rome had taken up Jewish practices without considering themselves, or being considered, Jews: the sabbath was widely observed, avoidance of certain meats would implicate vegetarians such as Pythagoreans, many gentiles might attend synagogues out of curiosity, even circumcision could be endured for non-Jewish reasons.[32] A sacrifice test like that used for Christians by Pliny might have worked, but despite its use at the instigation of a renegade Jew in Antioch in 67 CE (*BJ* 7. 50–1), it seems never to have been used against Jews by the Roman state.

Requesting individual Jewish communities themselves to identify which Jews were religiously observant would not have proved any more effective. Jews could not conceive of an ethnic Jew ceasing to be part of the nation with which God's covenant had been made, and they might readily claim as one of them a non-observant ethnic Jew, if only out of spite. Thus Josephus, unlike Tacitus, was clear about the Jewish origins of Tiberius Iulius Alexander, despite the fact that he lacked 'piety towards the god' and 'did not stay in the customs of his ancestors' (*AJ* 20. 100). It would in any case be difficult to decide which Jewish community in a town had the right to define its members. The only alternative, it seems to me, must be that Jews were taxed if, and only if, they declared themselves as Jews—that is, if they carried on their Jewish customs *professi*. The incentive to make such a declaration was presumably the freedom to carry on religious practices without odium, what Tertullian described rather enviously as '*vectigalis libertas*' (*Apol.* 18), freedom of worship brought at

---

[32] See in general Nolland, 'Do Romans Observe Jewish Customs?'.

the price of the Jewish tax. Such privileges as avoiding court cases on the sabbath and escaping prosecution for publicly boycotting civic cults were worth two denarii a year. Such a central role for the self-understanding of the persons involved in fixing their status was not foreign to Roman law. So, for instance, Roman citizenship was confined to the children of two citizen parents, but if a Roman citizen married a partner in the incorrect belief that he or she was a citizen, the offspring was granted citizenship in recognition of the intentions of the participants to contract a valid union for the production of citizen children.[33]

My hypothesis is that this new definition of Jewish identity by the Roman state may have resulted in an increased concern by Jews themselves to define who did and did not belong to their community, and to clarify the respective duties and rights of insiders and outsiders. The vagueness of earlier years, when gentiles on the fringes of the community might be left in uncertain status in Jewish eyes (see above, Ch. 3), was no longer tolerable when some of those gentiles chose to pay the tax, and to suffer concomitant social and political disabilities, while others did not. For Jews in the Roman empire the distinction between proselyte and friendly gentile was now regularly observable.

A second result of the imposition of the tax and Nerva's reform of its incidence was hardly less far-reaching and applies directly to the subject of the present chapter. The Roman state chose to define Jews by their religion, but that religion had been represented by the state since 70 CE as intrinsically hostile to civilization. The victory of Titus had been represented by the Flavians as the suppression by the Roman gods of an obnoxious cult portrayed as a form of atheism (see above, Ch. 3). Now after 96 CE liability to the *fiscus Judaicus* was confined to those who continued voluntarily and obstinately to express their adherence to those depraved religious customs. Some Jews, like Josephus, might respond to such attacks with the hurt assertion that Jews were happy to live in peace with their neighbours, and that nothing in Judaism precluded peaceful co-operation with

---

[33] Cohen, 'Matrilineal Principle', 43–4.

the Roman state. But other Jews might well react less eirenically. If Romans wished to portray them as not so much a nation with distinctive customs as a scattered group united only in a religious cult perceived by outsiders as at odds with the religious life of the rest of the civilized world, then so be it. There were attractions for Jews too in adopting such a self-image, as warriors for the Lord in a universal arena where true religion was at loggerheads with the idolatrous worship of false gods.

The best evidence for such an attitude by Jews outside the land of Israel may be found in the course of the diaspora revolt of 116–17 CE. The uprising was in part a rebellion against Rome by the Jews of Egypt, Cyrene, Cyprus, and Mesopotamia, but it was also partly an attack by those Jews on their Greek and native compatriots, and, most relevantly for the present discussion, it may also have constituted in some degree a religious crusade against paganism. Most of the evidence is to be found in Cyrene. The temples of Apollo, Zeus, Demeter, Artemis, and Isis, and the Caesareum were all apparently destroyed during the uprising; in some cases, signs of the destruction are, or once were, archaeologically visible, in other cases epigraphic evidence for rebuilding under Hadrian suggests a preceding catastrophe.[34] It is not impossible that these buildings fell victim to a general conflagration rather than a specific attack by the Jews, and the only inscription which *explicitly* links the destruction of a specific temple with the *tumultus Iudaicus* refers to the mishap which befell the Caesareum (*CJZC* 17), which, like the temple of Divus Claudius in Colchester destroyed by the rebels led by Boudicca in 60 CE (Tac. *Ann.* 14. 31–2), might have been the object of special hostility as a symbol of Roman power rather than as a pagan shrine. But the cumulative testimony for harm done to pagan cult places during the war is sufficient to make it very plausible that such damage was inflicted deliberately by the Jews.

So, for instance, a bilingual (Latin and Greek) inscription from the temple of Hecate in Cyrene refers to some

---

[34] Applebaum, *Jews and Greeks in Ancient Cyrene*, 269–85. For the inscriptions, see *CJZC* 17–25. For the arguments presented here, see Goodman, 'Diaspora Reactions'.

(unnamed) building which had been destroyed during the uprising (*CJZC* 21), and a second-century temple of Isis and Ammon in Eastern Cyrenaica contained fragments of statues deliberately mutilated. Appian (*B.Civ.* 2. 90) recorded the destruction of a sanctuary of Nemesis in Alexandria by the Jews, but since he wrote that it was destroyed 'for the requirements of the war', he may have implied that it was not demolished simply out of hostility, and in any case Jews had special reasons to attack the site because it was the burial place of Pompey, who long ago had desecrated the Temple in Jerusalem. The excavators of the Serapeum in the city suggested that it too was demolished at that time.[35] It was long ago noted that the epithet *anhosios*, 'impious', was attached to the Jews as a standard jibe in papyri written in Egypt during the rebellion.[36] The size of the Jewish community in the Egyptian countryside diminished so drastically after these events that it is not possible to know whether Egyptian Jews maintained their hostility to gentile paganism, but it would be rather surprising if some of them at least did not retain their hatred. Thus it may be significant that in the third century CE someone bothered to produce a translation (*CPJ* 520) of an anti-Jewish prophecy of the Hellenistic period which, according to an unpublished text of the same prophecy from Oxyrhynchus, asserted that Jews were impious people who would despoil the temples of the Egyptians.[37]

The remaining evidence for non-rabbinic hostility to pagan idolatry outside the Holy Land after 70 CE is either ambiguous or hard to date with certainty. Thus, for example, the author of the romance *Joseph and Asenath* included a fierce attack on the idolatry practised by Asenath before she met Joseph, but since the result of her abjuration of paganism was marriage to a Jew, it is clear that she was reckoned to have become not a righteous gentile but a proselyte—and the author's attitude to unconverted gentiles therefore remains obscure. In any case, since the date of the composition of this

[35] For the archaeological evidence, see Applebaum, *Jews and Greeks in Ancient Cyrene*, 261–344, esp. 290 and 295.

[36] Fuks, 'Jewish Revolt in Egypt', 157–8.

[37] On this document, see Frankfurter, 'Lest Egypt's City', 208–9.

work can only be placed to some time between the translation
of the Septuagint and the production of the Syriac version in
the sixth century CE, a date after 70 CE is no more probable
than a date before then.[38] Some of the fragments of verse
forged by a Jew in the name of Greek poets and of sages such
as Orpheus, which contained among other moral sentiments
some barbed attacks on idolatry, may have been composed at
any date before the first extant citation of their contents by
Pseudo-Justin and Clement of Alexandria in the late second
and third century CE[39] but it is impossible to find out whether
the sentiments there expressed constituted another example of
reactions to events at the end of the first century or an earlier
composition in which Hellenized Jews were confirmed in
their own avoidance of idolatry by the comforting assertion
that the greatest of the Greeks had espoused the same views
(see above, Ch. 4). Similar uncertainties apply to the recently
published fourth-century Latin document called the Letter of
'Anna' to Seneca, which has been ascribed to a Jewish author
because of its many quotations from Genesis and other books
of the Old Testament; the letter contains a strong attack on
polytheism, even in its philosophical forms.[40]

Rabbinic and non-rabbinic evidence thus converge to show
that after 100 CE some but not all Jews espoused a practical
denigration of gentile paganism wherever it occurred, a
denigration every bit as intense as that of early Christians. I
argued in Chapter 5 that Christians' hostility to paganism was
an essential element in the proselytizing approach of some
Christians to their fellow humans. In the next chapter I shall
consider whether hostility by some Jews to gentile paganism,
particularly as enshrined in the Noachide laws, ever had a
parallel effect on Jewish theology in the talmudic period.

---

[38] Schürer, *History*, iii. 546–52.   [39] Ibid. 656–71.
[40] Bischoff, *Anecdota novissima* (1984), 1–9. See the discussion in Momigliano,
Ottavo Contributo, 329–32.

7

Judaism in the Talmudic Period
Proselytes and Proselytizing

BEFORE 100 CE Jews accepted as proselytes those gentiles who applied to join their number, but they did not feel impelled to encourage such conversions (see above, Ch. 4). Their liberalism was generally reinforced by a belief that God was not offended by non-Jews continuing to worship their ancestral deities, provided that such worship did not affect Jews (above, Ch. 3). In the talmudic period some Jews began to take a harsher view of gentile paganism, wherever it took place, but other Jews moved in an opposite direction, recognizing in public the religious worth of gentiles sympathetic to Judaism even when those gentiles continued to indulge in pagan worship (above, Ch. 6). In this chapter I shall examine whether either of these shifts coincided with an increased enthusiasm among any Jews after 100 CE for winning proselytes.

Mutually contradictory but emphatic pronouncements on this question abound in modern scholarship. For Cohen in 1983, 'in the post-70 period . . . the gentiles were still eager to buy but the Jews . . . were no longer eager to sell'; for Goldenberg in 1988, there is 'ample evidence of active Jewish desire for converts . . . until Roman pressure made it impossible'; for Bamberger, in 1939 and still in the second edition of his book in 1968, rabbinic Jews at least retained a strong interest in a proselytizing mission until the end of antiquity; for Cohen in a more recent work, published in 1992, Judaism in antiquity was probably *never* missionary and was certainly not interested in proselytizing after 135 CE.[1]

---

[1] Cohen, 'Conversion to Judaism', 39; Goldenberg, 'Other religions', 30–1; Bamberger, *Proselytism*, 17; Cohen, 'Was Judaism Missionary?', esp. 21.

The evidence is due for a fresh consideration. Most of the relevant material will be found in rabbinic texts, but the laws passed by the Roman state, Greek and Latin inscriptions set up by Jews, and, more dubiously, religious tracts composed by Christians may shed some light onto the attitudes of non-rabbinic Jews.

One secure generalization can be made. There was no sudden, universal switch by all Jews to the sort of enthusiastic proselytizing found among some early Christians. Most of the varied views about gentiles found in Jewish texts composed before 100 CE can be found also in the rabbinic texts, all of which were redacted in the early third century or later. The biblical notion that God rules over all peoples but that his name rests specifically on Israel was still common (e.g. *MdRi Kaspa* 4, line 64). The rabbis assumed that it is a good thing for Jews to persuade gentiles to be monotheists, just as Abraham told all Babylon to acknowledge that there is only one God.[2] Many texts continue to take it for granted that prospective converts will normally offer themselves and that it is not part of a good Jew's role to try to increase their numbers. It is notorious that R. Helbo argued that proselytes actually delay the coming of the Messiah and are therefore, it must be presumed, to be turned away, or at least not actively to be sought (*b. Nidd.* 13b; *b. Yeb.* 109b, and parallels).[3] At *y. Yeb.* 8. 1, 8d, R. Isaac even reported a ruling in the name of R. Joshua b. Levi which seems to imply that in certain circumstances even the commonly accepted duty of Jews to convert gentile slaves in their ownership may be waived: 'everything should follow local custom.' The only duty to the gentile world which the rabbis blazoned forth explicitly was the need to be a light to the nations, to sanctify the name of God and proclaim his existence and glory to all men: thus *Lev. R.* 6: 5 (ed. Margulies, p. 142) interprets Lev. 5: 1 ('if he do not utter it, then he shall bear his iniquity') as 'if you will not proclaim me as God unto the nations of the world, I shall exact penalty from you'.

In theory the continuation of such earlier attitudes should

---

[2] The relevant midrashim are collated in Ginzberg, *Legends*, i. 193.

[3] On R. Helbo's dictum, see Bamberger, *Proselytism*, 163 ff.; Braude, *Jewish Proselyting*, 6–7 and n. 15, 42 ff.

cause no surprise: Jews, in this period as much as before, claimed that their theology derived from the same divinely inspired scriptures. But the changed attitudes to unconverted gentiles discussed in Chapter 6 might seem logically to require a shift in perspective when potential proselytes were considered. In theory at least, the crucial development was not so much the curious emergence of divergent views on whether gentiles could win divine approval while continuing in their paganism, as the apparently explicit agreement of almost all Jews that gentiles could, in one way or another, win divine approval without becoming Jewish.

This belief was of course enshrined in the rabbinic concept of the Noachide laws, but it was also a necessary element in the public recognition granted to gentile Godfearers by Jews in Aphrodisias and elsewhere in Asia Minor (above, p. 117). It may also be relevant that some rabbinic texts referred to certain gentiles as *yirei shamayim*, 'fearers of heaven', who were considered by them as distinct from full proselytes and in effect equivalent to the Godfearers known from Greek inscriptions: in *y. Meg.* 3. 2, 74a, it was claimed that 'even' fearers of heaven wear broken sandals on the Day of Atonement, so the onus on such individuals to keep the Law was evidently reckoned much less than the onus on ordinary Jews.[4] Whether these persons constituted any sort of formal group attached to Jewish communities is unknown and perhaps unlikely. So far as can be known from extant evidence, the rabbis were not concerned to evolve a special set of rules for gentiles who revered the Jewish God but did not convert. Presumably the laws which applied to other 'children of Noah' were also believed to apply to them, although God might be expected to look with special favour on those who paid him reverence.

I suspect that this category of Godfearers was not a phenomenon that the rabbis themselves sought or particularly desired but which they found established among some Jewish communities and decided (on the whole) not to condemn. This would explain the survival in rabbinic literature of a few statements markedly hostile to those unconverted gentiles

---

[4] Lieberman, *Greek in Jewish Palestine*, 78–80.

who practised some elements of the Jewish way of life but not all. Hence the assertion in *Deut. R.* 1. 21 (Mirkin, p. 23) that 'a pagan who observes the sabbath while he is still not circumcised deserves death', and the statement in *Exod. R.* 30: 12 that unless one has been circumcised one may not study the Torah. This latter ruling was in direct conflict with the practice at Aphrodisias as it was described by the editors of the Aphrodisias inscription, since they assumed that the three *theosebeis* mentioned on face *a* of the inscription were gentile, and that they were members of a Torah study group. In any case, the rabbis produced contradictory statements on this question of unconverted Judaizing gentiles, as on so many other issues. So, for instance, a statement in the Babylonian Talmud contrasts sharply with the condemnation quoted above: according to *b. B.K.* 38a, 'even a gentile who occupies himself in Torah is equal to the High Priest'.

The logical effect of Jews tending to give more formal recognition to gentile sympathizers after 100 CE should have been a strong disincentive to proselytizing. If Jews believed that gentiles could win divine approval and aid without taking upon themselves the requirements of the covenant between God and Israel, they had no altruistic reason to bring such gentiles into Judaism. If gentiles were told by Jews that it was sufficient to fear God, they would not wish to become proselytes, and any Jewish proselytizing mission that did occur would be undermined.

It is thus all the more striking that, despite this logic, some Jews at least did choose to proselytize in the same period that they or other Jews were honouring Godfearers who had deliberately elected not to cross over into Judaism. The rest of this chapter will examine the evidence for this curious behaviour and suggest possible reasons for it.

The continued existence of some proselytes in the Roman empire after 100 CE is attested by a wide variety of sources. Some scholars have asserted that the number of converts declined after the Bar Kokhba war,[5] but reliable statistics to support such an assertion have not and, I suspect, could not

---

[5] Moore, *Judaism*, i. 351.

ever be found. Apart from the general problem of the haphazard survival of evidence from the ancient world, many proselytes may be impossible to spot in Jewish inscriptions because they took on Jewish names and are thus indistinguishable from the native-born. Only rarely does the dual record of an individual's Jewish and gentile name, or an explicit designation as convert, permit modern scholars to chart a proselyte's progress, such as that of a certain Felicitas Peregrina, or Veturia Paulla who was renamed Sara, both explicitly described in funerary inscriptions as proselytes and both from Rome (*CIJ* 462 and 523).

Rabbinic sources took for granted the continued existence of proselytes, although they were named only seldom.[6] Of Christian writers, Irenaeus, *Ad. Haer.* 3. 21. 1 wrote about Aquila as a proselyte in the time of Hadrian. Tertullian, *Adv. Iudaeos* 1 made one of the participants in his reported dialogue a proselyte. Origen (*Comm. in Matth. series* 16, ed. Klostermann, p. 29) commented on Matt. 23: 15 that proselytes were often in his day more severe opponents of Christians than native-born Jews.

The probably fourth-century Christian forgery entitled the *Acts of Pilate* took for granted that 'proselyte' was a technical term for a gentile become Jew (*Acta Pilati*, 2. 4, Tischendorf, p. 226; see above, Ch. 4). In the second half of the fourth century a Christian moralizer, whose practical treatise entitled *Quaestiones Veteris et Novi Testamenti* was attributed in the manuscripts to Augustine but who is today more often identified with Ambrosiaster, remarked that 'when there is so great a multitude of Jews through all the world, none of them is changed to become a gentile, although we see some of the pagans become Jews, albeit rarely' (*cum videamus ex paganis, licet raro, fieri Iudaeos*) (*Quaestiones* 115, para. 14, ed. Souter, CSEL 50, p. 323). Ambrosiaster was accustomed to bolster his arguments by pointing to contemporary life; indeed, in the same *Quaestio* (no. 115, para. 12), he had supported his views on fate by referring to the recent spate of divorces since the divorce law had been changed by the apostate emperor Julian. Elsewhere in the same treatise he made clear what he

---

[6] Evidence is collected in Bamberger, *Proselytism*, ch. 11.

meant by 'becoming Jews': 'I do not refer to proselytes, who
it is agreed become Jews' (*non de proselitis dico, quos constat
fieri Iudaeos*) (*Quaestiones* 81, ed. Souter, CSEL 50, p. 137).

The same assumption that conversions to Judaism still took
place could be found also in the pagan Greek and Latin
sources composed after 100 CE. Epictetus in a discourse of
c.108 CE observed: 'Whenever we see a man halting between
two faiths, we are in the habit of saying, "He is not a Jew, he
is only acting the part." But when he adopts the attitude of
mind of the man who has been baptized [*sic*] and has made his
choice, then he both is a Jew in fact and also is called one . . .'
(Arrian, *Diss.* 2. 9. 20). Juvenal made a clear distinction
between gentile sympathizers who simply revere the sabbath
and those who adore nothing but clouds, avoid pork, get
circumcised and (crucially) despise the laws of Rome (*Sat.* 14.
96–104). Tacitus complained bitterly that gentiles who have
'crossed over into their customs' learn first to despise the
gods, disown their country, and treat their families with
contempt (*Hist.* 5. 5. 2). In the mid-second century the pagan
philosopher Celsus wrote that he found nothing wrong with
Jews who kept their own law, but 'rather we find fault with
those who have abandoned their own traditions and professed
those of the Jews' (Origen, *C. Celsum*, 5. 41). Cassius Dio in
the early third century observed that the name 'Jews' was
given to the inhabitants of Judaea but that 'it applies also to all
the rest of mankind, although of alien race, who affect their
customs' (37. 17. 1). Probably in the late fourth century, the
author of the *Historia Augusta* wrote, possibly fraudulently
but in that case reflecting conditions at the time when he was
writing, that Septimius Severus had forbidden (gentiles) 'to
become Jews' (*Iudaeos fieri* (*Sev.* 17. 1)); the expression was
the same as that used by the contemporary Christian author
Ambrosiaster to describe proselytes (see above).

A series of Roman laws in the fourth and fifth centuries
prohibited conversion to Judaism, particularly by Christians.[7]
In 329 CE Constantine declared that, 'if one of the people shall
approach their (the Jews') sect and join himself to their

---

[7] For discussion of all this legislation, see Linder, *Jews in Roman Legislation*, with
texts and comm.

conventicles', he will be punished (*Cod. Theod.* 16. 8. 1). This could just have been a prohibition against becoming a gentile sympathizer on the fringes of Judaism, although I doubt such an interpretation, but a law of 353 CE was unambiguous. Constantius II declared to his praetorian prefect that 'if someone shall become Jew from Christian [*ex Christiano Iudaeus effectus*] and shall be joined to sacrilegious assemblies', his property will be confiscated (*Cod. Theod.* 16. 8. 7). Similar clear prohibitions of conversion to Judaism were again re-enacted in the course of the next century (cf. *Cod. Theod.* 16. 7. 3 (383 CE); *Cod. Theod.* 16. 8. 19 (409 CE)). Reiteration and revision of the law suggests that the Roman authorities at least believed or feared that conversions continued to take place.

The precise nature of those conversions is less certain, not least because it cannot be taken for granted that these sources were all referring to the same phenomenon. Both Jews and gentiles after 96 CE may have evolved clear definitions of Jewish identity, but those definitions may have differed from one group to another. Some Jews may well have treated the male offspring of a Jewish father and a gentile mother as a proselyte if he behaved as a Jew, if some of their compatriots treated him as Jewish by right while others followed the eventual rabbinic view and treated him as a gentile. In Roman eyes such an individual might only have to declare his Jewishness to be accepted as a Jew—after all, it was in the interests of the state to adopt a wide definition of Jewishness in order to increase revenues from the special Jewish tax. Sensitivity to such ambiguity may solve some apparent oddities. Thus, three men were designated by the Jews of Aphrodisias as proselytes on the inscription erected in their synagogue. There has been some concern as to how the state's prohibition on the circumcision of non-Jews could be so blatantly flouted. Perhaps according to the Roman definition these individuals had always been Jews and it was only the local community that categorized them otherwise.[8]

There is, then, no reason to doubt that conversions to

---

[8] See Reynolds and Tannenbaum, *Jews and God-Fearers*, 43–5, with their attempt to explain such open defiance of the Roman state.

Judaism of some kind took place during this period, but the evidence so far has provided no clue as to the instigators of the process. Roman legal writers often assumed that proselytes, if they were free men, brought themselves to Judaism, and, by implication, that the recipient community played no role of importance. Thus would-be converts defined themselves as Jews: it was the convert who decided to become Jew from Christian (cf. *Cod. Theod.* 16. 8. 7). If non-Jews were circumcised the crime was theirs and their doctors: a lawyer wrote at the end of the third century, in a work later attributed to the jurist Paul (*Sent.* 5. 22. 3–4), that 'Roman citizens, who suffer that they themselves or their slaves be circumcised in accordance with the Jewish custom, are exiled perpetually to an island and their property confiscated; the doctors suffer capital punishment.' Presumably the doctor, like the physician who performed this service for the Adiabene king in the first century (above, p. 47), was not necessarily a Jew, let alone a missionary.

Rabbinic sources also generally envisaged that the impetus would derive from the prospective converts.[9] Even the rabbinic ceremony which marked conversion had the air of the recognition of a *fait accompli* rather than a contrived rite of passage. The actions required were minimal and existing pious Jews were expected to be involved more or less only as witnesses of the convert's statement of intent. In this respect little had changed since Izates in the first century chose to devote himself to Judaism without anything more than marginal connivance by any existing Jew (see above, Ch. 4).[10]

Perhaps, then, Jews still, as before 100 CE, did not in general see the winning of proselytes as their business. It is worth noting how little of the extensive rabbinic literature on conversion even alludes to the topic. Thus, for instance, the two great homilies on proselytes at *MdRi* Nezikin 18, lines 1–48, and at *Num. R.* 8 *passim* do not even refer to the problem of how converts come to consider becoming Jews in the first place. Numerous texts demonstrate that the rabbis normally welcomed those who sought them out, but, as I have stressed

---

[9] See Braude, *Jewish Proselyting*, 11–14.
[10] Cohen, 'Rabbinic Conversion Ceremony'.

throughout this study, a willingness to accept is quite different from a positive desire to acquire.[11] Rabbis did in general assume that a gentile living within a Jewish community (in the land of Israel?) is a potential convert (in halakhic terms, that a *ger toshav* is a potential *ger tzedek*, cf. *b. A. Zar.* 65a), but this did not imply any onus on Jews to take any action with regard to gentiles who lived elsewhere. As doves scent the food given to their fellow doves and come to partake, so proselytes are converted 'when the elder sits and preaches' (*Cant. R.* 4. 2, Dunsky, p. 99), but it was not suggested that such attraction of proselytes was the reason for the teaching in the first place. The remarkable assertion that God brought about the exile as a way of increasing the number of proselytes is found both in the name of the tanna R. Eleazar in some manuscripts of *b. Pes.* 87b and, ascribed to a Jewish acquaintance, in the writings of the third-century Christian writer Origen (*C. Celsum*, 1. 55), but the diaspora was brought about by God not humans, and no rabbi even hinted that a deliberate prolongation or extension of the exile would be desirable to further this mission to the nations.

Similar objections may be raised to some of the other material that has been put forward by one scholar or another as evidence for Jews as proselytizers in this period. Arguments based on synagogue architecture seem to me to have minimal value. It has been suggested that the peristyle around the Dura Europus synagogue, which was built in the mid-third century, and the easy visibility of the Sardis synagogue in the next century, may have been intended to entice gentiles into worshipping the Jewish God,[12] but such worshippers could have become gentile godfearers rather than proselytes. In any case large synagogues could express the defiance of the Jews when under political pressure from their neighbours as easily as they might reflect a proselytizing mission. Certainly that would be a better explanation of the decision of the Alexandrian Jews, who lived in near-constant tension with their Greek neighbours, to erect their great house of prayer

---

[11] For these texts see Braude, *Jewish Proselyting*, and Bamberger, *Proselytism*. Contrast their assumptions about proselytizing: Braude, *Jewish Proselyting*, 3 and 18; Bamberger, *Proselytism*, 290.

[12] Georgi, *Opponents*, 372; see Trebilco, *Jewish Communities*, 53, 159.

which was one of the wonders of the world (*t. Sukkah* 4: 6, L. p. 273).

More might be made out of the evidence enshrined in the corpus of laws about Jews and Judaism issued between the second and fifth centuries CE, but in practice the evidence in such laws for Jews as keen to convert non-Jewish free men and women to Judaism is at best ambiguous. The repetition of Roman legislation against the circumcision of non-Jewish males and, from the fourth century, conversion more generally expressed, clearly suggests that conversions took place but reveals nothing in itself about the motivation of the native Jews involved.[13] Thus the wording of the laws about circumcision is compatible with Jews' eagerness to circumcise others having extended only so far as would-be marriage partners or slaves, as in the Second Temple period. According to the early third century jurist Modestinus, quoted in the Digest (48. 8. 11), the emperor Antoninus Pius had ruled that 'Jews are permitted to circumcise only their sons . . .; if anyone shall commit it on one who is not of the same religion, he shall suffer the punishment of a castrator.' In the wording of a late third-century jurist, in the passage already quoted, attributed to Paul (*Sententiae*, 5. 22. 3–4), those who were to be punished when a Roman citizen or his slaves were circumcised were the citizen himself and the doctor, whereas 'if Jews shall circumcise purchased *slaves* of another nation, they shall be banished or suffer capital punishment'. A law promulgated by Constantine in 335 CE and almost fully preserved in *Constitutio Sirmondiana* 4 as well as in abbreviated form in the Theodosian Code (16. 9. 1) was again concerned about the circumcision of slaves by Jews: 'it shall not be lawful for a Jew who has circumcised a slave of the aforementioned kind to retain him in slavery's obedience.'

The reiteration of the ban on circumcision may have indicated more about Roman horror at mutilation of the flesh than it did about Jews' enthusiasm for converts. The original ban was introduced by Hadrian on analogy with the prohibition of castration. Its universal scope encompassed

---

[13] *Contra* Juster, *Juifs*, i. 259–63. See the very useful comments on all these laws by Linder, *Jews in Roman Legislation*, ad locc. Cohen, 'Was Judaism Missionary?', 21, states roundly that none of the Roman legislation attests Jewish mission.

many inhabitants of the empire apart from the Jews. The Christian heretic Bardaisan wrote, probably in the mid-second century, that 'Romans have recently conquered Arav (i.e. Arabia) and removed all their customs including circumcision.'[14] Origen wrote a century later that 'Sicarians' (better, Samaritans?) were still persecuted in his day for continuing to practice circumcision (*C. Celsum*, 2. 13). The Jews alone were exempted from the ban, and that was probably only in reaction to the awful conflagration of the Bar Kokhba war, of which the ban may have been a prime cause.[15]

Although many of these Roman laws which prohibited Jews from converting others in more general terms were primarily concerned about the fate of gentile, and specifically Christian, slaves owned by Jews, just occasionally emperors of the fourth and fifth centuries do seem to have assumed that Jews might be keen on proselytizing free men also. Thus Constantine pronounced to his praetorian prefect in 329 CE that the Jews should know that 'if one of the people shall approach their nefarious sect and join himself to their conventicles, he shall suffer *with them* the deserved punishments' (*Cod. Theod.* 16. 8. 1). For our purposes, the crucial words in this law are 'with them' (*cum ipsis*), with their implication that the Jews as well as the proselytes were to blame for what had happened. A law of 383 CE, which threatened with terrible penalties Christians who became pagans, Jews, or Manichaeans (*Cod. Theod.* 16. 7. 3), also threatened the instigators of such conversions, but in the law as it is preserved the individuals thus warned, described as *auctores persuasionis huius*, may have been not pagan or Jewish missionaries but only the Manichaeans, who were the subject of discussion in the previous sentence. About the missionary zeal of some Manichaeans there is no doubt (see below, Ch. 8).

Less ambiguous was a law of Honorius issued in 409 CE: 'Some people, moreover, oblivious of their life and their position, dare to transgress the Law to such an extent, that they force some to cease being Christian and to adopt the

---

[14] Drijvers (ed.), *Book of Laws*, 56.
[15] For the evidence, see Schäfer, *Bar Kokhba*, 38–50.

abominable and vile name of the Jews' (*Cod. Theod.* 16. 8. 19). But this law, with its allusions to the use of force by Jews, may possibly have referred only to Jews' treatment of their slaves or Jews who have apostatized to Christianity, rather than free gentile citizens. Six years later Theodosius II made explicit mention of Jewish circumcision of free men who had become converts in the law by which he stripped the rabbinic patriarch Gamaliel VI of most of his dignities (*Cod. Theod.* 16. 8. 22): 'If he himself, or one of the Jews, shall attempt to defile a Christian or a member of any sect whatsoever, slave and freeman alike, with the Jewish mark of infamy, he shall be subjected to the laws' severity'. But this does not show that Gamaliel was involved in proselytizing, only in accepting converts. The same emperor in 423 CE held 'the Jews' responsible for conversions (*Cod. Theod.* 16. 8. 26) when he proclaimed, 'Jews shall be condemned to confiscation of property and to perpetual exile, if it will be established that they have circumcised a man of our faith or ordered him to be circumcised', but, again, the initiative may have come from the convert. The state's attitude that proselytizing by Jews was possible seems clearest in Theodosius' *Novel* 3, issued in 438 CE and intended to clarify policy with regard to Jews, Samaritans, pagans, and heretics: 'We add to these, that whoever shall transfer a slave or a freeborn, against his will or with punishment-meriting persuasion, from the cult of the Christian religion to an abominable sect and rite, shall be punished by death and confiscation of property. . . . Furthermore, let him who overcame another man's faith with a perverse doctrine know that he shall be sentenced to confiscation of his property and to the death penalty.' But it is all too possible that the proselytizers whom Theodosius had in mind in this law were Christian heretics rather than Jews.

The evidence in Roman laws that any Jews were believed to have engaged in proselytizing free men and women is thus not in itself decisive, although nothing in the legal sources suggests a contrary assumption that Jews did not proselytize. Just one surviving law may point to an actual case when Jewish missionaries were in action but the details are too obscure for much to be built upon the surviving evidence. Constantine II wrote to the praetorian prefect Evagrius in 339

CE (*Cod. Theod.* 16. 8. 6): 'In regard to women formerly occupied in our weaving-establishment, whom the Jews led to their fellowship in turpitude (*quas Iudaei in turpitudinis suae duxere consortium*), it is resolved that they shall be restored to the weaving-establishment, and it shall be ensured, in the future, that they do not join Christian women to their deeds of disgrace, or, if they shall do so, they shall be subjected to capital punishment.' The problem here is to decide whether the *consortium* involved was marriage (hence these were free gentiles) or, as is more likely, religious fellowship, in which case the women were slaves. In either case, of course, no circumcision was involved since these were all women converts. If the general prohibition on conversion alleged by the author of the *Historia Augusta* to have been decreed by Septimius Severus be discounted as an invention by the late fourth-century author in the light of events in his own time (*V. Sev.* 17. 1), it may be that the Jews concerned in this case did not realize that they were doing wrong. Hence the wording of the law, which seems to have laid down rules for the future rather than complaining about the transgression of existing laws.[16]

The florid language of such fourth- and fifth-century legislation about religion hints at a general difficulty in evaluating Christian comments about Jews in this period. In many Christian texts down to the end of antiquity the biblical, both Old and New Testament, image of Jews predominated.[17] Since in the New Testament people called Jews were sometimes depicted as rivals for the souls of potential converts, it would be unsurprising if Jews were similarly pictured as rivals by the Church Fathers, particularly in the light of the occasional Christian use of the term 'Judaism' to abuse any allegedly over-literal form of Christianity of which the writer disapproved, so that some patristic references to Judaism may have actually reflected only an internal Christian argument.

Many patristic texts which have been claimed in the past as evidence for Jewish mission are thus not very convincing.

---

[16] On this law, see Bachrach, 'Jewish Community', 408–9; Linder, *Jews*, 148–50.

[17] Cf. Efroymson (1976); Richardson *et al.*, *Anti-Judaism in Early Christianity*. See now Taylor, 'Men of Straw'.

Justin Martyr complained in the dialogue with Trypho that the Jews sent messengers to every corner of the world to slander the Christians (*Dial.* 17), but the incidents to which he referred belonged to the Church tradition about the reaction of the Jewish authorities in Jerusalem to events immediately after the Crucifixion. Neither in Justin's text, nor in the reference made to it by Eusebius (*Hist. Eccl.* 4. 18. 7), was there any suggestion that these messengers were seeking converts to Judaism.[18] Justin elsewhere put into the mouth of his Jewish opponent Trypho the advice that he (the gentile Justin) should be circumcised, observe the sabbath, feasts, and new moons, 'in brief, fulfil the whole written law, and then, probably, you will experience the mercy of God' (*Dial.* 8). This sounds like a strong missionary statement, but it was more than somewhat diluted by Justin's Jew in the sentiments expressed immediately before: 'It would be better for you to concentrate on the philosophy of Plato or some other philosopher . . . for while you adhered to your former school of philosophy and lived a blameless life, there was hope of a better destiny for you, but when you have turned away from God and have placed your hope in man (i.e. Jesus), what hope of salvation do you have?' (*Dial.* 8). If Trypho was said to have taught that a moral pagan philosopher could achieve salvation, he cannot also have taught that everyone should become Jewish.

Justin's Jew was not very consistent in his attitudes. It is evident that he was to some extent an imaginary foil required for the dialogue form. So, for instance, the dialogue was probably set (perhaps fictitiously) in Ephesus in Asia Minor at a date not long before the synagogue inscription was set up in nearby Aphrodisias, but Justin appears to have known nothing about Jews' recognition of righteous pagans as Godfearers. According to him, Trypho understood Isaiah's description of the Jews as the light to the gentiles (Isaiah 49: 6) as a reference to the winning of proselytes (*Dial.* 121–2). I know of no Jewish text that interpreted this passage in this way. Trypho's version may have been invented by Justin to enable him to put the counter-proposal that Isaiah referred to

---

[18] Contra Simon, *Verus Israel*, 282; MacMullen, *Paganism*, 192.

converts to Christianity (*Dial.* 122).[19] Even in the fictional narrative Trypho's view is not put into his own mouth but into that of Justin, who claims that this is what 'you' (plural) think.

The testimony of other patristic authors is hardly more helpful. Origen referred in his commentary on Matthew 23: 15 to contemporary proselytes (see above, p. 133), but not to any contemporary equivalents to the missionary Pharisees described in the Gospel (*Comm. in Matt. Series* 16, ed. Klostermann, p. 29); Origen's failure to take such a promising opportunity to attack Jewish proselytizers suggests that he did not see them as a threat, but such an argument from silence has the usual weaknesses. Some of the Church Fathers, in particular John Chrysostom in late fourth-century Antioch, were evidently much concerned by the tendency of their flock to fraternize with the Jews by adopting Jewish customs and attending synagogue services. The tendency to 'Judaize' was almost endemic among Christians, since they all, apart from such heretics as Marcion and his followers, clung to the Old Testament as part of sacred scripture and thus faced a perennial problem of how to interpret laws which Christians no longer wished to obey. Whether the Antiochene or any other Jews saw such gentile hangers-on as proselytes is dubious. They might perhaps accord them status as God-fearers, but in any case the whole point of John Chrysostom's sermons was that it was Christians who sought out the Jews; he did not bother to relate whether the Jews also sought Christian converts.[20]

Also in the fourth century but further to the East, the Syriac Christian Ephraem used an allegory to interpret the story in 2 Kings 19: 9–14 of the letters sent by Sennacherib to Hezekiah, king of Judah, to warn him to submit to his power. These letters, according to Ephraem, denoted the writings of

---

[19] For rabbinic interpretations of Isaiah 49: 6, see Hyman, *Torah haKethubah veha Messurah*, ii. 162–3. Hyman gives only one reference from all early rabbinic literature, and the passage in question (from *y. Shebi.* 4. 10, 35c) does not allude to this part of the verse. On Justin's tendency to misread biblical texts as evidence for the desirability of mission, see Fredriksen, 'Judaism, Circumcision and Apocalyptic Hope', 547 n. 45 and 548, on Justin, *Dial.* 122–3.

[20] Wilken, *John Chrysostom and the Jews*, 91.

impious men who urged his (Ephraem's) flock to desert the Church of Christ and cross over to the synagogues of Satan (*Opera Syriaca*, ed. Mobarek 1. 558). These wicked individuals may have been proselytizing Jews engaged in the composition of missionary tracts about which nothing else is known, but it is not likely. The rhetorical abuse belongs better within the context of intra-Christian dispute. Similarly rhetorical was the image of Christians as sheep surrounded by fierce Jewish wolves which can be found both in the writings of John Chrysostom (*Adv. Jud.* 4. 1 (*PG* 48. 871)) and, uneasily combined with a reference to Jews as snakes, in a near-contemporary letter by Jerome (*Ep.* 93). This was stock invective and probably not even intended as an accurate depiction.[21]

Pagan writers were free of these particular biases, and in some ways their testimony may be more trustworthy. However, they had little to say about Jews as proselytizers, despite their numerous references to the fact of conversion (see above). The great exception is the account given in the early third century by Cassius Dio of the expulsion of the Jews from Rome during the reign of Tiberius. He stated there (57. 18. 5a), that 'as the Jews flocked to Rome in great numbers and were converting (*methistanton*) many of the natives to their ways, he (Tiberius) banished most of them'. I argued in Chapter 4 that this account, which differed considerably from Tacitus' and Josephus', misrepresented Jewish attitudes in the early first century. But if that is correct, Dio's mistake may well have been based on his beliefs about the Judaism of his own day, about which he wrote quite percipiently elsewhere in his history (37. 16. 5–17. 4).

The least ambiguous evidence that some Jews may have believed proselytizing to be desirable comes from the rabbinic texts, to which I turn last. The evidence for rabbinic approval of the winning of converts is indirect and allusive, but when it is laid out it may be seen to have some cumulative force.

The most persuasive evidence seems to me to lie in the common rabbinic depiction of Abraham as a missionary.[22]

---

[21] For parallels, see Wilken, *John Chrysostom and the Jews*, 118–19.

[22] See Bamberger, *Proselytism*, ch. 10; Braude, *Jewish Proselyting*, ch. 3.

Approving reference was made in many rabbinic passages (e.g. *ARNB*, ch. 26; *Num. R.* 14: 11; *Pes. R.* 43, ed. Friedmann, 181a, etc.) to the activities of Abraham and Sarah in Haran where, according to Gen. 12: 5, they had created souls. How, asked the rabbis, could humans create life? Already in the earliest extant reference to this problem, in the tannaitic midrash *Sifre Deut.* 32, the response was given that the expression 'created souls' means that Abraham and Sarah 'brought men and women under the wings of the Shekhinah'; this latter phrase possessed a semi-technical meaning, derived from its use in Ruth 2: 12, of converting someone to Judaism. In this passage in Sifre the implications of the actions of Israel's ancestors for contemporary Jews was made explicit. The words of Deut. 6: 5 ('you shall love the Lord your God') were interpreted by a shift of vowels to mean not 'you should love' but 'you should make the Lord your God be loved [by humanity]'; the reason given for this injunction was that this is what Abraham and Sarah did when they made proselytes (*megayaram*) in Haran. Since what they did was praiseworthy, all Jews should try to follow suit. Nor was the image of Abraham as missionary confined to discussion of his behaviour in Haran. Gen. 12: 8, which reads 'And he [Abraham] called upon the name of the Lord', was interpreted according to one view at *Gen. R.* 39: 16 (Theodor–Albeck, p. 381) as 'he summoned people to the name of the Lord' and taken to signify that he began to make converts.

This new status of Abraham as the great missionary is all the more striking because he lacked the role in the eyes of Philo and Josephus, let alone Artapanus (see above, Ch. 4). Of course, Abraham lived before the making of the covenant on Sinai, and if the biblical story is read in chronological order he should only have been converting others to monotheism. But that was not how the rabbis interpreted his actions. For them, Abraham was himself a prime example of a proselyte to Judaism. Such an interpretation was justified by the notion that the Torah pre-existed not just Abraham but the creation of the world (cf. *b. Pes.* 54a).

Other figures from the Bible were similarly portrayed in rabbinic texts as missionaries, evidently with approval. R. Hoshaya, a third-century amora from Palestine, cited R.

Judah b. Simon's reading of Gen. 37: 1 ('And Jacob dwelt in the land of his father's sojournings' (*megurei aviv*)) as *megayarei aviv*, with the implication that Isaac had made proselytes in that area—but whether this implied that he had undertaken deliberate proselytizing, I am not sure. In his interpretation of the Joseph story the late-third century Palestinian amora R. Abba b. Kahana alleged that Joseph inspired the Egyptians with a longing to be circumcised (*Gen. R.* 90: 6, Theodor–Albeck, p. 1106). In the same passage a certain R. Samuel (presumably some rabbi other than the great Mar Samuel) was said to have interpreted a curious reading in the biblical text to mean that Joseph gave the Egyptians life not only in this world but also in the world to come; in the eyes of the redactor of *Genesis Rabbah* at least, if not necessarily in the opinion of Abba b. Kahana, Joseph's insistence that the Egyptians be circumcised (cf. *Gen. R.* 91: 5, Theodor–Albeck, p. 1119) was intended to lead to their conversion to Judaism. Numerous texts portrayed Jethro as a missionary, just as they depicted him (contrary to the biblical account) as a proselyte. Exodus 18: 27 ('And Moses let his father-in-law (i.e. Jethro) depart; and he went his way into his own land') was glossed in the version of Ps.-Jonathan with the assertion that Jethro went home to convert all the inhabitants of his country; the same interpretation of this incident is found also at *MdRi Amalek* 4, lines 106–8 and *Sifre Zuta* to Num. 10: 30 (ed. Horovitz, p. 265). In *Sifre Num.* 80 (ed. Horowitz, p. 76) it seems that Jethro's ability to gain proselytes was given as a reason for *not* leaving the children of Israel, but here too proselytizing was seen as a self-evident good.

Apart from such commendation of alleged missionary figures from the past, other evidence for rabbinic approval of positive proselytizing was implicit rather than stated. The behaviour attributed to Rabbah bar Abbuha, of whom 'it is related that he said to those who came before him . . . "Go, sell all that you have and come and be converted" ' turns out on inspection of the context (*b. A. Zar.* 64a) to have been not an echo or parallel of Jesus' missionary call in Matt. 19: 21 and parallels but a practical injunction to gentiles who *already* intended to convert to sell before conversion those of their possessions which were connected with idolatry so that after the ceremony they might benefit with a good conscience from the purchase price.[23] But the more indirect evidence which is to be found is not without value. For instance, according to the fourth-century Rabin, citing the third-century Palestinian teacher Resh Lakish, the winning of converts is so desirable that it justifies the purchase of a heathen slave by a Jew from a gentile (*b. A. Zar.* 13b); Resh Lakish even taught that such purchases could be made at pagan fairs despite the danger of contact with immorality at such events (*y. A. Zar.* 1. 1. 39b). The ritual bath marking the conversion of a woman proselyte in Laodicea was an occasion of sufficient importance for the third-century patriarch R. Judan Nesiah to detain R. Joshua b. Levi in the town overnight for its sake, according to a rather inconsequential story attributed to R. Isaac b. Nahman (*y. Yeb.* 8. 1, 8d).

More tenuous was the implicit appeal to altruism for any Jew who might accept the tenet expressed at *b. Yeb.* 48b by an anonymous group of rabbis (probably of the third century, since either R. Abbahu or R. Hanina, both of whom lived late in that century, provided a scriptural proof for their view), that the sufferings of proselytes after conversion are a punishment for their delay in entering under the wings of the Shechinah, if such a Jew also accepted the opinion attributed to a fourth-century amora, R. Bun, that in practice converts come over only because the righteous go to seek them, as Joseph went to Asenath, Joshua to Rahab, Boaz to Ruth (!), and Moses to Hobab (*Eccl. R.* 8. 10). Altruism was in the forefront at *b. Ned.* 32a where R. Yohanan took Abraham to task for his behaviour, as described at Gen. 14: 21, in allowing the king of Sodom to demand the captives after their victory while he took the goods: such a decision was reprehensible, according to Yohanan, because 'he prevented sons of men from entering under the wings of the Shechinah'. It is not clear whether the sin with which Abraham was charged by an unspecified R. Judah at *Gen. R.* 40: 14 (Theodor–Albeck, p. 395)—his failure to make his nephew Lot cleave to God

---

[23] Urbach, *Sages*, 553 n. 17 (938 n. 17) is rather misleading in the use of this text, which he cites without giving the reference.

despite his success in persuading others—was seen by R. Judah as a failure of altruism or of duty to God. R. Ammi, a third-century Palestinian amora, prohibited the teaching of the Torah to idolaters (*b. Hag.* 13a), but such a teaching was evidently ignored at places like Aphrodisias (see also above, p. 132) and in any case would not necessarily inhibit proselytizing: according to the terms of the rabbinic conversion ceremony, the rabbis were content to leave prospective converts remarkably ignorant about their new religion until after they had crossed over into Judaism.[24]

By the third century, then, some Jews had begun to see proselytizing as a religious duty, but there was no unanimity on the subject, and much ambivalence even within the restricted society of the rabbis. Despite the evidence that many rabbis approved of proselytizing, there does not survive in any extant rabbinic text an explicit formulation of a theology of proselytizing mission. It seems that, in marked contrast to the detailed discussion and elaboration of the Noachide code for unconverted gentiles, and the minor posttalmudic tractate *Gerim* which dealt in full with the reception and status of converts, neither any general rabbinic doctrine nor any detailed halakha about the proselytization of the non-Jewish world was ever enunciated.

The paradox which led to this rabbinic ambivalence is too blatant to be ignored. On the one hand rabbis took for granted that conversion to Judaism is an advantage to the proselyte which it was desirable that a Jew should help him acquire. Thus, according to R. Huna, a minor incapable in law of giving consent may none the less be converted by a court on the grounds that a court has an absolute power to confer a benefit (*b. Ket.* 11a). On the other hand this view, despite its momentous potential consequence, was undercut by the rabbis' simultaneous espousal of precise requirements for pious gentiles who remained gentiles, since Jewish acceptance that such requirements are sufficient would appear to make conversion to Judaism irrelevant and any mission to win proselytes otiose. The paradox can be seen at its clearest in the statement (to which I alluded in the previous chapter,

---

[24] Cohen, 'Rabbinic Conversion Ceremony'.

p. 115) of the third-century Palestinian amora R. Yohanan, reported at *b. Meg.* 13a, that any gentile who spurns idolatry is called a Jew. Yohanan's assertion was doubtless a homiletical conceit, but his ability even to propose such a notion suggests a remarkable unawareness of the conflicting implications of the rabbinic attitudes of his time.

Rabbis assumed that all their slaves would be circumcised and thus become potential Jews but, despite the permission granted in *b. A. Zar.* 13b to take such action (see above), they never argued that, since buying up gentile slaves redeemed heathens from their blindness, Jews should purchase all the slaves they could.[25] Rabbis insisted reasonably that conversions must be made in the right spirit, thus not from a desire to facilitate marriage to a Jew, nor out of fear or for worldly advancement, but they sometimes added rather more strangely that conversion was invalidated if the motivation was a dream (*b. Yeb.* 24b).[26] Such a restriction was extraordinary in a religious climate in which all forms of behaviour, including the enthusiastic embrace of a particular cult, were inspired by divine visitations in dream visions. Thus Isis appeared to Lucius, the hero of Apuleius' novel, in a dream (*Met.* 11. 3–7), and it was in a dream that Josephus discovered that he would be following the divine will if he transferred his allegiance to the Roman side during the Jewish revolt (Joseph. *BJ* 3. 351–4).[27]

It is easier to chart these paradoxical beliefs than to show how they arose. It is tempting to assume that such contradictory attitudes must have been originally espoused by the rabbis either at different times or in different places, but it is not possible to be certain whether in fact this was so. It is possible, but not provable, that the Noachide laws were formulated by the rabbis rather earlier than a positive attitude towards proselytizing emerged. It has been noted above that the principle of the Noachide laws seems to have been already

[25] On rabbinic dicta about proselytizing slaves, see Bamberger, *Proselytism*, 124–32. Flesher, *Oxen, Women or Citizens*, emphasizes that the status of freedmen in the Mishnah was theoretically different from that of voluntary free proselytes, but the distinction does not seem to have had significant legal or religious consequences in the rabbinic tradition.   [26] Bamberger, *Proselytism*, 32.

[27] On dreams in ancient paganism, see Lane Fox, *Pagans and Christians*, 150–67; for dreams in Josephus, see Gray, *Prophetic Figures*.

accepted by the tannaim, although insistence on abstention
from idolatry appears not to have been universally held even
in the amoraic period. In contrast all of the comments which
imply approval of proselytizing are ascribed, when they are
ascribed at all, to Palestinian rabbis of the third or early
fourth centuries (*Gen. R.* 84: 4, Theodor–Albeck, p. 1004 (R.
Hoshaya, in the name of R. Judah b. R. Simon); *Gen. R.* 90:
6, Theodor–Albeck, p. 1106 (R. Abba b. Kahana); *Pes. R.* 43,
Friedmann, 181a (R. Eleazar b. Pedat, in the name of R. Yose
b. Zimra); *b. A. Zar.* 13b (Rabin, in the name of Resh Lakish);
b. Ned. 32a (R. Yohanan); *y. Yeb.* 8. 1, 8d (R. Isaac b.
Nahman, with a story about amoraim of the first generation);
y. A. Zar. 1. 1, 39b (Resh Lakish); *Eccl. R.* 8. 10 (R. Bun); *b.
Yeb.* 48b (R. Abbahu; 'some say' R. Hanina (b. Abbahu?))).
No amoraic text seems to ascribe approval of a proselytizing
mission to any second-century tanna apart from *y. Sanh.* 2. 6,
20c, where R. Yose b. Halafta, of the mid-second century, is
credited with attempting to explain Solomon's embarrassingly
excessive polygamy by the implausible claim that Solomon
multiplied his wives not from voluptuousness but to bring
them under the wings of the Shechinah. On the contrary, the
key teaching in *Sifre Deut.* 32 (see above, p. 145) is ascribed in
Pes. R. 43, ed. Friedmann, 181a to the third-century amoraim
R. Eleazar b. Pedat and R. Yose b. Zimra. It is therefore
possible that the anonymous reference to Abraham and Jethro
as missionaries in the tannaitic midrashim and Ps.-Jonathan
were composed by the last generation of the tannaim in the
early third century, and that the notion that proselytizing is
desirable was only first espoused by rabbis at that time,
although I am aware that any claim that, on the contrary, such
midrashic stories were already traditional by that time cannot
of course be disproved.

Wherever and whenever they *originated*, these contradictory notions seem to have been *held* in conjunction by
rabbis in the third and fourth centuries CE in both Palestine
and Babylonia, for all these ideas appear in both Talmuds.
Similarly, it may be correct to distinguish between the ideas
generated by the rabbis when they were teaching as aggadists
or story-tellers, and tended to adopt an idealist attitude to the
world, and the ideas of the same rabbis when they were

engaged as halakhists in laying down the law,[28] but rabbis did not generally preach sermons whose assumptions contradicted the halakha or law they themselves tried to uphold. It is better to assume that they were unaware of the contradictions in their beliefs (which is not impossible) or that they felt unable or unwilling to sort out this particular paradox. What seems certain is that this confused theology about gentiles was not the product of a sustained attempt to clarify the issue for its own sake.

In theory, one possible explanation of this messy theology could have been that Jews had been strongly missionary in the first century but, in fear of risking the ferocity of the Roman state by open proselytizing after the passage of legislation by Hadrian and his successors against the circumcision of non-Jews, justified their new restraint by evolving a theology which offered salvation to gentiles without conversion.[29] But I do not think that this explanation can be correct. State opposition might have been expected to spur missionaries to greater efforts rather than dampen their enthusiasm. This, after all, was what happened in the history of early Christianity, and Jews, too, knew the value of martyrdom, of dying 'for the sanctification of the Name'.[30] In any case I have argued in detail in Chapter 4 that Jews were not strongly missionary in the first century, and if I am correct, what needs to be explained is not the suppression of proselytizing enthusiasm in the second century but the emergence of such enthusiasm among some rabbis at that time despite the continuation of older, less missionary, assumptions.

No direct explanation of this phenomenon is likely to be provided by the rabbinic texts themselves, since the rabbis' espousal of contradictory notions about gentiles suggests that they never tried to probe the reasons for their particular attitudes. All that can be offered is a plausible reconstruction based on what evidence does survive.

The impetus for Jews to encourage non-Jews to take a respectful interest in Judaism may have increased after 70 CE

---

[28] Levi, 'Prosélytisme juif'.

[29] So Juster, *Juifs*, i. 259–63; Braude, *Jewish Proselyting*, 23.

[30] On the Jewish attitude to martyrdom, see *Enc. Jud.* x. 977–86, s.v. Kiddush ha-Shem. For criticism of Juster and Braude, see Simon, *Verus Israel*, 272–3.

when the attraction of gentiles to Judaism might help to bridge the gulf which separated Jews' belief in their election with the reality of their defeat and exile. But it was only in the third century that we can be certain that some rabbis began assuming the desirability of a mission to proselytize, which suggests that if proselytizing was a reaction to disaster, the reaction was extraordinarily slow. Only one obvious factor between 70 CE and the third century had altered to encourage this novel attitude. Rabbis in Palestine were by now well aware of the success of Christianity in winning pagans away from idolatry. In time the assumptions of rivals with whom debate and discussion were not uncommon, in for instance third-century Caesarea,[31] may have been adopted, perhaps unconsciously, by the rabbis themselves. If the rabbis paid any attention at all to the spread of the Church they will have known that it had succeeded thus far not by positing good behaviour for non-Christians but by encouraging outsiders into the Christian fold.

I am not suggesting here that the rabbis simply competed with the Church, but that the triumphs of the Church gradually changed the religious assumptions of some in the ancient world—not just Jews—until the notion of a mission to convert was taken for granted by those ancients who thought about religion at all, just as it is part of the common currency of modern society. As with much of the religious and social change in the late antique world, the rabbis could not keep themselves immune.

It is hardly surprising that the confused and ambivalent attitude to proselytizing found in the talmudic tradition lent itself to widely different interpretations in later ages. There is good evidence that conversions to Judaism continued through into the medieval period. The names of many individual proselytes are preserved, although most of those recorded were converted Christian clerics whose shift of allegiance caused major scandal.[32] It is possible that the populace as well as the rulers of the pagan Turkic kingdom of the Khazars, which was well known in medieval Jewish literature, did

---

[31] De Lange, *Origen and the Jews*.
[32] Blumenkrantz, *Juifs et Chrétiens*, 159–211; Golb, *Jewish Proselytism*.

indeed submit to a full rabbinic conversion to Judaism.[33] But it is much less clear whether these proselytes were stimulated by a Jewish mission or came of their own accord, for political, religious, or personal reasons. A certain Bodo, a Christian cleric known after his conversion to Judaism as Eleazar, apparently co-operated with the Muslims in Spain in 847 CE to insist that all Christians there turn either to Islam or to Judaism, but his incentive to such behaviour most probably came from his Christian background rather than from his new Jewish mentors, who would hardly be keen on the production of new Muslims.[34] A Christian author by the name of Amolon inveighed against the Jews for insisting that their debtors deny Christ,[35] but the charge, even if true, might reflect a desire to produce righteous Noachides rather than Jews, if Christianity was treated by these Jews, unlike some other Jews in the Middle Ages, as reprehensible idolatry.[36] Halakhic views as to whether winning converts is a positive religious duty varied in medieval times as much as in the talmudic period.[37]

The ambiguity still continues today. Conversion to orthodox Judaism has become notoriously difficult to achieve, particularly in this country, and the notion that Jews should *seek* converts, although not totally unknown, rarely even arises.[38] When a convert after long delay finally does enter the fold, he or she may be greeted with congratulations even though the approval of native Jews for his or her new status may be ambivalent or worse. The illogicalities of today reflect the confused formation of rabbinic attitudes in the second to fifth centuries CE.

---

[33] Golb, *Jewish Proselytism*, 38–49.

[34] Collins, *Early Medieval Spain*, 205.   [35] Ibid. 178.

[36] On medieval Jewish attitudes to Christians, see Novak, *Image of the Non-Jew*, 130–5.

[37] Wacholder, 'Halakah and the Proselyting of Slaves'; *idem*, 'Attitudes towards Proselytizing'.

[38] For a strong affirmation that Judaism should be missionary, see now Epstein, *Theory and Practice of Welcoming Converts*. But even he asserts (140) that any plan to welcome converts should specifically exclude non-Jews who do not voluntarily express an interest in learning more about Judaism.

8

The Consequences and Origins
of Proselytizing

THE suggestion that approval of universal proselytizing may
have arisen among some rabbinic Jews in reaction to the use
of the concept within the Church raises the possibility that
such mission may have been found also in other late antique
religions affected by Christianity. In this final chapter I shall
explore the possibility that pagans or others proselytized
under the influence of Christians. I shall then examine the
consequences of the notion of proselytizing mission on
religious behaviour in antiquity. Finally I shall investigate
some possible explanations for the emergence of the idea of
universal proselytizing in the history of the early Church.

In contrast to the rabbinic material surveyed in the previous
chapter, the evidence that any pagans advocated universal
proselytizing to their cults or to polytheism in general, even
when they were fully aware of Christian notions of mission,
is ambiguous at best. This fact is likely to be significant,
because it contrasts strikingly to the fact that other aspects of
Christianity certainly did infiltrate into the language and
assumptions of some pagans, particularly after the conversion
of Constantine. Thus in 376 CE the pagan philosopher
Aedesius copied Christian terminology when he claimed that
he had been 'reborn to eternity' through the rituals of a
mystery cult (CIL 6. 510), and the suggestion of the
hierophant of Eleusis, as recorded by the pagan scholar
Eunapius (VS 7. 3. 2–4) in the same period, that it would be
illegitimate for a worshipper of Mithras to succeed him as
hierophant of Eleusis, introduced elements of a concept
unusual in paganism and possibly derived from Christianity,

that membership of one cultic group precluded membership of another.[1] The best evidence of such influence by Christianity on aspects of paganism other than proselytizing comes from the brief period (361–3 CE) when Rome was ruled by the emperor Julian, who apostatized from Christianity to paganism only after a full education within the Church.[2] That Julian owed much of his vision of paganism to his Christian upbringing is well known. On the most basic level, the structures of the administration of the new revived paganism he promoted mimicked that of the Catholic Church, with high priests appointed from each province and local priests granted money to distribute charity to the poor on the Judaeo-Christian model. The emperor became the focus of prayer in the imperial cult rather than just worship, being turned into the pagan equivalent of Christian saint.[3] Just as significant, however, is the way Julian's vision of what pagan religion was *for* had been shaped by his Christian mentors. Julian's paganism was no longer simply a reflection of that part of ordinary life which especially concerned the gods, as in the old civic cults. His paganism was an abstraction, a system with its own carefully constructed and philosophically argued rationale based on the calculations of subtle Neoplatonists in imitation of the burgeoning and already vast technical theological literature of the Church Fathers.[4]

But despite this intellectual baggage carried over from Christianity, there is little to suggest that Julian brought into paganism the notion of universal proselytizing. When Julian decided soon after his elevation to power to mount a campaign against Persia he revived the old view that the power of Rome should extend over the inhabited world. According to the pagan writer Libanius in an oration composed on the occasion of Julian's early demise, victory in that campaign would have incorporated the Persians into the empire and would have caused them to take up such civilized Graeco-Roman cultural habits as rhetoric (*Or.* 18. 282).

---

[1] See Burkert, *Ancient Mystery Cults*, 50–1, who suggests a different, but more complicated, explanation of this attitude.

[2] See Bowersock *Julian the Apostate*.

[3] Nock, *Essays on Religion and the Ancient World*, ii. 833–46.

[4] This is the main contention of Athanassiadi–Fowden, *Julian and Hellenism*.

Presumably these Persians might have been encouraged to see themselves as participants in Julian's pagan theological system. Julian could have argued that local Persian cults, like local cults in the Mediterranean region, were all simply aspects of the single divinity who oversees everything in the cosmos. But there is no evidence that he ever used such arguments, nor that the encouragement of such cults played any part at all in his decision to mount his campaign.[5]

After Julian, no other pagan in antiquity found himself in a position to encourage the adoption of pagan polytheism or of any particular cult on such a wide scale. Surviving evidence produced by individual pagans in the late fourth and the fifth century under increasingly zealous Christian emperors suggests that their main concern was for tolerance.[6] One pagan might encourage the re-establishment of old cults which had fallen into disuse; thus Asclepiodotus, the pupil of Proclus, went as a 'missionary' for this purpose to Aphrodisias in Asia Minor in the fifth century.[7] But such behaviour was sporadic, defensive, and limited in its aim.

For blatant, explicit adoption in late antiquity of a proselytizing attitude akin to that of the early Church, the best evidence can be found not in such pagan polytheism but in the curious doctrines of the Manichaeans. Manichaeism was founded in Mesopotamia in the mid-third century CE by an Aramaic-speaking native, named Mani.[8] Mani had been educated within a Christian baptizing sect called the Elchasaites but experienced a revelation which, he was convinced, surpassed that of all preceding prophets. This revelation consisted in a complex mythology of the constant cosmic struggle of light against dark and good against evil, which required all men to strive to aid the light by careful conservation of the light particles in matter through the greatest possible asceticism. This revelation Mani determined to reveal to the whole world in order to persuade all mankind to join in the cosmic struggle, and with this intention he embarked on a series of journeys, mostly within the Sassanian

---

[5] For the claim that Julian's attack on Persia was part of a 'spiritual campaign', see Athanassiadi–Fowden, 192.   [6] Cf. Kaegi, 'Fifth-Century Twilight'.
[7] Geffcken, *Last Days of Paganism*, 235.
[8] On all the following, see most conveniently Lieu, *Manichaeism*, esp. 70–120.

empire, to win converts to the doctrines and way of life he proposed. By his death in *c*.280 CE his success had been remarkable, but since other Christians branded him a heretic, instead of a transformation of the Church, a new world religion was established.

Manichaeism was a missionary religion *par excellence.* Mani himself appointed disciples to go to the four corners of the earth to consolidate his own work and to spread the message to new fields, and by the fourth century the main *raison d'être* of the Manichaean elect was to spread the faith by a lifetime of travel and evangelism, existing in the most ascetic fashion. Even though such extensive travel was bound to injure the light particles in the ground simply by treading on them, the missionary urge was more important. The theological basis of this missionary drive was clear-cut. Only by changing the way of life of all men could sufficient light be released into the cosmos for the defeat of darkness to be achieved. To be sure, not everyone could undertake the supreme devotion to the light which characterized the Elect. So, for instance, all forms of agriculture were forbidden to the Elect out of deference to the light particles in the ground. But every individual *could* undertake to ensure the soteriological life-style of one of the Elect by undertaking as a Hearer, like Augustine did before his conversion back to Catholic Christianity, to see to the alimentary needs and the shelter of the extreme ascetics, while themselves preserving as much asceticism as the needs of preserving life would permit. It was such devotion, that of the Hearer, which Mani wished to persuade all men to undertake. Such a life-style involved a conversion parallel to that of converts to Judaism and mainstream Christianity. Like them, it involved the repudiation of pagan ritual; like the early Church, it early brought upon itself the wrath of the Roman state under Diocletian (*Mos. et Rom. Leg. Coll.* 15. 3. 4).

The origins and background of the curious Manichaean mythology are obscure and have been much debated,[9] but the origins of Mani's attitude to mission can be firmly sited within the Church. In some ways this was a negative reaction

[9] Cf. Lieu, *Manichaeism*, 7–32.

to Catholic Christians, for in proclaiming himself a prophet
to the whole world he specifically contrasted his role to that
of Jesus, who was a prophet only of the Jews as the Buddha
was the prophet of the Indians and Zoroaster that of the
Persians. By contrast Mani claimed that his own revelation
was definitive and final, transcending cultural and national
barriers; that this was so would be proved by the universal
recognition of its validity. More positively, Mani modelled
his own role consciously and deliberately on that of the
apostle Paul, as has become clear from his biography in the
recently deciphered fourth-century Cologne codex.[10]

The spectacular success of the Manichaeans in the first
century of their proselytizing testifies to their zeal. It also
reveals a good deal about their missionary methods, since the
new religion elicited not only a large internal literature, which
is often obscure since it was addressed to *cognoscenti*, but
also much Catholic Christian literature in opposition. The
methods used by the Manichaeans were the same as those of
the earliest Christian missionaries. So, for instance, the
Manichaean elect sometimes preferred to remain in one place
for a considerable time, consolidating their hold upon the
local population. Thus Mani in his lifetime commanded his
disciple Adda, who had been sent westwards into the Roman
empire, to remain there 'like a merchant who gathers in a
store'.[11] Manichaean missionaries travelled as, or with,
merchants, along the trade routes, using pictures and extensive
translations into the vernacular to get their literature across to
potential converts. Like Catholic Christians, Mani's followers
set up communities in scattered centres to nurture the truth
and entice outsiders into the alternative society they represented. Just as the Christian communities were often secretive
and Christian preachers rarely orated in public like the
popular philosophers, so too the Manichaeans operated from
closeted cells of close-knit brethren; in both cases, justified
fear of state persecution played a large part. Just as the
requirements to become an ordinary Christian required much

---

[10] Ibid. 88. On the Cologne codex, see Henrichs and Koenen, 'Ein griechischen
Mani-Codex', esp.114–15. On Manichaeans' awareness of the organization to which
they belonged, despite local diversity, cf. Lim, 'Unity and Diversity'.

[11] Lieu, *Manichaeism*, 98.

self-sacrifice in the denial of normal social bonds, so too did the asceticism demanded by the Manichees. In neither case did the underlying proselytizing drive suffer any check as a result.

But there are good grounds for treating Manichaean adoption of Christian missionary techniques not as imitation by one religion of a rival but as part of the internal history of the Church. Mani's theology was only in part grounded in Christian dogmas, but, at least in the Roman empire, Manichaeans portrayed their doctrines as an improved form of Christianity and were treated as heretics by Church and State for their pains.

The enthusiasm for mission found within the Manichaean offshoot of Christianity in the third and fourth centuries contrasts markedly with the more lukewarm attitude of many mainstream Christians. I discussed in Chapter 5 (above, p. 106) the rarity in patristic texts of explicit references to the desirability of universal proselytizing. There was no mechanism within the Church for organized mission, nor even any explicit policy to convert those individuals such as slaves on whom it would be easy for a Christian owner to bring pressure. The Church in the second and third centuries was often too involved with its own internal organization and survival to be concerned with a mission to the outside world. For much of the second century, many Christian communities were exercised in trying to defend their stance *vis-à-vis* each other, attacking those tendencies among fellow Christians which they defined as heretical. They seem in practice to have lacked much energy and interest in the conversion of outsiders.

But the enthusiasm and success of the Manichaeans were, at least in part, based upon traditions which they shared with other Christians. Because they were enshrined in an authoritative, sacred text, the teachings and example of St Paul were just as readily available to other Christians as to Mani, and could just as easily have spurred on them also to mission. I suggested in Chapter 5 (above, p. 107) that in fact most early Christians after the New Testament period accepted the desirability of universal proselytizing only implicitly, rather than making such a belief central to their faith. But even such a passive acceptance may have had quite a profound historical effect.

The explanation of the phenomenal spread and eventual victory of the Church within the Roman empire may not lie solely in the Christian message itself, or the social status of the first converts, or the religious uncertainties of the inhabitants of the Roman empire in the early centuries, or the personal whim of Constantine and later Christian emperors, important though all these factors were. It is not impossible that the Church conquered the Roman empire in part simply because among Christians, in contrast to the adherents of most of the religions of the empire, could be found some, even if only a few, enthusiasts who took it for granted that an increase in their number was a matter for rejoicing and that it was desirable for them to help bring about such an increase. For most of the period before Constantine's conversion, such Christians will have been running in a race of whose existence most of the other competitors were unaware. If that is so, it would not be so surprising that, with a clear notion both of their communal identity and the universality of their message, they should have emerged victorious.

Thus, although the search for the origin of this Christian notion of proselytizing is hazardous, the issue may be seen as sufficiently important to justify the risk. The huge scholarly literature about mission in the early Church has mostly been concerned with the nature and course of that mission rather than the reasons for it.[12] For most scholars the existence of mission of some sort has simply been taken for granted, and the few studies which have posed the question directly have been more successful in demonstrating that there is indeed a question to be answered than in providing a plausible answer.[13]

Two explanations often proposed either implicitly or explicitly can be quite easily dismissed in the light of Chapters

---

[12] See e.g. Hahn, *Mission*; Harnack, *Mission and Expansion*; Hengel, 'Origins of Christian Mission'.

[13] The main scholar to tackle the issue directly has been John Gager, in *Kingdom and Community* and 'Proselytism and Exclusivity'.

1 and 4 above. First, I do not believe that proselytizing is a natural religious instinct. Secondly, there is insufficient evidence that early Christians imitated or built on efforts by Jewish proselytizers. I hope that I have said enough to show that proselytizing is only an aspect of some religious groups at particular times, and that Jews probably did not seek gentile proselytes in the first century CE.

It is harder to find an alternative explanation which will prove any better. Books on Christian mission often assert that mission was triggered, 'albeit indirectly', by the ministry and person of Jesus.[14] It would obviously be helpful for modern missionaries if this could be demonstrated, but it is actually very hard to do. It is likely that Jesus' vision of the salvation of the gentiles was based on the centripetal concept that had been espoused by Isaiah, that in the end of days the nations would of their own accord come to Zion. Sayings such as 'I am sent only to the lost sheep of Israel' (Matt. 15: 24; cf. 10: 6) can only have survived in the tradition about Jesus if they actually reflected his teaching, since they ran directly counter to the trend of the early Church itself. According to Mark 13: 10 and 14: 9, Jesus taught that the Gospel *would* be published among all nations and throughout the whole world, but Jesus' own ministry seems to have been aimed almost exclusively at Jews, and it is clear from the whole narrative of the Acts of the Apostles that the desirability of a mission to gentiles was not self-evident to the first followers of Jesus after his death and resurrection.

Others have suggested that a proselytizing mission began not in imitation of Christ but in response to his direct call, as, perhaps, in the instruction issued by Jesus in Matt. 28: 19–20. Such a call was perhaps what distinguished the apostles, including Paul, from other missionaries: as the root meaning of their designation suggests (*apostello*), apostles were sent away to do God's will.[15] But this does not explain why some Christians who had not received such a call also believed that it was desirable for non-Christians to become Christian.

If proselytizing was not an obvious trait of religions in the

---

[14] Senior and Stuhlmueller, *Biblical Foundations*, 141–2; Hengel, 'Origins', 61–3.
[15] Schmithals, *Office of Apostle*, 24.

first century CE and it is unlikely that Christians adopted it in imitation of Jews or Jesus or in response to a divine injunction, an explanation is best sought either in what is known of the novel theological speculation by the first generation of Christians or in comparative studies of other religious groups which found themselves under the sort of pressure experienced by the early Church. In the end it may well require a combination of both methods to come up with a more or less satisfactory reconstruction of events and ideas.

In understanding the development of early Christian theology modern students are almost entirely restricted by the selection of writings preserved as authoritative around the end of the first century and (for the most part) enshrined in the New Testament. The letters of Paul in particular reveal just enough to demonstrate the variety of the theological stances adopted by some within the communities with which he corresponded, without clarifying what each stance was like.[16] It is not impossible, or even very unlikely, that cogent theological arguments for a world-wide proselytizing mission were propounded and accepted in the years immediately after the crucifixion and resurrection and that those arguments were simply lost and forgotten once the desirability of mission was acknowledged and unchallenged. So, for instance, early Christians may have felt that their exclusivist views about the damnation of those without the benefit of Christ imposed on them a simple sense of altruistic responsibility for the unevangelized world.[17] Such altruism might have benefits for the missionary, too—as the author of 2 Clement 15: 1 remarked with errant Christians in mind, there is 'no small reward if you turn a destroyed soul to salvation'. Thus the fact that altruism was not cited in any extant early Christian text as the incentive for proselytizing should not rule it out as the original justification cited by missionaries. Perhaps, indeed, altruism was too obvious a motive to need stressing. Alternatively, too explicit an emphasis on the need to save the unenlightened would raise the difficult issue of the fate of

---

[16] See e.g. Rowland, *Christian Origins*, 203–7.

[17] Gager, *Kingdom and Community*, 38; Green, *Evangelism*, 302. Gager, 'Proselytism and Exclusivity', 68, points out quite rightly that monotheism was never a cause of proselytizing for Christians any more than for Jews.

those unlucky enough not to be visited by any missionary and thus damned through no fault of their own (see above, Ch. 5).

Similarly, universal proselytizing might have been justified as the natural corollary of the new covenant between God and all humanity which replaced the old agreement between God and Israel. All humankind was to be united within the Church (Eph. 1: 10; cf. 2: 11–22; Rom. 3: 29). The new testament of Christ applied to all people, not just to Jews; the term used in Greek was *diatheke*, a word which also translated the Hebrew *brith*, meaning 'covenant'.[18] It could have reasonably been argued that if all humans owed allegiance to one God within one society, the whole future of humanity was imperilled if some failed to worship as they should. In other words, the old arguments in favour of religious uniformity within a society could have been applied on a world-wide scale. However in extant texts not only was no such argument put forward but it was actually undermined. Christian sinners were seen as bringing danger only on the *ecclesia*, not on non-Christians (see above, Ch. 5). As in the old covenant, God did indeed hope for some return for his favour: under the new dispensation, men were required to acknowledge Christ as Lord and to adjust their lifestyle accordingly. But the divine side of the bargain was made as a sort of freewill offering, that is, through grace. Christ did not make his demands on the grounds that all humanity had already agreed to the contract and must stick to it. There was no Christian myth about universal human acceptance of the new covenant to correspond to the elaborate myth of Israel's acceptance of the law on Mt. Sinai.[19]

Of the theological notions which can be deduced from extant early Christian writings the element most often cited as justification for proselytizing after the crucifixion is the special excitement produced by expectation of the imminent end of the world. At the very least the enthusiasm of missionaries like Paul must have been much augmented by hopes of such drastic divine intervention. But, although the

[18] See *Theological Dictionary of the New Testament*, s.v. *diatheke*.
[19] See, on the covenant motif in Judaism and Christianity, Sanders, *Paul and Palestinian Judaism*.

eschatological promise and the presence of salvation undoubtedly *shaped* the mission as described in the New Testament, I do not see how it can have *caused* it. Eschatological hopes in themselves did not invariably lead to mission in this or in any other period: expectation of the end often leads to an isolationist or quietist stance toward the outside world.[20] It was quite logical for those who believed that the end of the world was right now occurring and that all gentiles would repent and come to God to sit back and leave the spreading of the truth either to God's direct action or to a Messianic figure, which in the case of early Christians would of course happen with the Second Coming of Christ. There was no *need* to rush around trying to spread the Gospel— God could do that for you (as Romans 11: 25–32 assumes). Jews had for centuries believed that in the last days God would cause gentiles to come of their own accord to Jerusalem (see above, Ch. 4).[21] The author of the Acts of the Apostles stressed repeatedly that God intervened directly to widen the Christian mission from Jews to gentiles (e.g. Acts 10: 1–11: 17). If God could send a theologically significant vision to Cornelius and to Peter, he could do the same for all humans. The saying ascribed to Jesus by Mark (13: 10), that 'the Gospel must first be announced to the nations' before the end will come, is probably an invention of the later first-century Christian tradition, since it occurs in a passage which predicted the tribulations of the early Church,[22] but in any case it raises the serious question why Christ was not believed to have proclaimed the news to gentiles himself. Why prefer to leave so important a task to fallible humans? That he in any case controlled the process to some extent is stated explicitly at 2 Peter 3: 9: he deliberately delayed the timetable of the last days in order to give people opportunity to repent.

In sum, explanations of the Church's attitude to mission in terms of the experience of the resurrection or the expectation of the coming kingdom are, as John Gager has remarked, 'not

---

[20] Gager, *Kingdom and Community*, 39.

[21] See Fredriksen, 'Judaism, Circumcision and Apocalyptic Hope'.

[22] See comm. on Gospel of Mark, ch. 13, esp. 13: 9–13 (e.g. Hooker, *Gospel according to St. Mark*, 310–11).

really explanations at all'.[23] The same objection applies to claims that a sense of eschatological realization stimulated mission.[24] Too many problems remain unanswered. If all that was needed was to spread the news, why did early missionaries expend so much effort ensuring that gentiles did not just hear and understand but committed their lives to it within Christian communities? If eschatological hopes stimulated proselytizing why did any mission continue as those hopes declined? Alternatively, if Christians believed that they were already living in the last days, they might reasonably expect gentiles to sign up, but this does not explain why they felt it necessary to encourage them. In terms of ordinary Jewish theology, they would be attempting to induce a cause by producing its effect, like forcing oneself to laugh in the hope that one will thereby become happy.

A second common explanation for the universal mission of early Christianity derived from the extant literature is the peculiar personality, and the concomitant peculiar theology, of St Paul, partly perhaps because so much more can be known about his attitudes than about others in the early Church. According to his own account, Paul felt under compulsion to preach: 'Woe is unto me, if I preach not the Gospel' (1 Cor. 9: 16). He gloried in the fact that his world-wide mission was unprecedented.[25] His theology in at least one form made sense of his unrelenting activity through a new eschatological theory that gentiles must be 'won' to Christ because only once this was done would God bring about the salvation of Israel (Rom. 11: 25–32; cf. 15: 9–27); the number of gentiles thus to be won was fixed (cf. Rom. 11: 25: the 'full number'), but did not necessarily include everyone in the world.[26] How he came to such a theology is debatable, not least because his tendency to boastfulness left him little inclination to dwell on past failures. He himself made no reference in his own letters to having begun his mission by seeking to convert Jews (cf. Gal. 1: 13–2: 14), so if

---

[23] Gager, 'Proselytism and Exclusivity', 71.
[24] Wright, *New Testament and People of God*, 445.
[25] Hengel, 'Origins', 49.
[26] See Hengel, 'Origins', 50–1. On the originality of this theology, see Fredriksen, 'Judaism, Circumcision and Apocalyptic Hope', 561–2.

the picture in Acts of the beginning of his career is accurate, he was adept at concealing in his letters to gentiles his original attempts to win the Jews. It can thus only be a hypothesis (if a reasonable one) that for the first fourteen years after his conversion he preached to Jews without success, and that only after this long period did he decide to make a radical break and turn to the gentiles.[27]

Despite all the problems involved in reconstructing Paul's theological progress, this analysis is possible and, if true, would provide a partial explanation of his mission to the gentiles. But it is less satisfactory as a total explanation of Christian proselytizing. Paul himself expected God to do some of the work at the end, in saving Israel: 'And so all Israel shall be saved: as it is written, "There shall come out of Zion the Deliverer, and shall turn away ungodliness from Jacob" ' (Rom. 11: 26). Thus Paul's theology as much as that of traditional Judaism allowed for the possibility that God could have done everything Paul took upon himself. Since others also evidently had greater success than him in winning Jews to Christ, the reasons for Paul's adoption of the gentile mission will hardly have been compelling for anyone apart from Paul himself. Despite the extraordinary force of his personality, it can hardly be thought that his personal difficulties could have persuaded other followers of Christ into so drastic a religious innovation as universal mission.

It is actually rather striking that early Christian literature lacks explicit references to the purposes of mission apart from the few statements by St Paul just quoted. Such lack of explicit theological justification lends support to the theory that the real reason for mission was something that the participants did not wish openly to state. Thus it can and has been argued that Christians expected an imminent Second Coming and a dramatic end to the world. As the end was continually postponed, they reacted to the failure of reality to live up to expectations by seeking new adherents to their group: the fact that the newcomers wished to join them confirmed them in their beliefs despite the objective fact that

[27] So Hengel, ibid. For the view that the picture of Paul's career in Acts is totally fictitious and that Paul never went to the Jews at all, see Sanders, *Paul, the Law and the Jewish People*, 179–90.

what they had thought would happen had not come to pass. Missionary outreach was thus an antidote to doubt and uncertainty. Success in winning converts brought re-assurance.[28] Such an explanation is psychologically plausible and can be paralleled from the experience of other, more recent and thus better documented, eschatologically oriented groups. Because proselytizing was not generated by theology, it was not likely to be explicitly justified, hence the vagueness of terminology about proselytizing mission (see above, Ch. 5) and the lack of discussions about its purpose.

I think that it is likely that a general explanation of this kind will come closer to the truth of the origin of Christian mission than a search for explicit theology in the extant texts, but this theory also leaves some difficult questions unanswered. It is reasonable to suggest that Jesus' followers would react to the delay in the Second Coming by doing something energetic rather than allow themselves to become depressed by disappointment, but I cannot see why an active response to cognitive dissonance should necessarily consist in a search for proselytes. There are other ways to explain away the unsatisfactory nature of the world. Furthermore, the claim that success in winning converts was proof of the validity of the Christian message was double-edged, since the tradition was replete with stories of hostility to the early missionaries and rejection of their news. In any case, if Paul's mission was to the gentiles from the start (which, as I noted above, is disputed), he began that mission before disappointment had time to set in: the gap between the first missionary journeys of St Paul and the crucifixion may have been only a few months if the late date of 36 CE recently proposed for the latter event is correct.[29]

I am not going to pretend that I can supply a novel overarching explanation of the origins of Christian mission which will render all previous suggestions redundant. On the contrary, I believe it likely that eschatological fervour, the

---

[28] Gager, *Kingdom and Community*, reaffirmed in 'Proselytism and Exclusivity', 77.

[29] Kokkinos, 'Crucifixion in AD 36'; but his arguments are controversial. For the chronology of Paul's journeys, see e.g. Ogg, *Chronology*, 30.

peculiar personality of St Paul, and the gradual disappointment of early Christians waiting in vain for the Parousia, all
contributed to the enthusiasm of those believers to do
something; in such conditions, lack of action might too easily
lead to depression and loss of faith. But some extra factor was
needed to ensure that the direction taken by these enthusiasts
was the mission to the gentiles. In what follows I shall
suggest, with all due caution, what that extra factor may have
been.

The survival in the early Christian tradition of the belief
that Jesus' message was primarily for the Jews, despite the
later reversal of this priority, must reflect the early years of
the Jesus movement; hence the tenuous nature of the evidence
for any widespread mission to the gentiles before Paul or,
during his career, by Christians outside his circle (see above,
Ch. 5). As a revivalist sect preaching repentance within the
existing body of Jewish society, these early preachers faced
problems after the crucifixion in retaining their own identity
as a distinct group, particularly without the strong organization which seems to have emerged only slowly. Everyone in
the early Church believed that Jesus had risen from the dead,
but the significance of belief in the resurrection might vary
greatly for different individuals—after all, the Gospels themselves preserved the account of the resurrection of Lazarus
(John 11: 1–44) but this belief did not lead to Lazarus being
accorded any special role in early Christian faith. The peculiar
structure of the Gospels—that is, their status as biographical
narrative—betrays the most complete way in which this
identity was asserted from the beginning: not by particular
teachings about the Torah or about the nature of God, but by
continual emphasis on the charismatic individual who had
given the sect its *raison d'être*. Again and again both the
Gospels and St Paul stress that the first followers of Jesus
'preached Jesus Christ', or 'the Gospel of Jesus Christ' or 'in
the name of Jesus'; precisely *what* they preached was less
important than the direct link with their erstwhile leader.[30]

One effect of the continual stress that what really mattered

---

[30] For the shift from the message to the person of Christ, see Rowland, *Christian
Origins.*

was recognition of the life, death, and resurrection of Jesus was that, as Paul saw, it really did not matter whether a follower of Jesus was Jew or gentile. Within years, perhaps months, of the crucifixion and resurrection the news about Jesus had reached gentiles as well as Jews. Almost immediately a debate arose within the ranks of Jesus' followers as to whether such gentiles who joined them should be required to become Jewish proselytes. The problem may have been a simple one, namely the difficulties in keeping the Torah for Jewish followers of Christ if they were required regularly to share food with gentiles who might defile their common meals (Gal. 2: 12–13).[31]

At least in the diaspora the view of St Paul prevailed, that the grace of the Lord so outweighed all other considerations that the conversion of gentiles to Judaism was an irrelevance or worse. But this view naturally brought its own conflicts with those Jewish followers of Jesus who insisted on the circumcision of all gentile males who joined their community (cf. Galatians 6: 12; Romans 2–4), and presumably the conversion to Judaism by some other means of all females. It has been claimed in the past that the argument of these opponents of Paul was motivated by a desire to win salvation for such gentiles by their Judaization, but it is hard to see why they should have thought good gentiles needed to become Jews to win divine approval if that was not the normal attitude of other Jews in their time (see Ch. 3).

It is important to recognize that these early apostles of Jewish origin, including St Paul, clearly saw themselves as part of the community of Jews as well as part of the 'true Israel' who were the followers of Jesus. According to Paul's own claims about his actions he must have chosen deliberately to identify himself with the diaspora Jews in each city he visited, for, so he proudly averred, he suffered no less than five times the penalty of thirty-nine lashes at the hands of Jewish courts (2 Corinthians 11: 24). Such suffering must have been voluntary, for as a Roman citizen his person could

---

[31] On Jewish problems over gentile wine and oil, see above, Ch. 3. Sanders, 'Jewish Association with Gentiles', denies commensality was really a problem, but I am not convinced.

not be violated by the Jewish authorities unless he willingly accepted their jurisdiction. Proclaiming himself as a Jew, therefore, Paul introduced non-Jews as full members into his close-knit Jewish Christian communities.

The vehemence of the argument among Christians over the desirability of the acceptance of gentiles into the Church on such terms is widely reflected in the polemical letters of St Paul and in the apologetic *tendenz* of Luke's portrayal of the early missionaries in Acts, whom he showed preaching first to Jews and then, only when rejected, to gentiles. It would not be surprising if the trauma of the conflict left many scars on the ideology and self-understanding of the early Church, just as the radical break with non-Christian Judaism left its legacy of hostility towards Jews. It was natural for Christians to reinforce their current beliefs by attacking those doctrines they had rejected and by affirming those which had been attacked by others.

What I am suggesting is that Christians may have reacted to hostility inside their own ranks to the indiscriminate acceptance of gentiles by declaring that this was not only permitted, it was positively desirable. Gone were the hesitations displayed in the earliest Gospel tradition about whether any attention at all should be paid to the gentiles. Gone was the argument of the Jerusalem Church that at any rate such gentiles must become Jews before admission. Instead the author of the Gospel of Matthew attached to the very end of his work the resounding commission, ascribed to Jesus and addressed to the apostles, to baptize all humankind. And, just as Matthew produced his *ex post facto* justification of the mission to the gentiles, so Luke at much the same time composed in the Acts of the Apostles a similar rationalization of the universal mission of the Church.

Such a reconstruction is necessarily tentative, but it is possible to point to parallel religious developments within Judaism where the urge to insist that some behaviour is *permitted* led to the much stronger claim that it was desirable.

It was a characteristic of Judaism, unlike other religions in antiquity, that devotees expected to discover the divine will about correct human behaviour by argument. In other cults, the wishes of the gods were either revealed by some special means such as an oracle or a dream or were taken as obvious. Everyone knew, for instance, that the gods desire men to act justly, so argument among philosophers was confined to the definition of just acts. No pagans *argued* about the way that sacrifices should be brought. When Josephus compared Pharisees, Sadducees, and Essenes to Greek philosophical sects (*haireseis*), he accurately portrayed the vehemence of their disputes without adding the two main factors which made them different from such philosophies: first, that beneath their differences they were firmly united within Judaism, a creed whose 'unity and identity of religious belief' and 'perfect uniformity in habits and customs' were exceptional according to Josephus himself (Joseph. *C. Ap.* 2. 179–81); and secondly, that their disputes were not, or not only, on the level of abstract theory but concerned very practical questions of how men should behave towards the divinity.

It was a further characteristic of some elements of Judaism at least that fierce polemic might sometimes result in one side positively urging an action which they logically only wished to insist was permitted. Some of the best examples of such demonstrative behaviour may be found in the rabbinic traditions about the various groups in Judaism in the Second Temple period, such as the Pharisees and Sadducees. According to *m.Par.* 3: 7, 'they' (unspecified) used intentionally to render impure the priest who burnt the red heifer *precisely because* the Sadducees claimed that the priest who carried out the task had to wait until sunset to be pure. According to *m.Men.* 10: 3, the omer offering was made as publicly as possible even on the sabbath immediately following the first day of Passover precisely because the Boethusians claimed that this should not be done (cf. also *b. Men.* 65a–b). In *b. Hag.* 23a and *b. Zeb.* 21a the reason why 'they' took action as they did in intentionally defiling the priest who dealt with the heifer was elucidated with a revealing phrase. The Pharisees desired 'to remove [the idea] from the hearts of the Sadducees'. According to *b. Hag.* 16b, the rabbis believed that R. Judah b. Tabbai put a false witness to death (as soon as his sin was discovered) as a demonstration against the Sadducees, who said that such a criminal could only be executed if and when his victim had already suffered the death penalty.[32]

In other cases this didactic motive for what might be termed bloodymindedness can only be surmised. So, for instance, the rabbis insisted that it was not only legal for an uncle to marry his niece, but that it was positively praiseworthy to have such a union (*b. Yeb* 62b; cf. *t. Kidd.* 1. 4: 'a man should not take a wife until the daughter of his sister has grown up.') Their vehemence was probably connected to the fact that such marriages were expressly forbidden by other Jews, as the Qumran documents make clear (*CD* 5: 7–11 Rabin, p. 19).[33] Similarly, the biblical injunctions about the Day of Atonement lay down that you shall 'afflict your souls' not only on the tenth day of the seventh month (Lev. 23: 27) but also 'in the ninth of the month at even' (Lev. 23: 32), but the rabbis determined that, despite the plain meaning of the text, the fast should begin only on the evening of the tenth day; in a fine display of bloodymindedness they therefore decreed that it is a positive duty to feast on the ninth day: 'if one eats and drinks on the ninth, Scripture accounts it to him as if he had fasted on the ninth and the tenth' (*b. Yoma* 81b). Since all the explicit evidence of this type of argument is found in rabbinic texts compiled in the late second century CE or, as in the case of the Babylonian Talmud, much later in antiquity, it is possible that Jews began to adopt such methods only after the first century, but the specific attribution in the Mishnah of such arguments to the Pharisees and Sadducees (see above) creates a strong presumption that already before 70 CE some Jews might argue in this way.[34]

The epistles of St Paul, composed at the very beginning of Christian history, reveal how thoroughly the Jewish trait of

[32] The same story appears in the tannaitic source *Mekhilta* (*MdRi* Kaspa 3, lines 31–5), but with the main protagonists given opposite roles and without the crucial explanation that the execution was carried out to make a point to the Sadducees.
[33] See the note of Saul Lieberman, *Tosefta Ki-fshutah*, viii. 915, on the Tosefta passage. Lieberman both asserts that the rabbinic ruling was in deliberate opposition to the attitude taken by the sectarians at Qumran and observes that such contrariness in opposition to heretics was normal in rabbinic decisions about religious duties.
[34] Sussmann, 'History of *Halakha*', 67–8, n. 220, provides many other examples, and argues that such public demonstrations were prevalent before 70 over issues concerned with public worship.

arguing about the divine will was incorporated into the Church from the start. I suggest that the abundant enthusiasm of Jesus' followers after the crucifixion and resurrection may have taken the direction of a mission to the gentiles not because eschatological enthusiasm or concern at the delayed end of the world necessarily provoked proselytizing rather than some other energetic activity but because internal strife within their own ranks made the inclusion of gentiles the main issue of debate, overshadowing issues such as Christology which were later to become crucial.

The correct way to introduce gentiles into the Christian community occupies a disproportionately large part of the New Testament. The victorious party within the Church, following, perhaps, the demonstrative line of reasoning natural to them from their Jewish upbringing, insisted that the view for which they had fought was not only permitted but desirable. Since this view was that gentiles should be allowed to become Christians without also becoming Jewish, and since the definition of a gentile is the purely negative attribute that he or she is not Jewish, the implication of advocating that it was desirable for all gentiles as well as Jews to be brought into the Church as full members was the notion that the Church should embrace all humanity.

Once the injunction to bring all humankind to Christ had been promulgated it carried its own momentum. The ideology, however *ad hoc* its origin, was enshrined in what became the Church's sacred books during the second century. Like all teachings in all sacred books, universal proselytizing mission could be promoted to the forefront of Christian thinking or thrust into the background at any one time. As I noted in Chapter 5, it was—and is—possible for Christians to understand the meaning and implications of the Great Commission in the Gospel of Matthew in many different ways, just as both they and Jews can easily reinterpret the calls for social and economic justice elsewhere in the Bible. But the notion of universal proselytizing was always there, ready for the re-emphasis that a particular moment or individual might bring to it.

I began this book by arguing in some detail that comparisons with proselytizing in first-century Judaism have been wrongly used to explain the origins of mission in early Christianity. I do not wish to suggest that the history of the early Church should therefore be studied without reference to Jewish practices at the time. On the contrary, in this last chapter I have tried to reinstate the Jewish background of early Christianity on a different basis, as just one element in the causal chain which brought some Christians to seek the conversion of humanity to their creed. But I hope that I have also shown in the book as a whole that the causal chain was both complex and tangled, and that the motivation to proselytize, so important in the history of western religions in later centuries, was no more inevitable a part of early Christianity than of any other religious movement in the ancient world.

BIBLIOGRAPHY

ALLEN, W. C., 'On the meaning of προσήλυτος in the Septuagint', *Expositor*, 4: 10 (1894), 264–75.

—— *A Critical and Exegetical Commentary of the Gospel of St. Matthew* (International Critical Commentary, 2nd edn.; Edinburgh, 1907).

ALON, G., *Jews, Judaism and the Classical World* (ET; Jerusalem, 1977).

APPLEBAUM, S., *Jews and Greeks in Ancient Cyrene* (Leiden, 1979).

ATHANASSIADI-FOWDEN, P., *Julian and Hellenism: An Intellectual Biography* (Oxford, 1981).

BACHRACH, B. S., 'The Jewish Community of the Later Roman Empire as Seen in the *Codex Theodosianus*', in Neusner and Frerichs (eds.), *'To See Ourselves'*, 399–421.

BALDRY, H. C., *The Unity of Mankind in Greek Thought* (Cambridge, 1965).

BAMBERGER, B. J., *Proselytism in the Talmudic Period* (2nd edn.; New York, 1968).

BARON, S. W., *A Social and Religious History of the Jews* (2nd edn., 18 vols.; New York, 1952–93).

BAUER, W., *Orthodoxy and Heresy in Earliest Christianity* (ET; Philadelphia, 1979).

BAUMGARTEN, A., 'The Name of the Pharisees', *JBL* 102/3 (1983), 411–28.

BERTHOLET, A., *Die Stellung der Israeliten und der Juden zu den Fremden* (Freiburg, 1896).

BETZ, H. D. (ed.), *Plutarch's Theological Writings and Early Christian Literature* (Studia ad Corpus Hellenisticum Novi Testamenti 3; Leiden, 1975).

BICKERMAN, E., *Studies in Jewish and Christian History* (3 parts; Leiden, 1976–86).

—— 'The Altars of Gentiles', in *Studies in Jewish and Christian History*, pt. 2 (Leiden, 1980), 324–46.

BILDE, P., 'The Causes of the Jewish War according to Josephus', *JSJ* 10 (1979), 179–202.

—— *Flavius Josephus between Jerusalem and Rome: His Life, his Works and their Importance* (Sheffield, 1988).

BISCHOFF, C., *Anecdota novissima: Texte des vierten bis sechzehnten Jahrhunderts* (1984).

BLAUW, J., *The Missionary Nature of the Church* (1962).

BLUMENKRANZ, B., *Juifs et Chrétiens dans le Monde Occidental, 430–1096* (Paris, 1960).

BOWERS, P., 'Paul and Religious Propaganda in the First Century', *Novum Testamentum*, 22 (1980), 316–23.

BOWERSOCK, G., *Julian the Apostate* (London, 1978).

BRAUDE, W. G., *Jewish Proselyting in the First Five Centuries of the Common Era: The Age of the Tannaim and Amoraim* (Providence, RI, 1940).

BROWN, P., *The Making of Late Antiquity* (Cambridge, Mass., 1978).

—— *The Body and Society: Men, Women and Sexual Renunciation in Early Christianity* (London, 1988).

BURKERT, W., *Ancient Mystery Cults* (Cambridge, Mass., 1987).

BUSSMANN, C., *Themen der paulinischen Missionspredigt auf dem Hintergrund der spätjüdisch-hellenistisch Missionsliteratur* (Berne and Frankfurt, 1971).

CAMPBELL, L. A., *Mithraic Iconography and Ideology* (Leiden, 1968).

CHARLESWORTH, J. H. (ed.), *Old Testament Pseudepigrapha* (2 vols.; London, 1983–5).

CHESTNUTT, R. D., 'The Social Setting and Purpose of Joseph and Aseneth', *Journal for the Study of the Pseudepigrapha*, 2 (1988), 21–48.

CHILTON, C. W. (ed.), *Diogenes of Oenoanda: The Fragments. A Translation and Commentary* (London, 1971).

COHEN, S. J. D., 'Conversion to Judaism in Historical Perspective: From Biblical Israel to Post-Biblical Judaism', *Conservative Judaism*, 36: 4 (1983), 31–45.

—— 'From the Bible to the Talmud: The Prohibition of Intermarriage', *Hebrew Annual Review*, 7 (1983), 23–39.

—— 'The Significance of Yavneh', *HUCA* 55 (1984), 27–53.

—— 'The Origins of the Matrilineal Principle in Rabbinic Law', *AJS Review*, 10: 1 (1985), 19–53.

—— 'Respect for Judaism by Gentiles according to Josephus', *HTR* 80 (1987), 409–30.

—— 'Crossing the Boundary and Becoming a Jew', *HTR* 82 (1989), 13–33.

—— 'Rabbinic Conversion Ceremony', *JJS* 41 (1990), 177–203.

—— 'Religion, Ethnicity, and "Hellenism" in the Emergence of Jewish Identity in Maccabean Palestine', in P. Bilde, T. Engberg-Pedersen, L. Hannestad, and J. Zahle (eds.), *Religion and*

Religious Practice in the Seleucid Kingdom (Aarhus, 1990), 204–23.

—— 'Was Judaism in Antiquity a Missionary Religion?', in M. Mor (ed.), *Jewish Assimilation, Acculturation and Accommodation: Past Traditions, Current Issues and Future Prospects* (1992), 14–23.

COLLINS, J. J., *The Sibylline Oracles of Egyptian Judaism* (Missoula, 1974).

—— *Between Athens and Jerusalem: Jewish Identity in the Hellenistic Diaspora* (New York, 1983).

—— 'A Symbol of Otherness: Circumcision and Salvation in the First Century', in Neusner and Frerichs (eds.), *'To See Ourselves'*, 163–86.

COLLINS, R., *Early Medieval Spain: Unity in Diversity, 400–1000* (London, 1983).

CROUCH, J. E., *The Origin and Intention of the Colossian Haustafel* (Göttingen, 1972).

CULLMANN, O., 'Eschatology and Missions in the New Testament', in W. D. Davies and D. Daube (eds.), *The Background of the New Testament and its Eschatology: Studies in Honour of C. H. Dodd* (1956), Cambridge, 409–21.

CUMONT, F., *Textes et monuments figurés relatifs aux mystères de Mithra* (2 vols.; Brussels, 1896–99).

—— *Les religions orientales dans le paganisme romain* (4th edn.; Paris, 1929).

DALBERT, P., *Die Theologie der hellenistich-jüdischen Missionsliteratur unter Ausschluss von Philo und Josephus* (Hamburg, 1954).

DANIEL, S. (ed.), *Philo, De Specialibus Legibus I–II* (Paris, 1975).

DAUBE, D., *The New Testament and Rabbinic Judaism* (London, 1956; repr. New York, 1973).

DAVIES, W. D., *Paul and Rabbinic Judaism: Some Rabbinic Elements in Pauline Theology* (2nd edn.; London, 1955).

DE LANGE, N. R. M., *Origen and the Jews: Studies in Jewish–Christian Relations in Third-Century Palestine* (Cambridge, 1976).

DELLING, G., 'Josephus und die heidnischen Religionen', in *Studien zum Neuen Testament und zum hellenistichen Judentum* (1970), 45–52 (= *Klio*, 44 (1965), 263–9).

DERWACTER, F. M., *Preparing the Way for Paul: The Proselyte Movement in Later Judaism* (New York, 1930).

DE STE CROIX, G. E. M., 'Why Were the Early Christians Persecuted?', in M. I. Finley (ed.), *Studies in Ancient Society* (1974), 210–49.

178   Bibliography

DE WITT, N. W., 'Epicurean Contubernium', TAPhA 67 (1936) 55–63.

—— Epicurus and his Philosophy (Minneapolis, 1954).

DONALDSON, T. L., 'Proselytes or "Righteous Gentiles"? The Status of Gentiles in Eschatological Pilgrimage Patterns of Thought', Journal for the Study of the Pseudepigrapha 7 (1990), 3–27.

DRIJVERS, H. J. W. (ed.), The Book of the Laws of Countries: Dialogue on Fate of Bardaisan of Edessa (Assen, 1965).

DUDLEY, D. R., A History of Cynicism from Diogenes to the 6th century A.D. (London, 1937).

EASTERLING, P. E., and MUIR, J. V. (eds.), Greek Religion and Society (Cambridge, 1985).

EDWARDS, J. R., 'The Use of προσέρχεσθαι in the Gospel of Matthew', JBL 106 (1987), 65–74.

EFROYMSON, D. P., 'Tertullian's Anti-Judaism and its role in his Theology', Ph.D. thesis (Temple, 1976).

EPSTEIN, L. J., The Theory and Practice of Welcoming Converts to Judaism: Jewish Universalism (Lewiston, Queenston, and Lampeter, 1992).

FARRINGTON, B., The Faith of Epicurus (New York, 1967).

FELDMAN. L. H., ' "Jewish Sympathisers" in Classical Literature and Inscriptions', TAPhA 81 (1950), 200–8.

—— 'Abraham the Greek Philosopher in Josephus', TAPhA 99 (1968), 145–50.

—— 'The Omnipresence of the God-Fearers', BAR 12: 5 (Sept/Oct 1986), 58–63.

—— 'Proselytes and "Sympathizers" in the Light of the New Inscriptions from Aphrodisias', REJ 148 (1989), 265–305.

—— Jew and Gentile in the Ancient World: Attitudes and Interactions from Alexander to Justinian (Princeton, NJ, 1993).

FINN, T. M., 'The Godfearers Reconsidered', CBQ 47 (1985), 75–84.

FISHWICK, D., The Imperial Cult in the Latin West (2 vols.; Leiden, 1987–92).

FLESHER, P. V. M., Oxen, Women or Citizens: Slaves in the System of the Mishnah (Brown Judaic Studies, 143; Atlanta, 1988).

FLOWERS, H.J., 'Matthew xxiii 15', Expository Times, 73 (1961), 67–9.

FORNARO, P., Flavio Giuseppe, Tacito e l'Impero (Turin, 1980).

FOWDEN, G., 'Between Pagans and Christians', JRS 78 (1988), 173–82.

FRANKFURTER, D., 'Lest Egypt's City be Deserted: Religion and Ideology in the Egyptian Response to the Jewish Revolt (116–117 CE)', JJS 43 (1992), 203–20.

FREDRIKSEN, P., *From Jesus to Christ: The Origins of the New Testament Images of Jesus* (New Haven, Conn., 1989).

—— 'Judaism, the Circumcision of Gentiles, and Apocalyptic Hope: Another Look at Galatians 1 and 2', *JTS* 42 (1991), 532–64.

FREND, W. H. C., *The Rise of Christianity* (London, 1984).

FREY, J. B., *Corpus Inscriptionum Iudaicarum* (2 vols.; i, rev. B. Lifshitz, New York, 1975, ii, Rome, 1936).

FUKS, A., 'The Jewish Revolt in Egypt (A.D. 115–117) in the Light of the Papyri', *Aegyptus*, 33 (1953), 131–58.

GAGER, J. G., *Kingdom and Community: The Social World of Early Christianity* (Englewood Cliffs, NJ, 1975).

—— *The Origins of Anti-Semitism: Attitudes towards Judaism in Pagan and Christian Antiquity* (New York and Oxford, 1985).

—— 'Proselytism and Exclusivity in Early Christianity', in Marty and Greenspahn (eds.), *Pushing the Faith*, 67–77, 179–80.

GARLAND, D. E., *The Intention of Matthew 23* (Suppl. to Nov. Test. 52; Leiden, 1979).

GASTON, L., *Paul and the Torah* (Vancouver, 1987).

GEFFCKEN, J., *The Last Days of Greco-Roman Paganism* (ET; Amsterdam and Oxford, 1978).

GEORGI, D., *The Opponents of Paul in Second Corinthians* (ET; Edinburgh, 1986).

GINZBERG, L., *The Legends of the Jews* (7 vols.; Philadelphia, 1909–38).

GOLB, N., *Jewish Proselytism—a Phenomenon in the Religious History of Early Medieval Europe* (Tenth Annual Rabbi Louis Feinberg Memorial Lecture; Judaic Studies Program, University of Cincinnati, 3 March, 1987; Cincinatti, 1988).

GOLDENBERG, R., 'The Place of Other Religions in Ancient Jewish Thought, with Particular Reference to Early Rabbinic Judaism', in Marty and Greenspahn (eds.), *Pushing the Faith*, 27–40, 167–72.

GOODENOUGH, E. R., 'Philo's Exposition of the Law and his *De Vita Mosis*', *HTR* 26 (1933), 109–25.

GOODMAN, M., *State and Society in Roman Galilee, A.D. 132–212* (Totowa, NJ, 1983).

—— *The Ruling Class of Judaea: The Origins of the Jewish Revolt against Rome, A.D. 66–70* (Cambridge, 1987).

—— 'Proselytising in Rabbinic Judaism', *JJS* 40 (1989), 175–85.

—— 'Nerva, the *fiscus Judaicus* and Jewish Identity', *JRS* 79 (1989), 40–4.

—— 'Identity and Authority in Ancient Judaism', *Judaism*, 39 (1990), 192–201.

GOODMAN, M., 'Sacred Scripture and "Defiling the Hands" ', *JTS* 41 (1990), 99–107.

—— 'Kosher Olive Oil in Antiquity', in P. R. Davies and R. T. White (eds.), *A Tribute to Geza Vermes* (Sheffield, 1990), 227–45.

—— 'Jewish Proselytizing in the First Century', in Lieu, North, and Rajak (eds.), *Jews among Pagans and Christians*, 53–78.

—— 'The Roman State and the Jewish Patriarch in the Third Century', in L. I. Levine (ed.), *Galilee in Late Antiquity* (1992), 127–39.

—— 'Diaspora Reactions to the Destruction of the Temple', in J. D. G. Dunn (ed.), *Jews and Christians* (Tübingen, 1992), 27–38.

—— 'The Roman Identity of Roman Jews', *Menahem Stern Memorial Volume* (forthcoming).

GORDON, R., 'The Veil of Power: Emperors, Sacrificers, and Benefactors', in M. Beard and J. North (eds.), *Pagan Priests: Religion and Power in the Ancient World* (London, 1990), 201–31.

GRAY, R., *Prophetic Figures in Late Second Temple Jewish Palestine: The Evidence from Josephus* (New York and Oxford, 1993).

GREEN, M., *Evangelism in the Early Church* (London, 1977; new edn. Crowborough, 1984).

GRUEN, E. S., *Studies in Greek Culture and Roman Policy* (Leiden, 1990).

HAHN, F., *Mission in the New Testament* (1965).

HANFMANN, G. M. A., *Sardis from Prehistoric to Roman Times: Results of the Archaeological Exploration of Sardis 1958–1975* (Cambridge, Mass., 1983).

HARNACK, A. VON, *The Mission and Expansion of Christianity in the First Three Centuries* (2nd edn., 2 vols., Edinburgh, 1908) = *Die Mission und Ausbreitung des Christentums in den ersten drei Jahrhunderten* (4th edn.; Leipzig, 1924).

HARRINGTON, D. J., *Light of all Nations* (1982).

HENGEL, M., *Judaism and Hellenism: Studies in their Encounter in Palestine during the Early Hellenistic Period* (2 vols., ET; London, 1974).

—— *Acts and the History of Earliest Christianity* (London, 1979).

—— *Between Jesus and Paul: Studies in the Earliest History of Christianity* (ET; London, 1983).

—— 'The Origins of the Christian Mission', in id., *Between Jesus and Paul*, 48–64.

HENIG, M., *Religion in Roman Britain* (London, 1984).

HENNECKE, E., and SCHNEEMELCHER, W. (eds.), *New Testament Apocrypha* (2 vols., ET; London, 1963–5).

HENRICHS, A., and KOENEN, L., 'Ein griechischer Mani-Codex (P. Colon. Inv. nr. 4780)', *ZPE* 5 (1970), 97–216.

HERRIN, J., *The Formation of Christendom* (Oxford, 1987).

HOLLADAY, C. R., *Fragments from Hellenistic Jewish Authors*, i, *Historians* (Chico, Calif., 1983).

HOOKER, M. D., *A Commentary on the Gospel according to St. Mark* (London, 1991).

HOPKINS, K., *Conquerors and Slaves* (Cambridge, 1978).

HORSLEY, R. A., and HANSON, J. S., *Bandits, Prophets, and Messiahs: Popular Movements in the Time of Jesus* (Minneapolis, 1985).

HYMAN, A., *Torah hakethubah veha Messurah*, rev. and enlarged by A.B. Hyman (vol. ii; Tel Aviv, 1979).

JEREMIAS, J., *Jesus' Promise to the Nations* (ET; London and Nashville, 1958).

JONES, C. P., *Culture and Society in Lucian* (Cambridge, Mass., 1986).

JORDAN, M. D., 'Philosophic "Conversion" and Christian Conversion', *SC* 5: 2 (1985/6), 90–6.

JUSTER, J., *Les Juifs dans l'Empire romain: Leur condition juridique, économique et sociale* (2 vols.; Paris, 1914).

KAEGI, W. E., 'The Fifth-Century Twilight of Byzantine Paganism', *Classica et Mediaevalia*, 27 (1966), 243–75.

KASHER, A., *The Jews in Hellenistic and Roman Egypt: The Struggle for Equal Rights* (Tübingen, 1985).

—— *Jews, Idumaeans and Ancient Arabs: Relations of the Jews in Eretz-Israel with the Nations of the Frontier and the Desert during the Hellenistic and Roman Era (332 BCE–70 CE)* (Tübingen, 1988).

—— *Jews and Hellenistic Cities in Eretz-Israel: Relations of the Jews in Eretz-Israel with the Hellenistic Cities during the Second Temple Period (332 BCE–70 CE)* (Tübingen, 1990).

KING, N. Q., *The Emperor Theodosius and the Establishment of Christianity* (London, 1961).

KOKKINOS, N., 'Crucifixion in AD 36', in J. Vardaman and E. M. Yamauchi (eds.), *Chronos, Kairos, Christos (Studies presented to Jack Finegan)* (Winona Lake, Ind., 1989), 133–63.

KRAABEL, A. T., 'The Disappearance of the "God-Fearers" ', *Numen*, 28 (1981), 113–26.

—— 'The Roman Diaspora: Six Questionable Assumptions', *JJS* 33 (1982), 445–64 (= *Festschrift Yadin*).

KRAELING, C. H., *The Excavations at Dura-Europus: Final Report*, viii, pt. 1, *The Synagogue* (New Haven, Conn., 1956).

KRAFT, R. A., 'The Multiform Jewish Heritage of Early Christianity', in J. Neusner (ed.), *Christianity, Judaism and Other Greco-Roman Cults* (Leiden, 1975), pt. 3, 174–99.

LANE, E. N., 'Sabazius and the Jews in Valerius Maximus: A Re-examination', *JRS* 69 (1979), 35–8.

LANE FOX, R., *Pagans and Christians in the Mediterranean World from the Second Century A.D. to the Conversion of Constantine* (Harmondsworth, 1986).

LEON, H. J., *The Jews of Ancient Rome* (Philadelphia, 1960).

LEVI, I., 'Le prosélytisme juif', *REJ* 50 (1905), 1–9; 51 (1906), 1–31.

LEVINE, L. I. (ed.), *The Synagogue in Late Antiquity* (Philadelphia, 1987).

—— *The Rabbinic Class of Roman Palestine in Late Antiquity* (ET; Jerusalem and New York, 1989).

LIEBERMAN, S., *Greek in Jewish Palestine* (New York, 1942).

—— 'Palestine in the Third and Fourth Centuries', *JQR* 36 (1945–6), 329–70; 37 (1946–7), 31–54.

—— *Tosefta Ki-fshutah: A Comprehensive Commentary on the Tosefta* (10 vols.; New York, 1955–88).

LIEBESCHUETZ, J. H. W. G., *Continuity and Change in Roman Religion* (Oxford, 1979).

LIEU, J., NORTH, J., and RAJAK, T. (eds.), *The Jews among Pagans and Christians in the Roman Empire* (London, 1992).

LIEU, S. N. C., *Manichaeism in the Later Roman Empire and Medieval China: A Historical Survey* (2nd edn.; Manchester, 1992).

LIGHTSTONE, J. N., *Society, the Sacred and Scripture in Ancient Judaism: A Sociology of Knowledge* (Studies in Christianity and Judaism, no. 3) (Waterloo, Ont., 1988).

LIM, R., 'Unity and Diversity among Western Manichaeans: A Reconsideration of Mani's *sancta ecclesia*', *REA* 35 (1989), 231–50.

LINDER, A., *The Jews in Roman Imperial Legislation* (Detroit and Jerusalem, 1987).

LÜDERITZ, G., *Corpus jüdische Zeugnisse aus der Cyrenaika* (Wiesbaden, 1983).

MCELENEY, N. J., 'Conversion, Circumcision and the Law', *NTS* 20 (1974), 319–41.

MCKNIGHT, S., *A Light among the Gentiles: Jewish Missionary Activity in the Second Temple Period* (Minneapolis, 1991).

MACLENNAN, R. S., and KRAABEL, A. T., 'The God-fearers—A

Literary and Theological Invention', *BAR* 12: 5 (Sept./Oct. 1986), 46–53.

MACMULLEN, R., *Paganism in the Roman Empire* (New Haven, Conn., and London, 1981).

—— *Christianizing the Roman Empire (A.D. 100–400)* (New Haven, Conn., and London, 1984).

MALHERBE, A. J., 'Self-Definition among Epicureans and Cynics', in Sanders *et al.*, *Jewish and Christian Self-Definition*, iii, 47–59.

MARKUS, R. A., *Saeculum: History and Society in the Theology of St Augustine* (London, 1970).

—— 'The Problem of Self-Definition, from Sect to Church', in Sanders *et al.* (eds.), *Jewish and Christian Self-Definition*, i. 1–14.

MARTY, M. E., and GREENSPAHN, F. E. (eds.), *Pushing the Faith: Proselytism and Civility in a Pluralistic World* (New York, 1988).

MATTHEWS, J., *Western Aristocracies and Imperial Court, A.D. 364–425* (Oxford, 1975).

MEEK, T. J., 'The Translation of *Ger* in the Hexateuch and its Bearing on the Documentary Hypothesis', *JBL* 49 (1930), 172–80.

MEEKS, W. A., *The First Urban Christians: The Social World of the Apostle Paul* (New Haven, Conn., and London, 1983).

MENDELS, D., *The Land of Israel as a Political Concept in Hasmonean Literature: Resource to History in Second Century BCE Claims to the Holy Land* (Tübingen, 1987).

MOLES, J., ' "Honestius quam ambitiosius"? An Exploration of the Cynic's Attitude to Moral Corruption in his Fellow Men', *JHS* 103 (1983), 103–23.

MOMIGLIANO, A., *Ottavo Contributo alla Storia degli Studi Classici e del Mondo Antico* (Rome, 1987).

MOORE, G. F., *Judaism in the first Centuries of the Christian Era* (3 vols.; Cambridge, Mass., 1927–30).

MUNCK, J., *Paul and the Salvation of Mankind* (ET; London, 1959).

NEUSNER, J., *The Rabbinic Traditions about the Pharisees before 70* (3 vols.; Leiden, 1971).

NEUSNER, J., and FRERICHS, E. S. (eds.), *'To See Ourselves as Others See Us': Christians, Jews, 'others' in Late Antiquity* (Chico, Calif., 1985).

NEUSNER, J., GREEN, W. S., and FRERICHS, E. S. (eds.), *Judaisms and their Messiahs* (Cambridge, 1987).

NOCK, A. D., *Conversion: The Old and the New in Religion from Alexander the Great to Augustine of Hippo* (Oxford, 1933).

—— *Essays on Religion and the Ancient World*, ed. Z. Stewart (2 vols.; Oxford, 1972).

NOLLAND, J., 'Do Romans Observe Jewish Customs?', *VC* 33 (1979), 1–11.

—— 'Proselytism or Politics in Horace, *Satires*, I, 4, 138–143', *VC* 33 (1979), 347–55.

—— 'Uncircumcised Proselytes?', *JSJ* 12: 2 (1981), 173–94.

NORTH, J. A., 'Religious Toleration in Republican Rome', *PCPS* NS 25 (1979), 85–103.

—— 'Religion in Republican Rome', in *Cambridge Ancient History*, 2nd edn., vii. 2 (Cambridge, 1989), 573–624.

—— 'The Development of Religious Pluralism' in Lieu, North, and Rajak (eds.), *Jews among Pagans and Christians*, 174–93.

NOVAK, D., *The Image of the Non-Jew in Judaism: A Historical and Constructive Study of the Noachide Laws* (Toronto Studies in Theology, 14; New York and Toronto, 1983).

OGG, G., *The Chronology of the Life of Paul* (1968).

OHANA, M., 'Prosélytisme et targum palestinien: données nouvelles pour la datation de Néofiti 1', *Bib.* 55 (1974), 317–32.

OPPENHEIMER, A., *The Am Ha-aretz: A Study in the Social History of the Jewish People in the Hellenistic-Roman Period* (ET; Leiden, 1977).

OVERMAN, J. A., 'The Godfearers: Some Neglected Features', *JSNT* 32 (1988), 17–26.

PORTON, G. G., *Goyim: Gentiles and Israelites in Mishnah-Tosefta* (Atlanta, 1988).

PRICE, S. R. F., *Rituals and Power: The Roman Imperial Cult in Asia Minor* (Cambridge, 1984).

—— 'The Boundaries of Roman Religion', forthcoming as M. Beard, J. A. North, and S. R. F. Price, *Roman Religions* (Cambridge, forthcoming), ch. 5.

RAJAK, T., *Josephus: The Historian and his Society* (London, 1983).

—— 'Jews and Christians as Groups in a Pagan World', in Neusner and Frerichs (eds.), *'To See Ourselves'*, 247–61.

REYNOLDS, J., and TANNENBAUM, R., *Jews and God-Fearers at Aphrodisias* (Cambridge Philological Society, Suppl. vol. 12; Cambridge, 1987).

RICHARDSON, P., *et al.* (eds.), *Anti-Judaism in Early Christianity* (2 vols.; Waterloo, Ont., 1986).

RIST, J. M., 'Are you a Stoic? The Case of Marcus Aurelius', in Sanders *et al.*, *Jewish and Christian Self-Definition*, iii. 23–46.

ROBERT, L., *A travers l'Asie Mineure* (Paris, 1980), 393–421.

ROKEAH, D., 'On the Attitudes of the Sages towards Gentiles and Proselytes', *Mahalkhim*, 5 (1971), 72–3.

—— *Jews, Pagans and Christians in Conflict* (Jerusalem, 1982).

ROWLAND, C. C., *Christian Origins: An Account of the Setting and Character of the Most Important Messianic Sect of Judaism* (London, 1985).

RUETHER, R., *Faith and Fratricide: the Theological Roots of Anti-Semitism* (New York, 1974).

RUTHERFORD, R. B., *The Meditations of Marcus Aurelius: A Study* (Oxford, 1989).

SALDARINI, A. J., *Pharisees, Scribes and Sadducees in Palestinian Society* (Edinburgh, 1989).

SANDERS, E. P., 'The Covenant as a Soteriological Category and the Nature of Salvation in Palestinian and Hellenistic Judaism', in R. Hamerton-Kelly and R. Scroggs (eds.), *Jews, Greeks and Christians: Religious Cultures in Late Antiquity* (Leiden, 1976), 11–44.

—— *Paul and Palestinian Judaism: A Comparison of Patterns of Religion* (London, 1977).

—— *Paul, the Law and the Jewish People* (Philadelphia, 1983).

—— *Jesus and Judaism* (London and Philadelphia, 1985).

—— *Jewish Law from Jesus to the Mishnah: Five Studies* (London, 1990).

—— 'Jewish Association with Gentiles and Galatians 2: 11–14', in R. T. Fortna and B. R. Gaventa (eds.), *The Conversation Continues: Studies in Paul and John in honor of J. Louis Martyn* (Nashville, 1990), 170–88.

—— *Judaism: Practice and Belief, 63 BCE–66 CE* (London, 1992).

SANDERS, E. P. et al. (eds.), *Jewish and Christian Self-Definition* (3 vols.; London, 1980–2).

SANDMEL, S., *Philo's Place in Judaism: A Study of the Conceptions of Abraham in Jewish Literature* (Cincinatti, 1956).

—— *The First Christian Century in Judaism and Christianity: Certainties and Uncertainties* (New York, 1969).

SCHÄFER, P., *Der Bar Kokhba Aufstand: Studien zum zweiten jüdischen Krieg gegen Rom* (Tübingen, 1981).

SCHIFFMAN, L. H., 'The Conversion of the Royal House of Adiabene in Josephus and Rabbinic Sources', in L. H. Feldman and G. Hata (eds.), *Josephus, Judaism and Christianity* (Detroit, 1987), 293–312.

SCHMITHALS, W., *The Office of Apostle in the Early Church* (ET; London, 1971).

SCHOEDEL, W. R., 'Theological Norms and Social Perspectives in Ignatius of Antioch', in Sanders et al., *Jewish and Christian Self-Definition*, i. 30–55.

SCHÜRER, E., *Geschichte des Jüdischen Volkes im Zeitalter Jesus Christi*, 4th edn. (3 vols.; Leipzig, 1909).

SCHÜRER, E., *The History of the Jewish People in the Age of Jesus Christ*, rev. and ed. G. Vermes *et al.* (3 vols.; Edinburgh, 1973–87).

SCHÜSSLER-FIORENZA, E. (ed.), *Aspects of Religious Propaganda in Judaism and Early Christianity* (Notre Dame and London, 1976).

SEGAL, A. F., *Rebecca's Children: Judaism and Christianity in the Roman World* (Cambridge, Mass., 1986).

—— *Paul the Convert: The Apostolate and Apostasy of Saul the Pharisee* (New Haven, Conn., and London, 1990).

SELZER, R. M., 'Joining the Jewish People from Biblical to Modern Times', in Marty and Greenspahn (eds.), *Pushing the Faith*, 41–63, 172–9.

SENIOR, D., and STUHLMUELLER, C., *The Biblical Foundations for Mission* (London, 1983).

SEVENSTER, J. N., *The Roots of Pagan Anti-Semitism in the Ancient World* (Suppl. to Nov. Test. 41; Leiden, 1975).

SHERWIN-WHITE, A. N., *Roman Citizenship* (2nd edn.; Oxford, 1973).

SIEGERT, F., 'Gottesfürchtige und Sympathisanten', *JSJ* 4 (1973), 109–64.

SIMON, M., 'Sur les débuts du prosélytisme juif', in *Hommages à André Dupont-Sommer* (Paris, 1971), 509–20.

—— *Verus Israel: A Study of the Relations between Christians and Jews in the Roman Empire (135–425)* (ET; Oxford, 1986).

SMALLWOOD, E. M., 'Domitian's Attitude towards the Jews and Judaism', *Classical Philology*, 51 (1956), 1–13.

SMITH, J. Z., 'Fences and Neighbours: Some Contours of Early Judaism', in W. S. Green (ed.), *Approaches to Ancient Judaism*, ii (Chico, Calif., 1980), 1–25.

SMITH, M., 'Rome and the Maccabean conversions—Notes on I Macc. 8', in E. Bammel, C. K. Barrett, and W. D. Davies (eds.), *Donum Gentilicium: New Testament studies in honour of David Daube* (Oxford, 1978).

—— *Palestinian Parties that Shaped the Old Testament* (2nd edn.; London, 1987).

SMITH, W. C., *The Meaning and End of Religion* (New York, 1962; repub. London, 1978).

SPEIDEL, M. P., *The Religion of Iuppiter Dolichenus in the Roman Army* (Leiden, 1978).

STERN, M., *Greek and Latin Authors on Jews and Judaism* (3 vols; Jerusalem, 1974–84).

STERN, S., 'Jewish Identity in Early Rabbinic Writings', D.Phil. thesis (Oxford, 1992).

STRACK, H. L., and STEMBERGER, G., *Introduction to the Talmud and Midrash* (ET; Edinburgh, 1991).

SUSSMANN, Y., 'The History of *Halakha* and the Dead Sea Scrolls— A Preliminary to the Publication of 4QMMT', *Tarbiz* 59 (1990), 11–76 (Heb.).

TAYLOR, M., 'The Jews in the Writings of the Early Church Fathers (150–312): Men of Straw or Formidable Rivals?', D.Phil. thesis (Oxford, 1992).

TCHERIKOVER, V. A., 'Jewish Apologetic Literature Reconsidered', *Eos*, 48 (1956), 169–93.

TCHERIKOVER, V. A., FUKS, A., and STERN, M., *Corpus Papyrorum Judaicarum* (3 vols; Cambridge, Mass., 1957–64).

THOMPSON, L. A., 'Domitian and the Jewish Tax', *Historia*, 31 (1982), 329–42.

TOWLER, R., *Homo Religiosus: Sociological Problems in the Study of Religion* (London, 1974).

TREBILCO, P. R., *Jewish Communities in Asia Minor* (Cambridge, 1991).

URBACH, E. E., 'The Rabbinical Laws of Idolatry in the Second and Third Centuries in the Light of Archaeological and Historical Facts', *IEJ* 9 (1959), 149–65, 229–45.

—— 'Halakhot Regarding Slavery as a Source for the Social History of the Second Temple and the Talmudic Period', *Zion*, 25 (1960), 141–81 (Heb.).

—— *The Sages: Their Concepts and Beliefs* (ET; Cambridge, Mass., 1975).

VERKUYL, J., *Contemporary Missiology: An Introduction* (ET; Grand Rapids, Mich., 1978).

VERMASEREN, M. J., *Mithras, the Secret God* (London, 1963).

—— (ed.), *Die orientalischen Religionen im Römerreich* (Leiden, 1981).

—— and VAN ESSEN, C. C., *The Excavations in the Mithraeum of the Church of Santa Prisca in Rome* (Leiden, 1965).

VERMES, G., and GOODMAN, M., 'La littérature juive inter-testamentaire à la lumière d'un siècle de recherches et de découvertes', in R. Kuntzmann and J. Schlosser (eds.), *Études sur le Judaisme Hellénistique* (1984), 19–39.

VERSNEL, H. S. (ed.), *Faith, Hope and Worship: Aspects of Religious Mentality in the Ancient World* (Leiden, 1982).

—— *Inconsistencies in Greek and Roman Religion, I. Ter Unus: Isis, Dionysos, Hermes: Three Studies in Henotheism* (Leiden, 1990).

VEYNE, P., 'Une évolution du paganisme gréco-romain: injustice et piété des dieux, leurs orders ou "oracles" ', *Latomus*, 45 (1986), 259–83.

WACHOLDER, B. Z., 'The Halakah and the Proselyting of Slaves during the Gaonic Era', *Historia Judaica*, 18 (1956), 89–106.

—— 'Attitudes towards Proselytizing in the Classical Halakah', *Historia Judaica*, 20 (1958), 77–96.

WALBANK, F. W., *A Historical Commentary on Polybius* (3 vols.; Oxford, 1957–79).

WEST, M. L. (ed.), *Hesiod, Theogony* (Oxford, 1966).

WHITE, L. M., 'Adolf Harnack and the "Expansion" of Early Christianity: A Reappraisal of Social History', *SC* 5: 2 (1985/6), 97–127.

WHITTAKER, M., *Jews and Christians: Graeco-Roman Views* (Cambridge, 1984).

WILKEN, R. L., *John Chrysostom and the Jews: Rhetoric and Reality in the Late 4th Century* (Berkeley, Calif., and London, 1983).

WILL, E., and ORRIEUX, C., *'Prosélytisme juif'? Histoire d'une erreur* (Paris, 1992).

WITT, R. E., *Isis in the Graeco-Roman World* (London, 1971).

WRIGHT, N. T., *The New Testament and the People of God* (London, 1992).

ZEITLIN, S. , 'Slavery during the Second Commonwealth and the Tannaitic Period', *JQR* 53 (1962), 185–218.

INDEX

Abraham, image of 89,130,144–5,147–8
Achior 62
Acmonia 54–5
Acts of the Apostles 72, 93, 161, 164, 170
Acts of Pilate 74, 133
Acts of Thomas 93
Adda 158
adhesion 3, 27
Adiabene, royal family of 47, 63, 64, 65, 84, 136
Aedesius 154
Africa 119
aggadists 150–1
Agrippa II 77
Agrippa, M. Vipsanius 43
Alexander of Abonoteichos 29–30
Alexander Polyhistor 79–80
Alexandria 40, 88, 102, 127
   Jewish community in 85, 87, 88, 137–8
allegorists 67
allegory 40, 81–2
altruism 148, 162
Ambrosiaster 133–4
Amolon 153
Amos 50
Ananias 65, 84, 87
Anatolius, bishop 102
'Anna', Letter of 128
Antioch 143
   gentiles attached to Jewish community in 46, 63, 66, 87
   Jews in 85, 88, 124
Antiochus Epiphanes 64
antisemitism 57–8, 85
Antoninus Pius 6, 138
Aphrodisias 117–19, 131, 132, 135, 148
Apion 58
Apocrypha 64
Apollonius of Tyana 32
apologetic mission 4, 60–1, 86–8, 95–6, 130
Apollo 126

apostolate 106, 161
apostolic decree 53, 104
Apuleius 22, 26, 28, 149
Aquila (Christian) 106
Aquila (Jew) 79, 133
argument, as religious discourse 170–1
Aristeas, Ps.- 51, 56, 66, 79
Aristobulus 40, 66
Artapanus 52, 65, 89
Artemis 97, 126
Asclepiodotus 156
Asclepius 24, 30
Asia Minor 118–19
atheism 24, 44, 105
Augustus 6, 31
authority, lacking in Jewish society 47
avodah zarah 112, 114, 116

Baal 49
Babylonia 72
Bamberger 129
Bannus 104
baptism 67–8, 81, 105
Bardaisan 139
Bar Kokhba war 139
Barnabas, Epistle of 45
Bethsaida 99
Bible 39, 49–51, 53, 64
biblical figures, image in rabbinic texts 145–6
Bodo 153
Boethusians 171
Boudicca 126
bouleutai 118
b. Pes. 87b 137
Buddhism 2

Caesarea 67
calumnia 122–3
Capernaum 99
Cassius Dio 31–2
   on *fiscus Judaicus* 123
   on Jews 134
   on Jewish proselytizing 68, 83, 144

castration 138
catechumen 88, 105
Celsus 97, 107–8, 134
Celtic cults 28
census 47
Cerinthus 14
change in ancient religions 9–10
Charax Spasini 65, 87
charity, Jewish concept of 80, 84
Chorazin 99
Christian, definition of 91, 95, 100, 101, 159
Christian mission, motivation 83–4, 98, 161–74 (esp. 167–8).
Christian mission to Jews 91–2, 168
Christianity:
   effect of on Judaism 152
   success of 8, 18, 152, 160
Christianization 3, 7
Christology 168
Church, as institution 94, 95, 99–101, 163
churches 94, 96, 101–2, 103–4
Cicero 15, 21, 37, 74
circumcision 75, 138, 139, 169
   required for male converts to Judaism 67, 77, 81–2
citizenship 61
citizenship, Roman 12, 61, 76, 125, 169–70
   Christian attitudes to 14
   Jewish attitudes to 13
civic religion 16–17
Claudius 55
cognitive dissonance 166–7
Cohen, Shaye 63, 129
collegia 17
collegiality of gods 24–5
Commodian 119
communal rivalry 88
competition 18
Constantine 134–5, 138, 139, 160
Constantine II 140–1
Constantius II 135
control within society 5, 13, 18
conversion ceremony, Jewish 136, 148
conversion, to Christianity 103, 104
conversion, philosophical 35
conversion to Judaism:
   motivation for 149
   prohibited 135, 138–41, 151
converts, to Christianity, status of 86
Corinthians 97

Cornelius 164
covenant 115, 124, 163
cultural homogeneity, in Roman empire 20
Cynics 32–3, 34, 35, 36–7
Cyprian 98
Cyprus 106, 126
Cyrene 51, 106, 126

Damascus 103
Damascus Document 65
Day of Atonement 131, 172
Dead Sea scrolls 39, 40, 63, 65
Dead Sea sect 44, 172
Decius 5
decline of cults 26–7
Deliler 118
Delos 28
Demeter 126
Demetrius the Chronographer 65
demonstrative argument 171–2, 173
Deuteronomy 49
Deut. 4: 19 52, 116
diatheke 163
Diogenes Laertius 34–5
Diogenes of Oenoanda 35
Dionysus 23, 26, 51
   spread of worship in Italy 17, 22, 28–9, 83
divine intervention, expected by Christians 164, 166
Domitian 45, 122–4
dreams 26, 149
Dura-Europus 111, 137

ecclesia 13, 100, 163
   see also Church
Edom 77
educational mission 3, 5, 60–1, 86, 93, 95–6
Egypt 48, 56, 57, 87, 126–7
Elchasaites 156
Eleazar 65, 84
Eleusis 154
emperor cult 23, 30–2, 155
epelys 63, 72
Ephraem 143–4
Epictetus 67, 81, 134
Epicureans 32–4, 35–7, 97
Epicurus 33, 36, 37
eschatology 11, 55, 60–1, 80, 89
   in early Church 91, 94, 163–7
   in Judaism 97, 165

Essenes 71, 73, 109, 171
Esther, Book of 64
Ethiopian eunuch 96
Euhemerus 24
Eupolemus 65
Euripides 23, 26
Eusebius 6, 100, 101
exclusivism 17
   effects of, in Christianity 105, 162
   lack of, in ancient paganism 22
   varied attitudes to, in Christianity
     96–7
Exod. 22: 27 52, 116
exorcist 102
expulsions, of Jews from Rome 68, 82–3
Ezekiel the Tragedian 65–6
Ezra 46, 50

Felicitas Peregrina 133
fiscus Judaicus 46, 121–5
forced conversions to Judaism 64, 75–7

Gager, John 164–5
Gamaliel VI 140
Gehinnom 70
gentile, definition of 46–8
gentiles:
   disputed status of in early Church
     169–70, 172–3
   Jewish views of salvation of 115–16,
     169
ger 72–3, 137
Gerim (tractate) 148
ger toshab 113, 137
Glycon 30
Gnostics 96
Godfearers 47, 73, 87–8, 113, 117–19,
   131, 134, 135, 137
gods, pagan 25
   attitudes to humans 6, 23–5, 26
   collegiality 24–5
Goldenberg, R. 112 n. 7, 129
Gospels 168
great commission, *see* Matt. 28: 118–20

Habakkuk 3: 6 115
Hadrian 138–9, 151
Hasmonaeans 58, 64, 74, 75–7
Hecataeus, Ps.- 66, 79
Hecataeus of Abdera 58
Hecate 126–7
Helbo, R. 130

Hellenism, notion imitated by
   Hasmonaeans 76
Heracles 51
heretics 18
Hermas 13, 98, 99, 101, 103, 104
Hermes 51
Herod 51, 71
Herodian family 64–5, 77–8
Historia Augusta 134, 141
Holocaust 46
Holy Land 5, 49–50, 58, 76–7
homosexuality 54, 80
Honorius 139–40
Horace 68, 74

Iamblichus 34
identity, Jewish, *see* Jew, definition of
idolatry, in Bible 5
idols, Jewish attitude to 120
Idumaeans 64, 74, 75–6, 77, 86
Ignatius 102, 104
images:
   lack of in Jerusalem Temple 44
   in pagan cult 114
infanticide, Jewish attitudes to 80, 84
informative mission 3, 5
Isaiah 49: 6 142–3
Isis 26, 149
   temple of 126–7
   worship of 22, 23, 26, 27–8
Isocrates 33
isopoliteia 88
Israel, land of, *see* Holy Land
Ituraeans 64, 74
Izates 47, 65, 81, 136
   see also Adiabene

Jeremias, J. 60
Jerome 144
Jerusalem 42–4, 58
Jesus 69, 161, 168
   belief in 4, 64, 168
   Josephus on 41
Jethro, image of 146
Jew, definition of 13, 46–7, 62–3, 120–5,
   134, 135
Jewish Greek literature 48, 53, 65–6,
   78–81
Jews partipating in non–Jewish cult 51
Job 50–1
John 13
John Chrysostom 143, 144
John, Gospel of 98

John of Antioch 68, 83
John the Baptist 104
Joseph and Asenath 48, 78, 79, 127–8
Josephus 41, 149
  Against Apion 13, 41, 45, 57, 62
  Antiquities 41, 58, 62
  on Jewish sects 71, 109, 171
  Jewish War 41, 44–5, 62
  on Judaism 5–6, 171
  Life 41
  on other religions 52
  on proselytes 63–4, 68, 83, 85
  writings 40–1
Jubilees 53, 54
Judaism:
  as background to Christianity 7–8
  changes after 70 CE 44–6, 109–11,
    151–2
  effects of selected evidence for 39–40,
    48–9, 56
  evidence for 39–42, 111, 130, 141
  modern study of 8
  problems in studying 38–42
  variety within 39, 111
Julia Severa 55
Julian 22, 155–6
Julius Paris 82
Jupiter 51
Jupiter Capitolinus 121
Jupiter Sabazius 82
Juster, J. 60
Justin Martyr 36, 142–3
Juvenal 88, 134

Kerygma Petri 101
Khazars 152–3
knowledge, effects of 99

Laodicea 147
Lazarus 168
legislation, Roman about Jews 130,
  134–5, 136, 138–41
Leontopolis 82
Libanius 155
Livy 28–9
loyal sacrifices by Jews 43
Lucian 29–30, 32
Lucretius 15, 34, 36
Lyons 31

Maccabees 2 64
Maccabees 4 40, 79
mamzer 121

Manetho 57
Manichees 18, 139, 156–9
Marcion 143
Marcus Aurelius 37
Mark 16: 15–16 106
marriage, Jewish practice of 77–8
  see also mixed marriages
martyrdom:
  Christian 97, 151
  Jewish 151
matrilineal descent, in Judaism 120–1,
  135
Matt. 23: 15 69–74, 133, 143
Matt. 28: 18–20 92, 104, 106–7, 108,
  161, 170, 173
MdRi Nezikin 18 136
meals, in early Church 169
mediaeval Judaism 152–3
Mesopotamia 126
Metilius 82
Micah 50
Miletus 118
Mishnah 42, 45, 110
mission:
  definition of 3–4, 6, 95
  modern study of 7
  in nineteenth century 93–4
Mithraism 21, 23, 27
mixed marriages 47, 65, 77–8, 149
Modestinus 138
monotheism 23
Munck, J. 60
myths 16

Nabataeans 75
nasi 110–11
Nehemiah 46
neighbour, definition of 12
Nemesis 127
Nepotianus 82
Nerva 45–6, 122–4
Noachide laws 53, 112–16, 126, 131,
  148, 149–50
Nock, A. D. 2, 27
non–Christians, in Christian texts 14,
  103
Num. R. 8 136

oikoumene 12
Olbia 34
omer 171
On the Sublime 79
optional cults 17–18, 27

oracles 25
Origen 107–8, 122, 137, 139, 143
Orpheus 80
Orpheus, Ps.- 80, 128
Orphic teaching 34
Oxyrhynchus 127

paganism:
  changes in 9–10, 22–3, 26
  evidence for 10–11, 21–2
  mocked by Jews 49–50, 55, 116
  opposed by Christians 96–7
  study of 7, 20
pagan literature about Jews 57, 85
Pantaenus 108
Panticapaeum 118
patriarch, Jewish, see *nasi*
patristic comments on Jews 141
Paul (jurist) 136, 138
Paul, St:
  on altar to the unknown god 25
  copied by Manichaeans 159
  as Jew 42, 71, 169–70
  letters of 94, 162, 170, 172
  as missionary 85, 96, 103, 105–6,
    165–6, 167, 169–70
  as Roman citizen 13, 169–70
  taught that no salvation outside
    Christianity 98, 100
  teachings for gentile Christians 53–4,
    81, 92, 169, 173
  teachings for Jewish Christians 92
Pella 76
Pentateuch 39, 49
Peregrinus 33
persecution 5
Peter 95–6, 103, 164
Pharaoh 49
Pharisees 69–74, 109, 171–2
Philo 40, 66
  allegorical method 67, 81–2
  on extreme allegorists 67
  on other religions 52, 53
  on proselytes 63–4, 67, 72, 85
  on translation of Septuagint 68, 74–5
  universalistic traits 15
Philo the Elder 65
philosophy 32–7, 55
Phocylides, Ps.- 63
Pionios 118–19
Plato 26
Platonism 37, 40
Pliny 28, 97

pluralism 7
Plutarch 21, 23, 24, 25, 51
pollution of food, Jewish concern for
    65, 169
Polybius 16
Polycarp 102
pomerium 12
Pompeii 27
Pontus 29
Price, Simon 31
Prisca 106
private religion 18
propaganda, Flavian 43–5, 46, 125
prophets 6, 9
proselytes, Jewish 47, 54, 61–3, 133–6
  number of 64, 83, 84, 132–3
  status ambiguous in Judaism 85–6
proselytism, notion of in Judaism 61
proselytizing, date of rabbinic approval
    of 150
proselytos 70–4
pseudepigrapha 39
Ptolemy Philadelphus 75, 116
Pythagoreans 34, 124

Qumran, *see* Dead Sea sect

rabbinic authority 109–10
rabbinic Judaism 44, 51–2, 71–2, 109–10
red heifer 171
religion:
  function of 16, 17
  private 18
  separate sphere of activity 15, 17–18,
    22–3
  study of 10–11, 15–16
repentance 89
revivalism 6
revolts, Jewish 42, 48, 126–7
ritual 15–17
Rokeah, D. 60
Roma 23

sacred space, in Judaism 58
sacrifice test 124
Sadducees 109, 171–2
salvation:
  Jewish views on 115–16
  not found outside Church 98
Samaritans 47, 139, 140
Sanctus 14
Santa Prisca 27
Sardis 11, 118, 137

Schürer, E. 60
scribes 69, 70
scripture 11, 131, 173
semi-proselytes 88
Septimius Severus 141
Septuagint 52, 55, 63, 68, 72, 75, 116
  readership of 79, 80
Serapis 23, 28, 127
Sibylline Oracles 56, 66, 67–8, 80
Sidon 99, 103
Sifre Deut. 32 145, 150
slaves in Jewish society 65, 78
  converted to Judaism 65, 78, 130,
    138, 147, 149
  rabbis forbid return to heathen master
    116
Smyrna 118–19
society, definition of 12–14
  control within 13, 16, 18
Socrates 5
solitaries 104
Solomon 87
  image of 150
Spain 153
standards, Roman military 58
Stern, M. 60
Stoicism 34, 37, 40
Strabo 75–6
Suetonius 122–4
superstition 25, 101
sympathizer:
  of Christianity 102, 105
  of Judaism, *see* Godfearers
synagogues 66–7, 110, 111, 137–8
syncretism 28, 51

taboos, Christian 104–5
Tacitus 68, 134
Talmud 42
Tatian 80
Temple (in Jerusalem) 42–5, 46–7, 67,
  87
  destruction 42–3, 48, 109, 121
temples, pagan:
  destroyed by Jews 126
  rebuilt 43, 126
Tertullian 21, 105, 107, 119, 124–5

Testament of Abraham 54, 80
testes veritatis 92
Testimonium Flavianum 41
Theodosius I 18, 110
Theodosius II 140
third race, Christians as 100–1
Tiberius 6
Tiberius Iulius Alexander 123–4
Timagenes 76
Titus 43–4, 45
Tobit 55, 63
Torah:
  pre-existence of 145
  study of, by pagans 132, 148
Tosefta 110
Trajan 46
Tralles 118
triumph (in Rome) 44
Tyche 25
Tyre 99

unanimity, as desirable in Judaism 5,
  171
uncle, marriage to niece, in Judaism 172
unity of mankind 23
universalism 8–9
universalistic language 14–15

Valerius Maximus 68, 82–3
Varro 21
Vergil 31
Vespasian 43, 44, 121–2
Veturia Paulla 133

weaving factory 140–1
Wisdom of Solomon 40, 55–6, 66, 79
women proselytes 62
writing 11

Yabneh 45
yayin nesekh 114
yirei shamayim 113, 131
Yohanan b. Nappaha 114–15

Zeus 126
Zoilos 28